Ultimately Fiction

Ultimately Fiction

Design in Modern American Literary Biography

Dennis W. Petrie

Purdue University Press
West Lafayette, Indiana
1981

FTW
AES3599

Library of Congress Catalog Card
Number 80-84578
International Standard Book Number
0-911198-62-8
Printed in the United States of America

for
Edna Lear
and
Virgil C. Petrie

contents

acknowledgments

Jeffrey Cartwright, the putative author of Steven Millhauser's *Edwin Mullhouse,* insists in his preface that "there are none to thank besides myself," that he has "never received any encouragement at all from anyone about anything." Unlike Jeffrey, I have many to thank. For, in writing this book, I have incurred more debts than I can ever repay—or even acknowledge here. I wish to express my sincere thanks to all of my friends, colleagues, and mentors who have given me their support and loyal endurance.

My greatest debt is to William T. Stafford, who helped to initiate this study and who contributed his wise, patient, and enthusiastic guidance throughout its development; to him I offer my abiding gratitude.

I am also grateful to Margaret Church, Hugo M. Reichard, William Braswell, and William Epstein, all of whom kindly read my manuscript and provided suggestions for improving it.

To Robert C. Petersen I am immensely indebted for his extensive and judicious comments on my text just prior to its final revision, and for his preparation of the book's index. Likewise, I wish to thank Jacqueline E. Orsagh for effecting many stylistic changes in the manuscript, and especially for affording me the luxury of frequent conversations with a practicing literary biographer.

This book has benefited significantly from the editorial supervision of Verna Emery; I very much appreciate her help and understanding, and that of Anita Noble, who created the book's physical design.

Finally, I most gratefully acknowledge the special encouragement and assistance I have received from Sandra S. Ridlington, Thomas Tierney, Roberta Tierney, and Robert D. Briles.

introduction

"Truth"

ATruth—both the word and the idea—must be the point of departure in any serious discussion of biography. But crucial problems of definition can easily, swiftly overwhelm the theorist. Thus, in a 1925 *New Republic* article that defended the work of Lytton Strachey, Robert Littell recorded this bit of hypothetical dialogue:

> Novelist: We are dangerously near a discussion of the nature of truth itself.
>
> Biographer: . . . nothing could be more futile. But allow me to make a few footnotes.[1]

Since 1925, both biographers and critics have followed Littell's Biographer in continuing to offer their personal "few footnotes" about "the nature of truth," the character of the biographer's art, and the relationship of truth to the practice of biography. Yet they seem to have reached no real agreement in attempting to answer the basic question: What is biographical truth? Good biographers have usually begun their work by first confronting, simultaneously, the universal demand that it contain "truth" and the realization that "The Truth" is unattainable. But many other questions arise. Should biography, for instance, be something more than merely a vehicle for facts? Can it be art?

Some observers, while pointing to the often awkward nature of its craftsmanship, have attached enor-

1

mous importance to biography—have, in fact, seen it as a most significant device by which a kind of truth can be transmitted between people of different ages and lands. For example, Ralph Waldo Emerson made these notations in his journals:

> There is no history: There is only Biography.
>
> We are very clumsy writers of history.
>
> The great value of Biography consists in the perfect sympathy that exists between like minds. Space & time are an absolute nullity to this principle.[2]

F. Scott Fitzgerald, although he admitted biography to the ranks of art, nevertheless dubbed it "the falsest of the arts."[3] Even though Virginia Woolf produced some valuable and provocative articles on biography, she also managed to etch, with the small drops of satiric acid that she carefully placed throughout her novel-biography *Orlando,* a devastating portrait of the biographer as the proverbial "plodder": "The first duty of a biographer . . . is to plod, without looking to right or left, in the indelible footprints of truth; unenticed by flowers; regardless of shade; on and on methodically till we fall plump into the grave and write *finis* on the tombstones above our heads."[4] And long before she came to write a competent (but somewhat plodding) biography of one of her artist friends, Roger Fry, she expressed her distrust of biographers in general, basing her fears on the writer's inability to know the "real" truth about any person's life.

Quentin Bell, in his role as Virginia Woolf's biographer, recognizes her attitude. Bell quotes Woolf's diary entry for 4 September 1927:

> "A cold grey blowy day, made memorable by the sight of a kingfisher and by my sense, waking early, of being again visited by 'the spirit of delight.' 'Rarely, rarely, comest thou, spirit of delight.' That was I singing this time last year; and sang so poignantly that I have never forgotten it,

or my vision of a fin rising on a wide blank sea. No biographer could possibly guess this important fact about my life in the late summer of 1926. Yet biographers pretend they know people."

And he reacts in the following manner:

They don't, or at least they ought not to. All that they can claim is that they know a little more than does the public at large and that, by catching at a few indications given here and there in recollections and writings, they can correct some misconceptions and trace, if they are very skilful or very lucky, an outline that is consistent and convincing, but which, like all outlines, is but tenuously connected with the actual form of the sitter in all lights, poses, moods, and disguises.[5]

Luckily, Bell did have his subject's diary to help him catch more than a few "indications" about how to flesh out his own "outline," but he articulates well the modern attitude that biographical truth is never an absolute truth. Other life-writers and critics still debate even the meaning of "biography," however.

In the late seventeenth century, John Dryden, following the tradition of viewing biography as a special type of history, defined biography as "the history of particular men's lives."[6] The twentieth-century English historian Harold Nicolson followed the definition given by the *Oxford English Dictionary*: "the history of the lives of individual men as a branch of literature" (p. 7). And in *The Art of Biography*, Paul Murray Kendall insists that biography is in fact "not a branch of history"; rather, Kendall suggests, it is "the simulation, in words, of a man's life, from all that is known about that man."[7] But Leon Edel, biographer of Henry James and theorist of biography, has objected to Kendall's use of the word "simulation." The best definition, Edel claims, is probably the simplest: "a biography is the recounting of a life in narrative prose."[8] Writing in another instance, Edel manages also to catch a small bit of its mystery when he says that "a biography is a record, in words, of something that is as mercurial and as flowing, as compact of temperament and emotion, as the human spirit itself."[9]

All of these definitions are very broad. In fact, they could also apply to a special kind of biography which will not be considered in this study: the autobiography, i.e., the life that is recorded by the one who has lived it. In the eighteenth century, Samuel Johnson suggested that this form of biography was superior when he wrote in his *Idler*, No. 84 (24 November 1759) that "those relations are . . . commonly of most value in which the writer tells his own story. . . . The writer of his own life has, at least, the first qualification of an historian, the knowledge of the truth. . . . Certainty of knowledge not only excludes mistake, but fortifies veracity" (BA, pp. 44–45). A recent crusader for the cause of autobiography writes that "*only* the subject has full access to [the] material" which modern psychology can utilize.[10] Roy Pascal makes virtually the same point in his book on autobiography. Yet, in his conclusion, while repeating that "biography, . . . in seeing the person concerned as an object, misses the specific dynamic truth of the autobiography," Pascal admits, almost apologetically, that "there is no final and complete truth about a man."[11] Finally, Nicolson questions whether autobiographies are "essentially truthful" and states quite plainly, "I have not, as yet, read an autobiography by which I was absolutely convinced" (p. 15).

Even though Nicolson's argument here is somewhat vague, he begins to raise an interesting point. As L. P. Hartley states in the opening line of one of his novels, "The past is a foreign country: they do things differently there."[12] The truth for an old man looking back at the young man that he was in the past may be a radically changed truth. Indeed, autobiographies are, in essence, sometimes biographies. Autobiographies, Richard Altick writes,

> though more polished and continuous than such other forms of personal record as diaries and letters, are the products of sober second thought,

hindsight, and filtered memory; they very often represent episodes as they should have been rather than as they happened, and present youthful character as the mature man chooses to regard it as having been. They are influenced, in addition, by the writer's conscious or unconscious desire to control the impression his own and later generations would have of him. Often they throw more dependable light on their authors as they were at the time of composition than as they were at the time written about.[13]

Thus the best autobiographers often consciously select the form of biography. Such, of course, is the case with *The Education of Henry Adams,* whose author writes in the third person in his attempt—among other reasons, perhaps—to be more objective.[14] At the outset of his five-volume *Henry James,* Edel makes it clear that he will not "abdicate" in favor of autobiography, regardless of how masterly it may be; and he implies that he, the biographer, will use James's autobiographical writings in much the same way that he will use other extant James work.[15]

The concern in this book is exclusively with the narrative of a life which is lived by one person and written by another. However, merely to eliminate autobiography from consideration does not really make definition any easier. Perhaps valid definition is impossible—and unnecessary. In order to discuss individual biographies with any thoroughness, each critic must first offer a coherent personal theory of biography, "a few footnotes," by which these volumes may be evaluted. An attempt of this kind has been made by Joseph W. Reed, Jr., in the final chapter of his *English Biography in the Early Nineteenth Century, 1801–1838.* But at the beginning of his comments, Reed writes, "I certainly do not wish to attempt a definition of biography here. Biographical criticism already contains entirely too many fallen monuments of abandoned definitions and too few serious explorations of biography's problems."[16]

This study, then, also attempts to offer a "few serious explorations of biography's problems"—and biography's possibilities. First, though, a very brief survey (primarily in relation to authors' conceptions of truth) of some prominent examples of biography as it has been practiced since ancient times may suggest the various boundaries of the genre.

—————————— **I** ——————————

T. A. Dorsey, in his book on Latin biography, has noted that "biography has always been a popular literary genre—from the point of view of both the reader and the writer. There is something in human nature that makes men more interested in people than in events, and the details of the personal life and habits of eminent men have always fascinated the more ordinary members of the community. For the writer, the span of one man's life forms a compact literary unit."[17] Biography has, in fact, been produced in some form since the earliest times of man, for its roots "lie buried in man's search for immortality."[18] Historians have pointed out that various kinds of pictorial biographies often appear in the tombs of the Egyptians, and parts of the Bible qualify as types of eloquent biography. But carefully written accounts of lives were not plentiful in the ancient world, and even the Greeks failed to produce a substantial body of biographical work.

Certainly the most famous, and genuinely noteworthy, early writer of biography was Plutarch of Chaeronea, who died circa 120 A.D. A supreme moralist, Plutarch nevertheless shows himself also to be a fine artist in his *Lives of the Noble Grecians and Romans* (usually referred to as *Parallel Lives*), where he selects twenty-two famous Romans and as many celebrated

Greeks, pairs them, man to man, in portraits, and then draws moral conclusions in his comparisons, thus producing vibrant illustrations of his impression of truth in human endeavor. As Henry Seidel Canby has noted in his "Plutarchian" study of Mark Twain and Henry James, "the stories in Plutarch's lives are more effective than his final moralizing of them."[19] Indeed, Plutarch is perhaps best remembered for his technique of catching character in action and as, possibly, the real precursor of such modern fiction writers as Henry James. In his life of Alexander, Plutarch states his purpose in writing and beautifully defines his method:

> It must be borne in mind that my design is not to write Histories, but Lives. And the most glorious exploits do not always furnish us with the clearest signs of virtue or vice in men; sometimes a matter of less moment, an expression or a jest, informs us better of their characters and inclinations than the most famous sieges, the greatest armaments, or the bloodiest battles.[20]

The history of English biography is "a story of arrested development" (Nicolson, p. 16), for in spite of a few brilliant sparks such as Eadmer the monk of Canterbury's twelfth-century *Vita Anselmi*, it was a dark time for the genre before the eighteenth century. Hagiographers (writers of saints' lives) abounded, but their products had only one purpose: to praise their subjects. Truth for these biographers was any fact or fiction which allowed them to paint their monochromic portraits; truth was what should be true, within the proper religious context. Before the seventeenth century, critics can find very few biographies to praise besides William Roper's *Life of Sir Thomas More* (written circa 1535) and George Cavendish's *Life of Wolsey* (written 1554–57). Each of these biographers, who were close to their subjects (Roper was More's son-in-law; Cavendish was Wolsey's aide), manages to combine—each in his own way—reverence and attention to detail in a believable portrait.

The first glimmerings of a critical theory of biography did begin to show up in the seventeenth century, however. For example, in his *Life of Cowley* (1668), Thomas Sprat abhorred the printing of private letters in biographies: "In such letters the souls of men should appear undressed: and in that negligent habit, they may be fit to be seen by one or two in a chamber, but not to go abroad into the streets" (BA, p. 12). Earlier, Izaak Walton had made extensive use of such letters in the first parts of his series of *Lives* of John Donne, Sir Henry Wotton, Richard Hooker, George Herbert, and Robert Sanderson. These biographies, as a group or separately, have generally been considered the best that the century had to offer in the genre—although recently Walton has been harshly criticized for "tend[ing] to endow his subjects, even passionate John Donne, with something of the genteel and whimsical piety that so characterized himself. He smooths out too many wrinkles and planes off too many rough edges of his people" (Kendall, p. 98).

In addition, Vivian De Sola Pinto calls attention to the work of that compulsive note-taker John Aubrey and Bishop Gilbert Burnet in the seventeenth century, as well as to Dryden's valuable contribution in his short *Life of Plutarch*.[21] Whether Burnet's account of Rochester is "The Truth" may be forever debatable, but his life is a powerfully described personal version of truth, and it is compelling reading. In musing on his biographical urge, Aubrey once wrote to his friend Anthony à Wood that he recorded "nothing but the truth: the naked and plain truth, which is here exposed so bare that the *pudenda* are not covered, and affords many passages that would raise a blush in a young virgin's cheek. So that after your perusal, I must desire you to make a castration . . . and to sew-on some fig leaves—i.e., to be my *Index expurgatorius*" (BA, p. 15).

Harold Nicolson labels Dr. Johnson's *Life of Savage* (1744) "unquestionably . . . our first masterpiece in biography" (p. 76), and James Clifford views it as "the first genuinely three-dimensional biography, with psychological overtones, in the English language" (EECB, p. 80). Boswell records that Sir Joshua Reynolds "began to read it while he was standing with his arm leaning against a chimney-piece. It seized his attention so strongly, that, not being able to lay down the book till he had finished it, when he attempted to move, he found his arm totally benumbed."[22] Only Roger North's lives of his three brothers (written about 1715) even come close to rivaling Johnson's book in liveliness and importance in the first half of the eighteenth century. Both as a theorist and as a practitioner, Samuel Johnson led the way to the modern art of biography—both in spite of and because of his being a great moralist. In *The Rambler*, No. 60 (13 October 1750), he writes that "no species of writing seems more worthy of cultivation than biography, since none can be more delightful or more useful, none can more certainly enchain the heart by irresistible interest, or more widely diffuse instruction to every diversity of condition." Sounding very much like Plutarch, he continues: "The business of the biographer is often to pass slightly over those performances and incidents, which produce vulgar greatness, to lead the thoughts into domestic privacies, and display the minute details of daily life" (BA, pp. 40–41, 42). This was published after the *Life of Savage,* so for him practice preceded written theory.

What contributes most to the intriguing aspects of the *Life of Savage* is the fact that Johnson was a close friend of his subject; such was not the case with all of his subjects in Johnson's later (1781) *Lives of the Poets,* to which the *Savage* was added. Yet, in 1772 Johnson told Boswell that "nobody can write the life of a man, but those who have eat and drunk and lived in social intercourse with him." Even in his *Life of Addison,* he writes, "History may be formed from permanent monuments and records; but lives can only be written from personal knowledge" (BA, pp. 47, 46). So, for Johnson the capturing of moral truth seems to have been in some measure dependent upon the truth to be found in propinquity.

James Boswell's *Life of Johnson*, which was first published in 1791, is usually considered the living center, the touchstone, of all study of the art of biography today. Essentially, Boswell followed Johnson's biographical principles, if not his practical example.[23] He was, of course, a close friend of his subject, and, in general, he studied and recorded not only the major events in Johnson's life but also the minutiae.[24] Here is how Boswell describes, in the introduction to the *Life*, his biographical method; although few biographers have had the opportunity to use this method to the extent which Boswell did, it has nevertheless posed a powerful challenge for all biographers since that time:

> Indeed I cannot conceive a more perfect mode of writing any man's life, than not only relating all the most important events of it in their order, but interweaving what he privately wrote, and said, and thought; by which mankind are enabled as it were to see him live, and to "live o'er each scene" with him, as he actually advanced through the several stages of his life. Had his other friends been as diligent and ardent as I was, he might have been almost entirely preserved.

Boswell's idealism about the possibilities for catching the true essence of a man is apparent here. He continues:

> As it is, I will venture to say that he will be seen in this work more completely than any man who has ever yet lived.
> And he will be seen as he really was; for I profess to write, not his panegyrick, which must be all praise, but his Life; which, great and good as he was, must not be supposed to be entirely perfect. . . . [I]n every picture there should be shade as well as light, and when I delineate him without reserve, I do what he himself recommended, both by his precept and his example.[25]

So goes Boswell's explanation. But as James Clifford has recently shown, Dr. Johnson, late in life, "reluctantly confessed himself willing to postpone telling the whole truth"; and even Boswell, in actual practice, "did not himself attempt to give the whole truth" (EECB, pp. 83, 84). For even the kind and quantity of truth which Boswell chose to tell in his writings before the *Life of Johnson* were apparently enough to evoke blushes and to set the tongues, and pens, of Mrs. Montagu and others in motion against him and his techniques (EECB, p. 87). Later biographies, like Boswell's book, have often raised the now-standard question, How much should a biographer tell? Ultimately it is merely a small part of the question that involves larger truths. Not even twentieth-century minds have been able to answer it more effectively than Johnson and Boswell. Clifford's own conclusion, after a lively and intelligent discussion of the problem, is feeble: "All I have been able to do is to show how little the eighteenth century thought about biographical problems, and how impossible it was for practicing life-writers to be completely honest."[26]

Telling just part of the truth, but telling it unslanted, was also too much for the Victorians. According to most commentators on the art of biography, the period between 1838, when the last volume of John Gibson Lockhart's *Life of Scott* appeared, and 1882, when James Anthony Froude's *Life of Carlyle* was published, is a vast wasteland for biographical writing. Lockhart caused quite a furor with his revealing work, but his subject, who was his father-in-law, had insisted that both the "shades and lights" be "accurately" given.[27] Meanwhile, only James Stanfield (in his clumsy but important *Essay on the Study and Composition of Biography* in 1816) and Thomas Carlyle seemed seriously concerned about the art.[28]

Carlyle was one of the few people who defended the revelations in Lockhart's *Scott*. With characteristic force, he wrote, "How delicate, how decent is English biography, bless its mealy mouth! A Damocles Sword of

Respectability hangs for ever over the poor English life-writer . . . and reduces him to the verge of paralysis" (quoted in Nicolson, p. 125). And when, in turn, Froude came to write the life of Carlyle, he "had to choose between the alternative of giving a truthful and as such a disagreeable representation of Carlyle, and that of writing no biography at all. He chose the former alternative, and a yell of dismay rose from the Victorians."[29]

In 1903, Edmund Gosse, later the author of the much touted *Father and Son* and the ironically muted *Swinburne*, wrote an essay entitled "The Ethics of Biography"; here he set up a flexible principle that has, generally, been adhered to in the writing of "respectable" biography since that time. He suggested that mention of certain shady aspects of a subject's life better be omitted completely than permit respect for "the legitimate scruples of private persons" to "extend so far as to the telling of a deliberate lie" (BA, p. 119). Gosse's "ethics" lead one directly to Lytton Strachey and his work.

Here it is necessary to pause for a look backward. Perhaps, in choosing to survey Boswell, Lockhart, and Froude in terms of "how much" truth they told, one gives false impressions about what is important in biography. But a realization of how critics and the public could so often become obsessed with what should have been little more than quick-lived literary gossip may help us to understand why it took the English-speaking world so long to become concerned with the more formal elements of biography—style and structure, for example: aesthetic truth. Boswell, Lockhart, and Froude were each attempting to capture the fullest possible portrait of his subject. Consequently, their books are big; and critics charge, justifiably perhaps, that they are fundamentally unstructured. Since the time of Plutarch, the chronological, birth-to-death structure had been used, and the most direct style had been considered the best. Strachey began his work by trimming away at the girth of traditional biography. Manifested obsession with style became Strachey's forte.

Virtually everyone agrees that Strachey is extremely important in the history of biography, but some disagree concerning exactly how "true"—in several senses of that word—his work is. "Every biographer since 1918, from the producer of weighty 'definitive' lives to the confector of romantic trifles, has necessarily written in the shadow of Strachey" (Altick, p. 283). In the preface to his revolutionary work, *Eminent Victorians*, Strachey penned his manifesto:

> The art of biography seems to have fallen on evil times in England. . . . [T]he most delicate and humane of all the branches of the art of writing has been relegated to the journeymen of letters; we do not reflect that it is perhaps as difficult to write a good life as to live one. Those two fat volumes, with which it is our custom to commemorate the dead—who does not know them, with their ill-digested masses of material, their slipshod style, their tone of tedious panegyric, their lamentable lack of selection, of detachment, of design? They are as familiar as the cortege of the undertaker, and wear the same air of slow, funereal barbarism. One is tempted to suppose, of some of them, that they were composed by that functionary, as the final item of his job. . . . To preserve . . . becoming brevity . . . which excludes everything that is redundant and nothing that is significant—that, surely, is the true duty of the biographer.[30]

The whole argument of "how much" finally hangs, of course, upon one's interpretation of "significant." Strachey enjoyed the satisfaction of being greatly applauded for this volume and for such subsequent, and perhaps better, work as his *Queen Victoria* (1921); and he endured the frustration of watching the appearance of poor imitations that resulted from the popularity of his manner. Discoveries that Strachey did in fact sometimes use his materials with malice and even falsify the facts to obtain the precise shading that he desired in a portrait (e.g., Altick, p. 286) have tended to lessen his popularity, if not his real influence.

Thus biography entered the modern age in England. But what about its condition in America? According to Paul Murray Kendall, "distinguished American writers from Washington Irving and Nathaniel Hawthorne to Henry James published biographies, but they are of no importance. Until the First World War the United States is, biographically speaking, virtually a blank" (p. 100).[31] Even at this point the art was young in America; "the only American of his era who steadfastly regarded biography as a high art and dedicated his life to its practice was . . . Gamaliel Bradford" (1863–1932), who specialized in finely-drawn psychological portraits which he termed "psychographs." But "it was intuition, rather than methodical induction from all the facts, which guided Bradford's judgment. Only in the loosest sense, therefore, can he be called a biographer" (Altick, p. 277).

Still, attempts to discover inner truth by the application of psychological principles in biography became more and more common with the growth of Freud's influence and popularity in America. Too often such applications were amateurish and reckless, but there remains today a literary interest in a few of the psychological biographies produced during the twenties and thirties. Some notable examples include Joseph Wood Krutch's study of Poe (1926), Lewis Mumford's *Herman Melville* (1929), and Van Wyck Brooks's examination of Mark Twain (1933).

But because the art of biography was still young in America, biographers had many lessons to learn; in general, they wielded an uneasy command of their craft. For example, many subsequent Melville scholars have maintained that Raymond Weaver's pioneering *Herman Melville: Mystic and Mariner* (1921) was an illustration of the biographical fallacy in action — that Weaver sometimes, especially in his treatment of *Typee*, *Omoo*, *Redburn*, and *White-Jacket*, confused his subject with his subject's fictional characters.[32] "Throughout the early 1930's the biographical fallacy grew, with inevitable Freudian accretions"; Weaver's errors (committed most probably because of the scarcity of factual material available about Melville at the time of Weaver's composition) encouraged later biographers and critics—including John Freeman (1926), Mumford, and Ellery Sedgwick in the 1940s—to continue the tradition.[33] The publicity which accompanied the full revelation in the 1940s of Rufus W. Griswold's long-hidden biographical crimes against Poe further underscored the necessity for complete honesty and thoroughness on the part of all biographers (Altick, p. 269). Yet other problems, which involved more than just authenticity, remained for biographers and critics alike in the second half of the century.

II

During the past twenty-five years, a few biographers have written books to explain the problems and joys they have experienced with their writing, and these works can certainly contain value for the critic.[34] But criticism of biography should be interested mainly in evaluating the achievement in the finished product, not in examining its often painful process of becoming finished. Such criticism at present consists almost entirely of brief historical surveys, printed lectures, collections of miscellaneous writings on the subject, and random general critical comments appearing at the beginnings and/or ends of newspaper, magazine, and journal reviews of newly-published biographies. In many ways, biographical theory is still in its adolescence—not much further advanced, say, than film theory.

In his essay "The Strategies of Biography and Some Eighteenth-Century Examples," Frank Brady posits an interesting hypothesis to explain the problem. "The rudimentary state of biographical theory," he writes, "can be blamed on biography's anomalous status among literary forms. It is based on fact, and modern criticism hardly knows what to do with the factual." Brady goes on to lament the naïveté of modern biographers who refuse to utilize the so-called techniques of fiction to wed the "truth of facts" with the "truth of the imagination." He continues: "Since the biographer himself seems so often unaware that his work has either formal aspects or a general strategy, it is not surprising that the critic usually appears ignorant of many formal aspects in biography comparable to those he could at once specify in a novel or poem."[35] In the introduction to the last volume of his *Henry James*, Leon Edel echoes Brady's frustration:

> I believe biography to be the most taken for granted—and the least discussed—of all the branches of literature. Biographies are widely read, but they are treated as if they came ready-made. Our explicating critics seem to find little in them to explicate; and many indeed read the lives of poets and then hide them, as if they were ashamed of them, insisting on the sanctity of the work of art. Small wonder that Stephen Spender has asked criticism to restore the poet to his poem. Critics tell us every Monday or Friday that the novel is dying or dead thereby showing a genuine concern for that form of literature. But biographies are accepted as they come and relished for their revelations. Biographers themselves have not on the whole been helpful. . . . Questions of form, composition, structure are seldom raised.[36]

"Truth" in a biography can involve both the life of the subject and the art of the biographer. In each case, however, the word "design" might be employed in describing this involvement. In the first instance, the word would refer to something which is often viewed as a sinister scheme on the biographer's part: either the absence of literal truth or the inclusion of too much literal truth is "design." Design might, on the other hand, also mean the "formal aspects of biography" which Brady mentions. Although criticism should concern itself less with the historical authenticity of a biography's facts *per se* and more with the manner in which the biographer has presented them, the two factors are—and should be—irrevocably entwined. And a biographer's purpose will surely affect the structure and style of his work. For example, hagiographers violate facts to achieve their adulatory aims; and directly because of this, their art becomes pattern-moulded and cliché-ridden. On the other extreme, Lytton Strachey manipulates literal truth to construct brilliantly formalized, compact portraits of subjects whom he loathes.[37] Thus, the circumference of truth in biography is always design—design in function, form, and fashion.[38] Ideally, the biographer can wrestle with the problems that these three elements encompass and manage to strike a fair and pleasing equilibrium.

Certainly the best biographies have always provided their readers with the excitement that one has come to expect from the best fiction—and they have been as finely and as carefully wrought. In recent years, when writers have used the phrase "nonfiction novel" frequently, biography's popularity seems to have grown. We have entered a new age of biography. And perhaps the most fascinating and popular type of biography is literary biography—i.e., biography that has as its subject a person who is an imaginative writer himself. In his history of literary biography, Richard Altick tries to account for and analyze the appeal which this subgenre has for readers; the life of the artist, he says, is always intriguing, primarily because of the artist's roles as the outsider and the rebel. "The peculiar attraction of literary biography is essentially that of the psychological novel and the confessional lyric. Like them, it opens the windows of the soul." Such a book is also a "quest for the creator behind the creation. All books about artists imply an attempt to shed light on the mystery of the artistic process, but literary biographies as a class are more successful than others because they are couched in the language of the art with which they deal" (p. xi). Further, Altick says, "vicariously [reading literary biography] makes authors of us all" (p. xii).

Biographies of artists differ from those of warriors, statesmen, businessmen, etc., in ways besides the degree of their popularity. For example, in literary biography there is, in addition to the life, the art of the subject to contend with. The facts of the subject's life and works must somehow be balanced out with the overwhelming, sometimes contradictory, spirits of these two domains. Some authors—notably Dickens, James, Faulkner—have long been notorious for their attempts to protect their private lives by trying to separate them from the lives of their writings. W. H. Auden illustrates this attitude well when he begins the foreword to his *A Certain World: A Commonplace Book* (which, he finally admits, constitutes a kind of autobiography itself) by stating:

> Biographies of writers, whether written by others or by themselves, are always superfluous and usually in bad taste. A writer is a maker, not a man of action. To be sure, some, in a sense all, of his works are transmutations of his personal experiences, but no knowledge of the raw ingredients will explain the peculiar flavor of the verbal dishes he invites the public to taste: his private life is, or should be, of no concern to anybody except himself, his family and his friends.[39]

The New Critics, of course, ostensibly supported this conviction with their critical theory. There will always be people who, as Edel says, insist upon the sanctity of the work of art—who prefer to see no bond between the artist and his art. They, like Auden, will characteristically argue, out of a personal taste which is to be respected, "But you should not be looking for a bond between the artist's life and the artist's work in the first place; one is private, the other is public; one should be left alone, the other should be able to stand alone." Other modern writers, though, have spoken out in opposition to this argument. As early as 1918, Amy Lowell was writing:

> Criticism is not merely an interpretation of technique: it is a tracing of mental bias, a tracking of angles of thought to their starting points, a realization of the roots from which the flowers spring . . . . A knowledge of the man illumines his art if we mean by "knowledge" a realization of his psychology and its shock against the world in which he lived. This in no way militates against the aesthetic consideration of his art *per se* but leads in the end more directly towards it.[40]

Since that time, artists as diverse as Stephen Spender, Norman Mailer, and James Dickey have seemingly continued to encourage this attitude through statements in the media, "advertisements for themselves," and publication of private journals and "self-interviews."[41]

But even if this bond is viewed as inherent, still other questions remain: Is it really the task of the biographer to delineate this important but enigmatic relationship between a writer's life experiences and his artistic expression? Should it be left completely to the critic? If so, how should the biographer treat the writings of an author whom he has chosen to examine solely as a man or a woman? And, in turn, must the critic then become a kind of biographer even if his main interest is in the creative works? Ultimately, what should be the primary reason for and the center of a biography of an author? The man himself? His writings? A synthesis of the two? Should the works be used to illuminate the life, or vice-versa? Should biography have an even higher aim? The stimulus for this book derives from questions such as these.

III

The subtitle of this study suggests some of the arbitrary limitations which have been of necessity imposed upon the book's scope in order to achieve a more manageable focus. First, only biographies of American writers and by American biographers have been considered. Second, the word "modern" means not only that the major American writer-subjects treated here all worked within the twentieth century but, as it turns out, that only biographies written since 1950 have been included.

My purpose here is to examine both utilitarian and aesthetic problems and possibilities in the field of modern American literary biography. My method is to analyze sample biographies which contain intrinsic merit (either because they are standard source books of reliable information or because they are artistically satisfying, or both) and are also representatives of particular types of literary biography. In the past twenty-five years in America, a tremendous boom has occurred in the production of biographies of writers. Although many modern American literary figures still have not been treated with any thoroughness, many others have been recorded with what sometimes seems to the reader to be exhausting exhaustiveness. Eugene O'Neill, for example, has been afforded two mammoth biographies, in three volumes, by three biographers. Playwrights and poets have often enough been taken as subjects,[42] but certainly the most flourishing activity has involved modern American novelists. Thus, again for focus, I have chosen my primary samples from available biographies of novelists.

Many of the biographies mentioned in the preceding historical survey just happen to be literary biographies. This fact possibly suggests how this subgenre has provided the most paradigms of quality and originality in conception and technique for the entire genre of biography. But literary biography has its own special demand, and this should be taken into consideration in setting up any classification system of its types. Leon Edel and James L. Clifford have dealt intelligently and rewardingly with the myriad problems of literary biography, but they have not stressed sufficiently this special demand in defining their own systems, which they both have attempted to make broad enough to encompass all biography.

Actually, critic-biographers have described many ways that biography in general may be divided and its types named. Nicolson simply splits the genre into parts "pure" and "impure." Elements which make pure biography impure include "the desire to celebrate the dead," "the desire to compose the life of an individual as an illustration of some extraneous theory or conception," and "undue subjectivity in the writer" (pp. 9–10). Kendall says that "modern biographies display an infinity of gradations," and he proceeds to differentiate among "eight perceptible types":

> On the radical left appears the novel-as-biography, almost wholly imaginary. Then come the extensive and often marshy reaches of fictionized biography, which stretch from outright romancing to more or less serious biographical intentions. This popular form merges into the more carefully controlled and sometimes remarkably able genre, interpretative biography, running to the center of the scale. The Lives on the other side, all of them true to the biographic oath, range from the chief exemplars of modern life-writing, with the best scholarly biographies on the right flank, through the increasingly dense "research" biography, the "life-and-times" biography, what I venture to call the "Behemoth biography," and so to works of such high specific gravity that they are little more than compilations of source-materials. Hovering above the center of the scale appears the radiant-plumaged "super-biography," which seeks to be both ultimately literary and ultimately scientific. (pp. 126–27)

Edel, for whose *Henry James* Kendall has apparently
coined his derisive term "super-biography," in the middle of discussing literary biography specifically, distin-
guishes "three main Architectural Ideas . . . in the
structure of biographies [in general]": "The traditional
documentary biography," in which "the voice of the subject [is] to be heard constantly"; "the creation, in words,
of something akin to the painter's portrait"; and "one in
which the materials are melted down and in which the
biographer is present in the work as omniscient narrator." He further explains, "The first type of biography
might be said to be chronicle; the second pictorial; the
third narrative-pictorial or novelistic" (LB, p. 125).

In chapter seven of *From Puzzles to Portraits*,
James L. Clifford is likewise supposedly dealing with
literary biography, for his subtitle is *Problems of a Literary Biographer*, and he states in his preface that his book
is aimed primarily at the person who may wish to write
a literary biography. But, after briefly noting other
possibilities and being careful to avoid placing his types
on a fixed spacial scale in the manner of Kendall, he sets
up a "series of five categories for *biography* [my italics],
beginning with the so-called 'objective' and ending with
the 'subjective.'" He stresses this word "so-called" in
setting up his first ("objective") category by showing
that even a work such as Jay Leyda's *Melville Log* (used
by Leon Howard as a source book in writing his *Herman
Melville*), which consists almost completely of facts, still
"represents only partial, or selective objectivity" because
of possible omissions or the obligatory juxtaposition of
materials. Clifford's other divisions of biography are
"scholarly-historical" (which approximates Edel's first
type, except that Clifford sees the biographer taking a
more visible part in it: "the chief point is that few risks
are taken"); "artistic-scholarly" (a duplicate of Edel's
third type); "narrative" (enthusiastically imaginative —
but not pure fiction); and "fictional" (about real figures
for whom we have sketchy documentation). The emphasis in his narration of the biographer's problems in

writing is on the "artistic-scholarly" type—"the one," he says, "most appealing to the creative biographer"; for examples of this type he uses his own *Young Sam Johnson* and Edel's *Henry James.*[43]

Later in his chapter, Clifford does allot three pages to a discussion of how the biographer may deal with a writer-subject's writings (the special demand of literary biography noted above)—"whether they should be made subsidiary throughout, or should dominate the stage." At this point, he acknowledges the possibility of leaving out critical mention of the writings altogether. But he admits that he personally does not think this approach is best, and he then suggests two self-explanatory methods of integrating strictly factual materials and critical materials: the "stop and go" method and the "interwoven" method. He ends this brief section, and the chapter, by observing that "there is no easy answer. But at least this is an area which needs much more detailed discussion."[44]

The following system of classification for types of literary biography employs ideas from both Edel and Clifford, but it also emphasizes that distinct factor which I believe should be of great concern in criticism of literary biography: the biographer's chosen function regarding both the life and the works.[45] Instead of focusing purely upon method, as Edel and Clifford seem to have done, one who wishes to examine modern American literary biography needs also to consider the purpose which has generated this method. At present, few "objective" biographies comparable to Leyda's work are being published; and, in light of the masses of information that are readily available about most modern authors, the "fictional" biography type has little reason for existence (although the *roman à clef* about literary figures continues to be produced). The remaining types are here labelled "Monument of the Famous Writer," "Portrait of the Author as a Man or Woman," and "Vision of the Artist."

When a biographer chooses to write the first type

of literary biography (which seems to be the most prevalent type today), his chief concern is usually historical; he wishes to preserve, in a very orderly, scholarly manner, what are, in essence, the archives of a celebrated author—and these include interviews with virtually every person with whom the artist came into close personal and professional contact. Focus here is upon the subject's role as the Famous Writer, so both the individual and the works are treated—at least superficially. It is not strictly a chronicle in the manner of Edel's first type, for the materials are in fact selected, "melted down"; but the biographer, as Clifford observes of his first type, takes few risks with those materials which are presented. In the second type, the portrait of the author as a human being, the biographer intends to emphasize the individual qualities of the person—who just happens to have been a writer; this type, too, requires careful scholarship. Finally, in the third type, the biographer considers himself an artist; his primary desire is to employ a scholarly knowledge of both the writer and his works to transmit, finally, his own vision of the artist; he aspires to infuse in his own work the radiance, harmony, and wholeness of true art.[46]

The systematizing of literature tends to be worthwhile only when the process is not too rigidly restrictive and when it somehow manages to enhance, rather than obstruct, the reader's understanding of both a genre as a whole and the particular works of that genre under consideration. Thus, I wish to stress at this point that my own categorizing of literary biographies is purely for illustration, not limitation. Further, this study is intended to be heuristic, not in any way exhaustive.

The following chapter presents a theory of literary biography—or, at least, "a few footnotes" toward a personal theory. Chapters Two, Three, and Four examine and evaluate—in view of the discussion in Chapter One—the three types of literary biographies just described. Although numerous biographies of authors are mentioned throughout this study, the analysis focuses upon recent biographies of four major modern American novelists: Joseph Blotner's *Faulkner* (1974); Andrew Turnbull's *Scott Fitzgerald* (1962); W. A. Swanberg's *Dreiser* (1965); and Leon Edel's *Henry James* (1953–72). Aside from their having intrinsic value and their being representatives of various types, these four literary biographies comprise a broad survey of modern American literature. For they treat the lives of authors whose combined creative production covers the years from 1875, when James published *Roderick Hudson,* to 1962, when Faulkner's *The Reivers* appeared.

chapter one

The Literary Biographer's Design: "A Few Footnotes"

Any biographer who is working at even the lowest level of professional competency should, first, gather all the facts available about his or her subject from all sources, including various kinds of written documents and, if the subject has lived recently, other mass media materials, as well as interviews with his relatives, friends, and acquaintances. Second, the biographer should formulate from these facts a personal vision of this other human being and communicate it with style. The order of these two processes is significant, of course, for the biographer must not know and prove for show; instead, he must search to discover. The biographer must search for truth in all its varieties. As Marchette Chute has emphasized, "you will never succeed in getting at the truth if you think you know, ahead of time, what the truth ought to be" (BA, p. 194).

And often this search must reach beyond the boundaries of the subject's life. "The danger of writing biography," warns Louis Sheaffer, the most recent biographer of Eugene O'Neill, "is that you may project yourself onto your subject."[1] This statement implies that the biographer may superimpose the truth of his own life upon the facts of his subject's. To avoid this error, every good biographer, before beginning to write, should examine all his reasons for choosing his particular subject. Thus, the biographer is both the analyzer and the analyzed. This shifting of roles does not stop here, however, because biography is necessarily a tripartite affair. Not two, but three lives are involved: the subject's, the biographer's, and the reader's.

Self-analysis is inevitable for any reader of biography who automatically reevaluates his own existence as he evaluates both the life of the subject of the biography and the biographer's treatment of it. But in spite of this apparent interaction among the three, the figure which these participants make is actually linear rather than triangular, since the articulated vision of the biographer always stands firmly between the capturable essence of the subject and the understanding of the reader. A good biography itself belongs solely to the biographer: it is "*his* vision, *his* arrangement, *his* picture" (LB, p. 12). Ultimately, "the critical reader looks at the subject through the biographer's eyes and judges the biography according to the respect which he believes the biographer's vision and insights merit."[2] Virtually every major commentary on biography since 1932 has noted Desmond MacCarthy's dictum that the biographer is "an artist who is on oath."[3] The truth, the whole truth, and nothing but the truth, though, must be limited to the biographer's own particular version of the truth; he should swear, then, to withstand all threats to and assaults upon his artistic integrity.

Thus, the uniqueness of each individual biographer is no less important than the uniqueness of each individual subject of biography. For this reason, the method of no successful biographer, not even of Boswell, as many critics have pointed out, can be copied in its entirety. Certainly, critics, using various criteria to examine the genre as a whole, may group biographies together, noting similarities and naming types; but when a biographer discovers the precisely right reasons for writing the life story of a man and when he does adopt the strikingly appropriate form and fashion, we should celebrate, first of all, his most individual achievement. The particular pattern which he has created is—and should be viewed as—*sui generis*, as original as a fingerprint. And when he has failed in his task, even slightly, he should likewise be informed by the critic.

In this context, then, biography *may* be an art, and the biographer *may* be an artist. But theorists have often disagreed on this point. Paul Murray Kendall writes that "biography is the craft-science-art of the impossible" which "must always be a flawed achievement and the biographer, a man who fails before he begins" (pp. x–xi). As early as 1928, Harold Nicolson predicted that biography as a science, "specialised and technical," might someday overpower biography as literature, as art (p. 154); in the previous year, Virginia Woolf, observing the so-called "New Biography" of her friend Strachey, stated that the biographer "has become an artist" (BA, p. 127). But by 1939, Woolf had shifted her opinion: "And thus we come to the conclusion that [the biographer] is a craftsman, not an artist; and his work is not a work of art, but something betwixt and between."[4] Although Woolf has high praise for biography in other respects, it is her uneasiness about the biographer's mixing of novelistic truth and biographical truth—that same squeamishness which Frank Brady abhors—that seemingly provokes this final judgment. More recently, Leon Edel, while stressing that the bulk of available materials often threatens to overpower the modern biographer, sees no real panacea in the use of scientific methods (notwithstanding Nicolson's prediction). "If you press me," Edel writes, "I will say that much more art than science is involved in the process" of biography.[5]

Ralph Rader's questions about "how works whose primary commitment is distinctly non-literary nevertheless become literature" have given us a good clue concerning how literary biography may be an art. Rader believes that some biographies become "literature" by "transcending while fulfilling the usual purpose of history and biography" (EECB, p. 4). And he writes that Boswell chose to make the subject of his *Life of Johnson* "not the life of Johnson but the *character* of Johnson as revealed in the facts of his life." "Boswell's image of Johnson," he says, "is the selective, constructive, and controlling principle of the *Life*, the omnipresent element which vivifies and is made vivid in the whole. The image is the unity—the real and living unity—of the *Life*" (EECB, pp. 6, 9). There can be no doubt that, in this view of the book, the creator of the most famous biography in English is an artist. Frederick A. Pottle, biographer of Boswell, has reenforced the idea: "A biographer who aims at this kind of unity (that is, who aims at literature) must win and keep control of his book. The view of the subject's character presented must be *his* view, not the subject's."[6] Although the biographer must take into consideration the order which the subject apparently saw within the chaos of his own life, the biographer also has the advantage of being able to discern, perhaps, gradations of order whose existence the subject did not realize.

It should be recognized at this point, however, that if the artist-biographer begins to shift the real focus of his work from the subject to himself, if he pushes out the boundaries of his role as artist to make his book primarily a vehicle for self-expression, then he will produce a work that might serve to illustrate James Clifford's fifth ("fictional") type of biography. Such a book might resemble André Maurois's early *Ariel: The Life of Shelley*.[7] Undoubtedly the existence of such "novelized" lives as this obliges some critics to retain a somewhat narrow conception of the biographer's role. Kendall states flatly that "the biographer must be the servant, and the subject, the master, of the life being simulated . . . . In trying to be more of an artist, he becomes less of a biographer."[8]

The Marchesa Iris Origo, another commentator on the genre, likewise appears to advocate a rather selfless role for the biographer: "The judgment of character still remains the central problem of biography. But insofar as a biographer is also a historian, he should, I think, be very careful not to drown his subject's voice with his own." Finally, however, her ideas seem very close to Pottle's; she continues: "The biographer's true function—the transmission of personality—may also be, within its own pattern, an act of creation, giving shape, in Virginia Woolf's phrase, to a man after his death and endowing him with what is, when we come to think of it, a very odd form of immortality" (Davenport, pp. 374–75, 377).

Thus, as James Flexner suggests, the artist-biographer is a kind of magical "juggler, expert at keeping many bright balls circling in the air. Fact and imagination, sober scholarship and dramatic writing, character study and sound history, a sympathetic understanding of his hero and yet a judicial lack of special pleading, these are a few of the balls that must for ever fly around his head without colliding or dropping to the floor" (BA, pp. 183–84). Overemphasis in his use of either fact or imagination may result in such works as the all-inclusive, often multivolumed monstrosity which Richard Altick calls the "*omnium gatherum*" (p. 372) or the biased, terse, ironic portrait which Lytton Strachey's most vociferous critics accuse him of having produced. Recognition of these two objective-subjective poles begins to permit one to measure the horizonal expanses, if not the depths, of literary biography.

In trying to measure these depths, one must attempt to examine also literary biography's more intricate utilitarian and aesthetic problems, difficulties which may be found among the three interrelated elements of design that I briefly identified in my introductory chapter: problems arising from the biographer's chosen function, those manifested in the results of his search for an appropriate form, and those related to the style with which he has fashioned the presentation of his vision. Problems of purpose, structure, and style—these must be the major interests of the critic who believes that literary biography, as a specifically literary art, is worthy of receiving the same exacting kind of analysis which fiction receives.

Of course, one might first remember that many successful works of fiction have been cast in the form of biography or autobiography. Daniel Defoe comes quickly to mind as an author who has used the method; Swift, Sterne, Dickens, and, in America, Washington Irving and John Barth, are others. In addition, books which have been written expressly as biographies have sometimes been discussed by critics as works of fiction. For instance, Johnson's *Life of Savage* has been referred to by critics as being "in the fictional mode" and was included by Cyril Connolly in his anthology *Great English Short Novels*.[9] Another type of book is simultaneously a work of fiction, a "biography," and a satiric examination of biography. For example, Leon Edel has pointed out that embedded in Virginia Woolf's fantasy, *Orlando: A Biography*, "is a full-fledged theory of biography and that the book seems to be saying a great deal about this art or science or craft. . . . It is a fable—a fable for biographers" (LB, p. 139).

One possible method of defining these major problems of purpose, structure, and style, then, is to examine another such novel-biography-satire, Steven Millhauser's *Edwin Mullhouse: The Life and Death of an American Writer, 1943–1954, by Jeffrey Cartwright,* which appeared in 1972. For this work, too, is a "fable for biographers." It is a beautifully-written piece of fiction, a satire of modern American literary biography which is "balanced on the fine thin line of loving parody"[10]—and ultimately it contains a very serious critical commentary about the genre which it parodies. For, as Aldous Huxley, the master satirist, states it in *Point Counter Point*, "parodies . . . are the most penetrating of criticisms."[11] As a perfectly articulated chronicle of the joys and pains of childhood, *Edwin Mullhouse* is splendid. As a mock biography, the novel reveals to us the problems of literary biography in action. Concomitantly, its author, in the voice of the putative biographer, provides a running series of explanations about and apologies for his art. Conveniently, it is also a humorous, but wonderfully admirable, attempt to incorporate in one volume all three of the types of literary biography which I identified in my introductory chapter. What one of the novel's reviewers writes regarding its evocation of childhood applies equally to its parody: *Edwin Mullhouse* "offers a substantial amount of truth disguised as elegant artifice."[12]

Northrop Frye, in the "Mythos of Winter" section of his *Anatomy of Criticism*, says that "two things . . . are essential to satire; one is wit or humor founded on fantasy or a sense of the grotesque or absurd, the other is an object of attack."[13] The object of Steven Millhauser's clever attack, literary biography, is made absurd because of a matter of degree, first of all. Here we have the method of the writer of the mock-heroic parody, who treats large, traditionally important subjects and techniques in an ironical, trivially serious manner.[14] Millhauser's novel is ostensibly the biography of an American writer, Edwin Mullhouse, who produced his masterpiece, a novel entitled *Cartoons*, at the age of ten and then died mysteriously at exactly the age of eleven. The fictitious biographer, Jeffrey Cartwright, writing at the age of twelve, was a neighbor, classmate, and close friend of Edwin—and apparently the only person who recognized Edwin's rare genius while he was still alive. In the manner of Swift, Millhauser offers a pedantic "Introductory Note" to "this new edition of a major American biography."[15] Its author, we are led to believe, is one Walter Logan White, a scholar who is eminently qualified for his job because he was a sixth-grade classmate of the biographer (although White never really knew him) while Jeffrey was writing his book.

As most reviewers have noted, there is a definite resemblance between *Edwin Mullhouse* and Nabokov's *Pale Fire* (1962); the characters of both White and Jeffrey have affinities with Nabokov's Charles Kinbote, and verbal wit abounds in both books.[16] Certainly subtle, multidirectional satire prevades all aspects of *Edwin Mullhouse*, but it is the explicit statements about biography and the role of the biographer from Jeffrey's pen that are usually the most forceful. For example, in this passage, Jeffrey is comparing the respective tasks of the novelist and the biographer:

> God pity the poor novelist. Standing on his omniscient cliff, with painful ingenuity he must contrive to drop bits of important information into the swift current of his allpowerful plot, where they are swept along like so many popsicle sticks, turning and turning. He dare not delay for one second, not even for one-tenth of a second, for then the busy and impatient reader will yawn and lay aside the book and pick up the nearest newspaper, with all those slender columns that remind you of nothing so much as the sides of cereal boxes. The modest biographer, fortunately, is under no such obligation. Calmly and methodically, in one fell swoop, in a way impossible for the harried novelist who is always trying to do a hundred things at once, he can simply say what he has to say, ticking off each item with his right hand on the successively raised fingers of his left.
> (p. 54)

First, "modest" is hardly the word for this particular biographer, considering what he writes in his "Preface to the First Edition." There Jeffrey expresses his disdain for "those smug adult prefaces" and announces, "Let me say at once that in this instance there are none to thank besides myself" (p. xi). Beyond this, the word "simply" is the key to the whole statement. It is used in much the same way that Virginia Woolf uses "plod"—to tip the reader off about the absurdity of the argument.[17] The most serious thrust of Millhauser's satiric fiction is, in fact, ridicule of modern literary biography for supposing that it is "under no such obligation" to attend to the formal aspects of any well-told, interesting story.

Let us look now at the particular light which *Edwin Mullhouse* sheds on the problems of design in literary biography.

———————— **I** ————————

In his discussion of *Orlando* in *Literary Biography*, Leon Edel says that its "central and gentlest mockery is of time and history" (p. 139). In *Edwin Mullhouse*, this same derision of the limitations of structure occurs, but here the principal mockery is related to the biographer's purposes. At this point, one might say that the critic of biography should not even be interested in matters of purpose; one might suggest that these are problems involving only the biographer previous to and during the process of composition. If one uses "purposes" to mean the biographer's most inchoate motivations, then this objection would be a valid one. However, one may also use the word to apply to the function which the biographer selects for himself and which he usually defines quite explicitly in the text of his book (or, at least, in a preface or afterword). Before imposing his own vision of how the biographer *might* or *should* have written his book, the critic should first accept this chosen function as his *donnée* and then evaluate the finished book in light of his own understanding of it. Without first taking this factor into consideration, the critic is merely imposing his own moral judgment upon the life-writer and his work and, worse, upon the subject of the biography. Both biographer and critic should try at all times to understand, not judge, the subject. (Of course, judgment of the biographer's methods is an unavoidable and necessary operation.)

Certainly there is always the danger that the biographer himself may be standing in judgment of his subject. In recent years, reviewers have complained that such works as Mark Schorer's *Sinclair Lewis: An American Life* and Lawrence Thompson's *Robert Frost* have contained evidence that these biographers hated their subjects (or came to hate them as they came to know them better through their research). Or, on the other extreme, a biographer may make his work "impure" by being too sympathetic.[18]

In *Edwin Mullhouse*, Jeffrey Cartwright's attitude toward his subject is one of clear-eyed admiration, for he is well aware of Edwin's shortcomings. Sounding like a pint-sized version of William Faulkner, Edwin Mullhouse says, "The only thing that doesn't interest me is facts." Then he adds, "Jot that down, Jeffrey" (p. 3), and the pint-sized modern Boswell obeys, for he intends to miss nothing regarding his subject—nothing, from the variegated gurgles of the newborn baby (which are philologically analyzed, for this book also constitutes a theory of language[19]) to the most minute details about the mysterious demise of the novelist. Indeed, Jeffrey, although he was only a few months old himself, was present on the very day on which Edwin was born; and he writes, "Luckily for literary history my senses were immensely alive to the importance of that occasion, that bright August morning" (p. 13). Since Jeffrey has the opportunity to observe and analyze his subject at such close range, the biographer's responsibility for self-analysis is most acute. Hence, the biography also becomes an autobiography of the biographer, who nevertheless makes it perfectly clear that "it is with no desire of thrusting myself forward, but only of presenting the pertinent details . . ., that I must intrude my personal history into these pages" (p. 13).

Because the biographer attempts to be both objective observer and participant, Jeffrey's book is an attempt to make a magnificent fusion of art and life. At one point, Jeffrey suggests that Edwin is an artist who is in need of a "watcher" (p. 24); this companion-biographer fulfills that need. But, unfortunately, there is no one to watch Jeffrey—except, of course, the reader, who learns quickly enough that he also is needed for "watching." For besides expanding his scope to include lengthy descriptions of his own dreams (pp. 93, 171), the biographer here displays his own neuroses in action. For example, Jeffrey is obsessively neat; one of his purposes is to put a meticulous order in all things with which he comes in contact. This fact is most evident in the shape and ornamentation of his book. Thus, when Millhauser divides the book into sections ("The Early Years," "The Middle Years," and "The Late Years"), he is simultaneously satirizing one of the conventions of scholarly literary biography and also giving Jeffrey's personality a perfect means of expression. Within his narration, Jeffrey further reveals his obsessions. At one point, for instance, in describing Edwin's room, Jeffrey writes: "To the right of the window stood the large gray bookcase. . . . To the left of the window, in an imbalance so unendurable that I would have invented a second gray bookcase if I had not known one was coming, stood a blackboard on an easel. . ." (p. 69). But with Jeffrey, obsession is, after all, a virtue; he pauses early in his book for a special reminder to his reader:

> I wonder if I have sufficiently emphasized a major theme of this biography. I refer to Edwin's naturalness, his distinct lack of what is usually called genius. . . . The important thing to remember is that everyone resembles Edwin; his gift was simply the stubbornness of his fancy, his unwillingness to give anything up. . . . For what is genius, I ask you, but the capacity to be obsessed? Every normal child has that capacity; we have all been geniuses, you and I; but sooner or later it is beaten out of us, the glory faded, and by the age of seven most of us are nothing but wretched little adults. So that genius, more accurately, is the retention of the capacity to be obsessed. (pp. 74–75)

Embedded in this statement about his subject, then, is not only the biographer's bold-faced bid for the reader's good graces but also his announcement that he, certainly, has retained his genius.

Nevertheless, Jeffrey is solicitous toward his subject, and he tries always to be objective in considering his materials. After Edwin has finished the awesome task of writing his novel, Jeffrey takes one hundred hours to peck out the manuscript on a typewriter so as to "read a copy free from the distracting personality of a particular handwriting" (p. 268). Of one of Edwin's girl friends, the inspiration for the aborted Rose Dorn sequence of poems, Jeffrey writes, "I never liked Rose Dorn; but I do not wish to temper the strict truthfulness of this biography by painting her one stroke blacker than she was" (p. 176). And the biographer never ceases his crucial questioning. Such scrupulousness (one of Jeffrey's favorite words) should be repaid—and thus Jeffrey is amazed when Edwin exclaims, near the end of his life, "Phew! A biographer is a devil" (p. 274).

Steven Millhauser plays devilish tricks on the reader—and on Jeffrey—throughout *Edwin Mullhouse*. One such trick occurs during a walk which Jeffrey takes with Edwin. Jeffrey seems to record a conception of the inexplicable human personality that resembles the 4 September 1927 entry in Virginia Woolf's diary; he is looking down on Edwin from a cliff:

> Suddenly as I watched I was filled with the sense of his remoteness, it was as if I did not know him at all and had never known him, it was as if he were as impenetrable to my knowledge as the hard tree shading me and pressing into me with its ridges of bark, it was as if, standing there with his back to me, he were as forever unseeable as a transparent negative, which when turned around does not show the other side but the same side reversed; and I wanted to run down to him and again spin him around and make sure he was there. (p. 80)

The irony, of course, comes when Jeffrey goes closer. He finds that he has not been looking at Edwin after all; it is actually another little boy. Likewise, the main plot device in Millhauser's novel is a trick. Besides being a mock biography, the book is also a mystery story of sorts.

Near the end, Edwin, in a playful-somber mood, plans his suicide with a pistol, at almost the exact minute of the eleventh anniversary of his birth. Edwin even composes a suicide note in which he relates, among other profundities, "P. S. Goodbye, life. I aspire to the condition of fiction" (Jeffrey obligingly contributes this sentence—i.e., the biographer believes that the creature in his biography should be presented through those narrative techniques which we most often term "fictional") (pp. 279, 296). But at the last second, when Edwin hesitates with the gun, Jeffrey, who is in attendance, rushes out of control and, gripping the weapon, turns jocularly contemplated suicide into murder—or at least assisted suicide. Millhauser thus satirically extends the old biographical question, "How much should a biographer tell?" to suggest another one regarding the real "life-relationship" that is increasingly more often involved in modern literary biography: "How much should a biographer *do*?" (In these terms, of course, James Boswell, in his role as subject-friend manipulator, qualifies as a most modern biographer.)

Edwin Mullhouse's death was thus viewed as suicide—at least until Jeffrey made his book public. Walter Logan White notes that even while he writes his new preface, "the search for Jeffrey Cartwright continues. I, for one, hope they never find him" (p. viii). But contrary to what Jeffrey maintains, his own actions are hardly unpremeditated; rather, they are merely the carrying through of his purposes as a literary biographer.

When Jeffrey first tells Edwin that he is going to write his biography, the novelist virtually ignores him, saying, "Anyway, how can you write my biography? I'm not dead." Looking back on the remark, Jeffrey remembers: "'You don't have to be dead,' I sneered, though as it turned out I was mistaken" (pp. 269–70). Later, when Edwin finally acknowledges that his future biographer has helped him to see a pattern in his life, to see his life as a biography, "a design with a beginning, middle and end . . . I [Jeffrey] replied that strictly speaking his life could not be considered a design with beginning, middle and end until it had ended" (p. 102). The scene in which Jeffrey "perceived dimly that the design [of his biography] was marred somewhat by Edwin's indefinitely continued existence" (p. 246) has affinities, certainly, with the passage in Richard Ellmann's book of biographical essays, *Golden Codgers*, in which Joyce's biographer notes laconically that "it's always better to wait until the subject of your biography is dead, . . . since it reduces the possibility of authoritative refutation."[20] Finally, Jeffrey writes, "At times, I confess, I found myself thinking of Edwin as recently deceased" (p. 281). And he ultimately goes so far as to refer to "the final month of Edwin's pre-posthumous life" (p. 282)!

II

As humorous as it is, all of this is a fictional, exaggerated indication of part of what a real biographer must think about in choosing his subject and gathering his materials. It is perhaps also a ridiculously epitomized portrait of Every Biographer's secret motivations in setting out to write the life of a modern literary figure. But criticism can only begin to analyze real biographies at the point where their authors divulge their goals in terms of ground to be covered and methods to be used — in other words, where biographers indicate what they think should be the focus of biography.

Even though Jeffrey treats the Great Author who deserves to be famous (he calls Edwin America's "most gifted writer") and attempts to present — with many sensory details[21] — a portrait of the writer as a physical man (or boy, in this case), he also defines his own more ambitious aims at the beginning of his biography: "The true biographer . . ., an artist in his own right, is interested solely in destiny's secret designs. Indeed, I hope these diagrams will lead the reader to reflect upon the nature and meaning of true biography; for it is the purpose of this history to trace not the mere outlines of a life but the inner plan, not the external markings but the secret soul" (p. 22). Here again are the essentials (even some of the identical terms — "outlines," for example) of the Virginia Woolf-Quentin Bell dialogue, except this time the meanings are reversed for satiric effect. But Jeffrey's idea of trying to capture the "secret soul" is also a distinguished and challenging one. In fact, it is the theme that binds together the various parts of *Golden Codgers*.

On his opening page, Ellmann says that he is interested in the "secret or at least tacit life," "the inner life," "the obscure life" of each of his biographical subjects. And basically, Ellmann implies the same question which many other critics and reviewers have asked outright: "How satisfactory can the biography of a writer be if the author is unwilling (or unable) to grapple with the crucial facts of [the artist's] imaginative life?"[22] Edgar Johnson, a biographer of Dickens and a historian of biography, believes that the idea expressed in this question may be used as a major criterion in defining what is "modern" in twentieth-century literary biography. He writes: "The nineteenth century was interested in the man, and it was interested in his work, but it seldom occurred to the biographer to attempt any penetrating analysis of how, in what vital way, they were related to each other."[23]

Actually, Ellmann carries his demands on the literary biographer a bit further: "Ultimately what the biographer seeks to elicit is less the events of a writer's life than the 'mysterious armature,' as Mallarmé called it, which binds the creative work. But writers' lives have their mysterious armature as well. Affection for one leads to interest in the other, the two sentiments tend to join, and the results of affection and interest often illuminate both the fiery clay and the wrought jar" (GC, p. x). And the novelist and critic William Gass sees an even

more integral relationship between the life and the work
than Ellmann's phrase "the results of affection and interest" suggests. In discussing Henry James, Gass writes
that "the lines he put upon paper were the lines he
chose for his face. The history of such a man must
somehow contrive to be the history of his imagination—
what feeds it, what it does with what it gains, how it
embodies itself in its work—since his words were those
servants who did his living for him; and consequently
every sign of significant change in the nature of that
imagination will mark an important moment in the life
of its owner."[24] We could infer here that Gass might
apply this requisite, in varying degree, to all biographies
of creative writers.

Naturally, many dissenters from this view believe,
as does Floyd C. Watkins, that it is the critic's job, not
the biographer's, to attempt "the enormously difficult
task of determining whatever complex relationships may
exist between the author's world and the world of his
fiction," and say that "the way fiction emerges from reality may be an impenetrable mystery unknowable even
in the imagination of the creator."[25] But, as John
Livingston Lowes reminded us long ago in his critical-
biographical study *The Road to Xanadu*, the immediate
ways of the imagination need not always be approached
in such an awestruck manner. Lowes observed that "the
imagination never operates in a vacuum. Its stuff is always fact of some order, somehow experienced; its
product is that fact transmuted."[26] Certainly it would be
too much to expect each biographer of a creative writer
to perform so exhaustive a search as that carried out by
Lowes for what began as a work of criticism of two
poems by Samuel Taylor Coleridge. The mere bulk of
such an undertaking would be staggering, especially to
the reader. However, any biographer is irresponsible
who fails at least to attempt to erect the rigging for the
necessary drilling into the sources of his subject's
imagination—into what Lowes calls the "Well." In his

metaphorical fashion, Lowes states that "there enter into imaginative creation three factors which reciprocally interplay: the Well, and the Vision, and the Will" (p. 395).

Now, as Watkins intimates, the essence of the "Vision" and the "Will" may very well be lost to both the biographer and the critic. But Lowes is correct in insisting that the substance of this "Well" is available to the diligent scholar. And the creative results of the imagination may surely be examined alongside the physical stimuli found in this "Well" in order to try to arrive at a definition of the artistic interaction which has occurred between the two. Both the critic and the biographer might have an interest here: the former because he needs to assess the full accomplishment in the finished work, the latter because he is obliged to consider all available information in constructing his account of a forming personality. In this limited sense, then, Leon Edel is right when he says that "the literary biographer . . . must at every moment of his task be a critic. His is an act of continual and unceasing criticism" (LB, 52).

On the other hand, however, Malcolm Cowley is justified when he hints repeatedly in his reviews of literary biographies that each individual reader should be expected to do most of the work of interpretation, of connecting source with result.[27] Even if this is the case, without an articulate, coherent presentation of the "facts" of both the life and the art, there is, effectively, no biography. Furthermore, in addition to providing the materials for placing emphasis upon the "secret of creation" (that factor which Ellmann and Gass and other biographers and theoricians wish to see firmly stationed near the center of biography's purposes), the biographer must give his reader the sense of coming into contact with a living, breathing, physical person; if we are dealing in concentric circles, this is an outer ring.

The most important thing, then, in literary biography, is that both the artist's life and his work must be dealt with. Somehow, a thorough knowledge of the life must inform a thorough knowledge of the work, and vice-versa. In most cases, it is, after all, the creative work which provides the most legitimate (and potentially profitable) attraction for the literary biographer; and it is perhaps the creative work which should thus provide the starting point for this mutually informing process.[28] If, for example, it is the biographer's chosen purpose to make explicit connections between the life and work, then he might more safely decide, first of all, to use the facts of his subject's life to illuminate the works. The inverse technique—using facts from the work to explain or justify the subject's life—is much more risky.[29]

In *Edwin Mullhouse,* Jeffrey Cartwright relates that he has "sometimes wondered whether all the murderers and criminals in this evil world are nothing but tormented authors, writing their unwritable books in blood. I, for one, can testify that even a modest biographer may be driven to strange devices for the sake of his throbbing book" (p. 257). One of Jeffrey's most "throbbing" problems in his own book seems to concern how to treat *Cartoons* (and, of course, the early short stories and poems: "At least as early as the third grade [Edwin] had a distinct sense of having produced juvenilia" [p. 5]). The manner in which Jeffrey treats both Edwin's life and his work might best be described with Clifford's term "interwoven"; but at one point in the biography, Jeffrey does stop to examine the "major" novel in more detail.

First, he summarizes the novel ("for the sake of those unhappy readers who may not have read it . . . and in order to provide fuel, so to speak, for the fiery remarks that follow"). Next, he gives notice of his critical intentions: "Let others beat against the rich red brick of Edwin's art their heads. There are many things that I might say about his work, but I shall limit myself to a small number of major insights." Finally, he presents his critical theory of "scrupulous distortion" ("the reader . . .

must under no circumstances forget one simple fact: *distortion implies that which is distorted*"). Having perpetrated this pedantic act of criticism, Jeffrey proceeds to connect its implications with the facts of Edwin's life and, more ambitiously, to "the false images that feed our American dreams" (pp. 261–67).

If Jeffrey Cartwright's purpose is to fathom the "secret soul" of his subject, then he must delve deeply not only into Edwin's creative work, but also into Edwin's personality. Although Millhauser's precocious biographer intimates throughout his biography that he is more than capable of analyzing the psychology of his subject with considerable completeness, Jeffrey is very scrupulous in his avoidance of psychological jargon. For example, in his discussion of Edwin's unrequited love for Rose Dorn (pp. 164–71), Jeffrey just gives his readers the facts and explains them "simply" (as he might say). Perhaps Millhauser is satirizing the simplistic psychological assessments that literary biographers have been known to make of their subjects, but at the same time, he is permitting his biographer to practice psychological interpretation in accordance with a kind of moderation which has become respectable in the genre.

Some faint forms of psychologizing by biographers have been considered acceptable for many years. At the end of a short chapter on personality in *The Nature of Biography*, John Garraty seems to summarize the attitude of many commentators on the subject of biography and psychology: "The use of psychological techniques by biographers should result in the reconciliation of many seeming contradictions in their subjects' characters, leading not to simplification, but to understanding."[30] The use of deeper, psychoanalytical techniques, however, has often drawn harsh censure from reviewers and critics. Bernard De Voto, for instance, published his objections in 1933: "The obligation of a biographer is to find facts. When he employs psychoanalysis he cannot arrive at facts but only at 'interpretations,' which is to say theory, which is to say nonsense" (Davenport, pp. 284–85). Recently, though, Richard Altick has been able to make this announcement:

> The truth is that, despite all the excesses and foolishness that marked the flirtation years, the advent of depth psychology momentously expanded the scope and art of biography as a whole; and the union may now be taken as permanent, and healthily fruitful. . . . [I]n literary biography the greatest advance which psychoanalytic concepts made possible was that toward a tighter and more comprehensive bond between the artist and his art. (pp. 342–43)

And Richard Ellmann can now write that "the battle to use Freudian techniques has been won; but victory has not been conclusive because while techniques are needed, these remain . . . difficult to convert for lay purposes" (GC, p. 4).

Perhaps Ellmann is here misstating the problem. Perhaps the crux of the problem still involves the question of whether these "lay purposes" should in fact exist. Ellmann, of course, thinks that they should, but his requirement is that we see "the biographer manipulating psychological theory, not allowing psychological theory to manipulate him" (GC, p. 13). James Clifford approaches the issue more cautiously, finally falling backwards, in a sense, by invoking the example of Dr. Johnson in his *Life of Savage:* "This, I should say, is what a biographer ought to do. Be sensitive to possible psychological quirks of character, and give all of the relevant evidence, but make no attempts at technical analysis."[31]

Leon Edel (with whom Clifford says he is in agreement "on many points") is more confident about the possibilities for the lay biographer's use of depth psychology. Despite the attractiveness of the greater caution of Clifford, Edel's statements, which are themselves seasoned with large amounts of caution, are more persuasive:

> The literary biographer [Edel writes], when he
> borrows the psychoanalyst's code, is obliged to
> decipher it and render it into the language proper
> to literature and literary discussion. . . . Literature
> and psychology are not necessarily antagonistic,
> as they have been made to seem. They meet on
> common ground. . . . [I]n our time, when creative
> writers have been exposed directly to the works of
> Freud and Jung and their disciples and use them
> in their writings, we must treat them for the
> sources that they are. . . . The answer to the mis-
> guided use of psychoanalysis is not to close our
> ears, but to ask ourselves: how are we to handle
> this difficult material while remaining true to our
> own disciplines — and avoid making complete
> fools of ourselves? . . . Critics who babble of the
> Oedipus complex and who plant psychoanalytical
> clichés higgledy-piggledy in their writings do a
> disservice both to literature and to psycho-
> analysis. (LB, pp. 97–98)

Finally, the degree to which a lay literary biographer
should utilize psychoanalytic techniques may vary in
individual cases. The applications to biography which
practicing psychoanalysts may make of their professional knowledge, however, seem more clear-cut. If such
applications are done well, they can be both quite valid
and most valuable.

A model for this type of quasi-biographical work
might be Dr. John Cody's fine study, *After Great Pain:
The Inner Life of Emily Dickinson* (1971). The introduction to this book constitutes a carefully-argued case for
the usefulness of such an examination as Cody's, which
is neither conventional literary criticism nor literary
biography. In addition, it offers some significant guide-
lines which might well be adopted by conventional lay
biographers who attempt to use psychoanalytical tools.
Cody, like Edel, stresses caution, first and last. "It is important," he warns, "that psychoanalytic explorations
not overstep their inherent limits. They cannot explain
talent, much less genius. Psychoanalytic methodology

also cannot establish *concrete* facts. . . . That is the function of the historian. The unique contribution of the psychoanalytic biographer is to generate a deepened insight into personality by making explicit the unconscious emotional connections among events." The reasonable, sensible nature of Cody's whole approach is exemplified in this statement of what is perhaps his major guideline: "The question is what has any of this [a discussion of Emily Dickinson's psychiatric problems] got to do with literature? Can such investigations lead to a greater appreciation of the poems or help define Emily Dickinson's stature as a poet? That is, after all, what really matters."[32]

One important point regarding purpose in literary biography remains to be made. Jeffrey Cartwright begins to articulate it well:

> The fatal flaw of all biography, according to its enemies, is its helpless conformity to the laws of fiction. Each date, each incident, each casual remark contributes to an elaborate plot that slowly and cunningly builds to a foreknown climax: the hero's celebrated deed. All the details of the hero's life are necessarily related to this central image, which suffuses them with a glow of interest they lack by themselves, as firelight enchants the familiar items of a living room; an interest, moreover, that was probably quite different for the hero himself, sporting in his meadow outside the future cage of his biography. (p. 100)

An element of this supposed "flaw" is exemplified by passages in *Edwin Mullhouse.* Jeffrey informs his reader in the paragraph immediately preceding the one quoted above that "as his sixth birthday approached, [Edwin, the Author] was quite unaware that more than half his life was over." But Millhauser uses Jeffrey's voice to exaggerate the point, just as André Maurois overstates it in *Aspects of Biography* when he says, "It is always a mistake, in a biography, to anticipate. 'This great states-

man was born in a small village . . .' No baby is a great
statesman. Every man discovers successively the ages
and aspects of life."[33]

In his *Time, Form, and Style in Boswell's Life of
Johnson*, David Passler writes that "the hero of the *Life*
has a static character. As the episodes and details ac-
cumulate, Boswell holds Johnson up for our view and
slowly rotates him, like a huge cut gem, to display his
many facets."[34] Richard Ellmann likewise points out this
static presentation, and he claims that it is antimodern.
"More than anything else," Ellmann asserts, "we want in
modern biography to see the character forming, its
peculiarities taking shape—but Boswell prefers to give
it to us already formed." Yet Ellmann also predicts that
the best biographies "will offer speculations, conjec-
tures, hypotheses" (GC, pp. 3, 15). These two requirements, however, appear antithetical—unless one other
requisite is granted: that this picture of "the character
forming" must be presented completely as the picture
conceived by the biographer; that it is not, in other
words, shoved upon the reader as a picture that was
supposedly formed from the viewpoint of the subject,
which can never be recaptured. In this sense, then, the
biographer, who must wield complete speculative control of his book, can—indeed, must—validly anticipate.
Only if he loses sight of his own personal vision of the
whole life will his anticipation be detrimental to the
biography. He must, as A. O. J. Cockshut suggests, give
us "a clear view of the actual variety and unexpected-
ness of life, while keeping the main lines of his interpretation unchanging."[35] For certainly the most wonderful
advantage which any biographer, literary or otherwise,
has over his subject is that he is permitted to function as
an interpreter of a life seen not merely in its parts, but in
its entirety.

Thus, perhaps there is, after all, more truth than
fun in Jeffrey Cartwright's dictum that a "life could not
be considered a design with beginning, middle, and end

until it had ended." However, the real biographer's design should primarily consist not of a "sinister scheme," but of a "right form."

III

My Introduction suggests the intricate reciprocal relationships which exist among purpose, structure, and style in biography. Recent critics of the *Life of Johnson* have produced studies that examine some of these relationships in Boswell's book. William R. Siebenschuh, for example, basing his work upon that of Ralph Rader, has shown that Boswell used a technique of "selective dramatization" to shape his book and that he was "a genuinely interpretive biographer"—that "dramatic choices in the development of materials about Johnson's action *mean* interpretation."[36] Form, therefore, not only follows but also "means" function. In his more substantial study, David L. Passler charges that Rader "is guilty of investing Boswell with too much perspicacity and self-conscious literary craftsmanship"; but Passler himself nevertheless demonstrates that the function that Boswell has chosen for himself determines the formal aspects of his biography. Boswell's deliberate "wavering between inclusiveness and commentary," Passler maintains, "is what generates the temporal restlessness and mixture of styles in the work."[37] By searching among the facts of a subject's whole life, the biographer tries to discover thematic patterns in that life; he must then endeavor to translate these themes into the patterns of form[38] in his book. In good literary biography, as in all good literature, formal scheme should somehow mirror theme.

Certainly the question of form involves many factors for the biographer. As Frank Brady reminds us, "the

handling of plot and point of view . . . make up part of
the grander strategy every good biographer must settle
upon in shaping his material." These elements, of
course, are parts of form in fiction also, but the novelist's
approach must differ slightly from the biographer's: "In
loose analogy, the painter can choose his materials
freely, while the sculptor must be more conscious of the
'resistance' of his material."[39]

Obviously, the element of time must be another
important formal consideration for the biographer no
less than for the novelist. Any serious discussion of a
novelist's attitudes toward and uses of time demands
complex critical tools; but, in a sense, any such discussion involving biography becomes perhaps even more
complicated because of this "resistance" of the biographer's "life" materials.[40] The life-writer's respon-
sibilities toward the chronology of actual events create
one level of difficulty in his task; his own need to give
order to his biography surely creates another. Should he
attempt to adhere to straight birth-to-death chronology
in telling his story? Or can he legitimately violate "clock
time" in producing lines of narrative that primarily involve "mind time"? Such questions have caused violent
disagreements among both critics of biography and biographers themselves.[41] No real settlement may ever be
made in these arguments. Possibly the best solution we
may hope for is that each individual biographer will
make a significant effort to match as closely as possible
his own methods of dealing with time with the kinds of
meaning that he finds in his subject's life.

Under the guise of satire, some notable ideas
about form in biography are introduced in Steven Millhauser's novel.[42] Jeffrey Cartwright, biographical
theorist, worries out loud at various points in his biography about the problem of time. Early in the book, for
example, he stops his narrative to declare that

> memory and chronology simply do not make
> good bedfellows. Indeed it sometimes seems to

me that I should abandon the madness of
chronology altogether and simply follow my
whims. . . . And yet, after all, no. My task does not
resemble the making of a jigsaw puzzle. . . . [L]et
chronology be the meter of my biography, memory my rhythm: now matching so closely as to be
barely distinguishable, now tugging against one
another, now drifting so far apart that the reader
begins to frown and tug at his chin, now coming
together with a bang. Where was I? (p. 41)

Later, Jeffrey waxes even more eloquent on the
subject of clock time versus mind time in biography. It is
worthwhile to listen to him at some length:

But again my memory refuses to behave, again my
biography escapes its frame, and I am reminded
of certain pictures in Edwin's beloved comic
books in which a horse's nose protrudes over the
edge into the margin of the page or the hero's toes
come over the bottom of the frame as if he were
about to step into your lap, brandishing his
sword. A curse on chronology! And again: a curse
on chronology! I do not refer to the hyprocrisy of
it all, the stupid wretched pretense that one thing
follows from another thing, as if on Saturday a
man should hang himself because on Friday he
was melancholy, whereas perhaps his melancholy
had nothing to do with his suicide, perhaps he
hanged himself out of sheer exuberance. Nor do I
refer to the vulgar itch to get to the good part, the
desire to leave out everything and plunge at once
into the bloody horrors of Edwin's end. No, I refer
simply to the difficulty of the thing, the im-
possibility of fitting everything into its proper
niche. And if I were to let myself go! If I were to
let the horse step completely out of its frame! (pp.
78–79)

Undoubtedly most readers wish sometimes to find, so to
speak, the horse stepping completely out of its frame;
desire to be given a glimpse into the truth which the
biographer may discern beyond the impediments of

mere factual, chronologically-presented details; want to see applied to biography "the principle which Ford Madox Ford always insisted upon: an event sifted through the crucible of memory and imagination can give a truer *impression* of what happens than the actual facts"—and "this is not so much a matter of lying as dramatizing the truth."[43] Not all modern literary biographers are fortunate enough to have the element of personal "memory" at their disposal, since many of them have never even met their subjects. But "imagination" can be utilized—for form, if not for facts.

Passler has noted in the final sentence of his book that often the "amiable mixture of the general and the concrete [in the *Life of Johnson*] becomes teasingly and unpredictably present in our minds, and it is always disconcerting when books insist this way on spilling over into our lives."[44] We might well use Passler's observation to explain some readers' emotional objections to any mixture of chronology and mind time in biography. But conceivably the final word is said by Millhauser through Jeffrey:

> The false fusions of memory may reveal truths beyond chronology, and the fearless biographer, in his tireless pursuit of the past, must be willing to heed the kind of evidence contradicted by clocks. Which is not to say . . . that memory is merely one form of imagination. The true course of events must always be carefully distinguished from memory's false fusions, lest biography degenerate into fiction. (p. 172)

The "fearless" literary biographer must have other concerns also. In his finished biography, for instance, he must show that he has dealt effectively with matters of style. First of all, his own writing style, like the architectonics which he has chosen to use, should complement or approximate his purposes in writing and, in turn, the meaning that he finds in his subject's life. Style determines the tone of any work, and tone designates the author's attitude toward his work and his reader, and literary biography in general. Second, using his own style, the biographer must examine his subject's lifestyle, a process which he may accomplish, at least in part, through analyzing his subject's *writing* style. As Leon Edel has written in *Literary Biography*,

> there is no poet or prose writer who forges a style and achieves transcendent utterance without stamping his effigy on both sides of every coin he mints. A style, it has been said, is a writer's passport to posterity. This is another way, I suppose, of saying that the style is the man. The biographer can thus argue, with equal validity, that the man is the style. Indeed this is what he is always trying to show. (p. 53)

In this sense, all biographies, not merely the pseudo-biographical *Edwin Mullhouse*, are also autobiographies of their authors. To this degree, also, all biographies take on a doubleness of conception and execution that always makes the biographer and his subject partners within a book, no matter how far they may be separated in time.

The critic of any biography might thus engage himself in numerous practical investigations into the biographer's writing style. For instance, any hypothetical critic of Jeffrey Cartwright's hypothetical biography might be obligated to analyze carefully the prose style in selected passages from the book—fascinating passages such as this one:

> We developed an intimate speechless friendship. Through the mist of years I look back upon that time as upon a green island of silence from which I set forth forever onto a tempestuous sea. In green and blue August we stared at one another through the lacquered bars of his crib. In orange and blue October we rode side by side in our carriages along Benjamin Street; a yellow leaf came down out of the sky onto Edwin's blanket. In white and blue December I gave him a snowball, which he tried to eat. He liked his father to hold

him upside down and blow on his feet. On my
first birthday (February is a gray month) I gave
him a piece of cake; he threw it up in the air,
where I shall leave it. April showers bring May
flowers. Time, as Edwin would never have said,
passed. (p. 16)

Diction, sentence structure and variety, tense, rhythmi-
cal movement of the language, metaphor—these are a
few of the many elements which might generate critical
comments about Jeffrey's style here. Considering what
we already know about the biographer's personality in
this case, such a discussion might be quite entertaining,
if not particularly useful. But similar examinations into
the styles—along with the purposes and forms—chosen
by representative modern American literary biographers
should suggest some illuminating conclusions about the
state of the genre.

IV

To paraphrase James Boswell, Jeffrey Cartwright
in *Edwin Mullhouse* is "strongly impregnated with the
Mullhousian aether." Yet the imagery which Jeffrey con-
jures up in trying to suggest certain aspects of his subject's psychology often creates an impression which is
far from laudatory. Jeffrey writes, for example, "Like so
many creative people, Edwin was not impressive as a
thinker; his brain resembled a murky aquarium, occasionally illuminated by the flickers of a faulty electrical
system" (p. 101). This simile (satirically reminiscent,
perhaps, of some of Boswell's images for Dr. Johnson's
vast mind) is employed by Jeffrey for some swift short-
circuiting of his own. He has always found Edwin's
ideas about biography quite silly; and although he feels
obligated to record them "in the strict interests of bio-

graphical accuracy," he wishes to dispose of them as quickly as possible to save the reader the trouble of working his way through this "typical mixture of subtlety and inanity." But *pace* Jeffrey, Edwin's ideas may finally be worth a brief review.

Jeffrey quotes Edwin's statement exactly: "Biography is so simple. All you do is put in everything." Then, without noticing how the word "simple" gives it a certain kinship with some of his own pronouncements, the biographer continues to tell us that Edwin was one of the aforementioned "enemies" of biography—that he claimed

> that the very notion of biography was hopelessly fictional, since unlike real life, which presents us with question marks, censored passages, blank spaces, rows of asterisks, omitted paragraphs, and numberless sequences of three dots trailing into whiteness, biography provides an illusion of completeness, a vast pattern of details organized by an omniscient biographer whose occasional assertions of ignorance or uncertainty deceive us no more than the polite protestations of a hostess who, during the sixth course of an elaborate feast, assures us that really, it was no trouble at all. And since Edwin claimed that good stories always struck him as true, he found himself in the curious position of believing absolutely in the Mock Turtle and the Mad Hatter but experiencing Lewis Carroll, about whom his father [a college English professor] used to tell affectionate anecdotes, as an implausible invention. (p. 101)

Edwin, of course, is correct in saying that "good stories" are always "true." Unquestionably, they are "true" in biography if they are historically accurate; but in another sense, they are also "true" if they are worthy of our belief because they are well-told, because, for example, their shapes are aesthetically pleasing. Edwin says simply "put in everything," but he (and Jeffrey—and Steven Millhauser) is also calling for more expertise from the biographer. Ironically, as reported by Jeffrey in that final sentence, what Edwin is finally suggesting, I believe, is that biography, since it is already "hopelessly fictional," should endeavor to be more "fictional," that is, should utilize the (so-called) techniques of fiction more effectively to tell "good stories," "true" ones.

Without appearing to know it, Jeffrey, then, is in basic agreement with Edwin. Finally, in a brilliant burst of irony, Jeffrey says:

> It is not worthwhile, therefore, to break our heads over his useless opinions concerning the fictionality of biography. But I take this opportunity to ask Edwin, wherever he is: isn't it true that the biographer performs a function nearly as great as, or precisely as great as, or actually greater by far than the function performed by the artist himself? For the artist creates the work of art, but the biographer, so to speak, creates the artist. Which is to say: without me, would you exist at all, Edwin? (pp. 101–2)

Admittedly, it is stated here in absurd hyperbole, but this idea that the biographer does, in his own way, "create" his subject is a central part of the conception of literary biography to be explored in subsequent sections of this book. Regardless of the type of biography which the literary biographer chooses to write, it is his own point of view, it is his own artistry, ultimately, which "creates" (or more properly, perhaps, "re-creates") the Public Writer, the private man or woman, or the artist who created the literature.

Recently, the novelist Vance Bourjaily, reviewing a biography of a celebrated modern American novelist, concluded that "whatever its faults of movement, tone and focus, it seems very nearly complete and absolutely trustworthy as a record." But, in closing his review, he questioned whether it is "a fair test of biography to feel that one should be able to say: 'The book is interesting, even if you know and care very little about its subject to begin with.'"[45] In my view, it is indeed a fair test if biography is to be considered an art form. Evaluations of "good stories" do not begin with their being certified "absolutely trustworthy as a record." Surely fiction is not needed to make interesting the life of even the most obscure human, but "fictional" techniques are needed. Literary biography should indeed "aspire to the condition of fiction" in its aesthetic design.

chapter two

Monument of the Famous Writer

"We suffer inflation." Thus begins George Steiner in the brief survey of modern literary biography that prefaces his review of the novelist Sybille Bedford's "leviathan" *Aldous Huxley*. Like many reviewers, Steiner desires to register his concern about the large number and the enormous girth of recent biographies of authors, and he does so by posing a question: "Why this plethora?" His answer, though certainly overly simplified, is enlightening. "We inhabit a gossip culture," he maintains, which idolizes our great artists not merely because of their works but also because of the fact that we can so frequently view their private lives and condescend to them in spite of their great creations. We thus ironically explain and reward their "major performance" by scrutinizing their "private indignities." Moreover, we "read *about* more often than we read: reviews rather than books, the critic rather than the poem." Modern literary biographers, Steiner seems to suggest, often cater to this "gossip culture," first of all, by hastening to chronicle our writers almost as quickly as they expire, and, secondly, by embellishing their chronicles with as many intimate details as possible. Even though Steiner apparently believes that literary biographies should ideally bring the reader back to the work, in the particular case of Mrs. Bedford's biography, the spotlight, he says, is exclusively upon the man. And, finally, "the literal dimensions of this book . . . diminish its object.

Largesse betrays. A smaller biography would have left a greater man."[1]

Steiner is correct in his implication that societal pressure may be credited, at least in part, for the shape and texture of modern literary biography in general. Significantly, this theory is mirrored by A. O. J. Cockshut, who views, in *Truth to Life*, most noteworthy nineteenth-century English biographies as intricately related to Victorian England's concern with and/or revolt against Evangelical Protestantism.[2] All modern literary biographies, though, are not exclusively concerned with the man or woman; and the "inflation" in the genre is not caused merely by a "plethora" of details about the subjects' private lives. In fact, unlike Mrs. Bedford, a majority of modern American literary biographers seem to write the type of biography which deals with both the literature and the life—at least superficially. Consequently, their real focus is upon some point between the two. But this point is not often the Artist; rather, it is the Famous Writer, Steiner's observed object of public condescension and idolatry. External details about the creations as well as external details about the creator fill out these huge volumes, which become quite literally monuments of—not to or for—the Famous Writer. The basic building block for these monuments is the historical fact; the mortar, the archival impulse.

Because his attention is so feverishly occupied by historical facts, the literary biographer who makes a Monument of the Famous Writer may very often fail to construct, at the same time, the aesthetic edifice of Edwin Mullhouse's "good story." Regardless of his success or failure in this area, however, the modern American monument-maker usually produces a solid utilitarian foundation of scholarly documentation. Since documentation is generally a matter of great natural concern for such a literary biographer, it might be worthwhile to pause briefly here to ask precisely how useful the methods of documentation are which have been chosen by recent biographers.

Any method of documentation, of course, is unsuitable to the reader who is mainly interested in the story; for him all methods constitute intrusions upon narrative. Ironically, in his rush to achieve an antipedantic modernity and a peculiar kind of economy, the modern American literary biographer has usually exiled his documentation, important as it is, to the back of the volume(s). Those biographers who do at least retain the old system of using footnote numbers—for example, Lawrance Thompson in his three-volume *Robert Frost* (1966, 1970, 1976) and Arthur Mizener in *The Far Side of Paradise: A Biography of F. Scott Fitzgerald* (1951; revised 1965)—remain considerate of readers who wish or demand to be easily informed of sources and invited on peripheral excursions (Thompson's copious notes, in fact, are frequently more interesting than his text).[3] More prevalent, though, are those biographers who conduct, in essence, intricate games with the reader in recording their sources.

For example, Carlos Baker, in *Ernest Hemingway: A Life Story* (1969), requires the reader to make a great flourish of turning pages back and forth, trying to match passages in the text with topic titles and, finally, listed sources in the rear of the book. Part of the problem here appears to have been solved, either through choice or necessity, by John Unterecker in *Voyager: A Life of Hart Crane* (1969). In the opening note to his biography, Unterecker advises that he and his publisher "agreed that the most readable format would be a text free of footnote numbers, the documentation to be published separately." Thus, a person may conveniently read *Voyager* side by side with its companion sourcebook. A major drawback to this method in Unterecker's particular case, however, is the fact that this separate documentation is not sold with the biography: "readers wishing a copy" must, unfortunately, write to the author at his Columbia University address, where they may be told that the supply is severely limited or depleted.[4]

Perhaps the most burdensome system of docu-

mentation in modern literary biography has been
adopted by Joseph Blotner for his *Faulkner: A Biography*
(1974). Here the factual references listed in narrow columns at the back of each of Blotner's two vast volumes
are given numbers which supposedly correspond with
the lines on the pages of the text. Between flipping pages
back and forth—from the notes to the key to abbrevia-
tions used (stationed rather awkwardly at the beginning
of the notes in each volume) to the text itself—and
counting lines, the reader, however patient at the outset,
can easily be driven to academic distraction before he
finally reaches the final page, page 1846.

If all this bother about documentation—including
mention here of its methods—finally seems unbearably
pedantic, it is nevertheless important. It is remarkably
indicative of the purpose chosen by the writer of this
type of literary biography. For here documenation and
the abundant details of the text are necessarily made the
foundation above which all else appears, at times, to be
superficial superstructure. Certainly one must not dis-
miss a healthy respect for the historical fact. Unquestionably, it is wise for writers and critics of biography to
remember the premise regarding all history with which
David Levin begins his defense of "historical literature":
"In formal history the highest literary art is that combination of clear understanding and exposition which
brings us closest to a just evaluation of the past now
present to us. Bad history can be written with grace and
wit, but so long as it is 'bad' its art cannot be consummate."[5] But when biographers too often expect cold historical facts, like the mute stones that make up the
countenance of the pyramids, to furnish, alone, this "just
evaluation"; when they too often relinquish "grace and
wit" in their earnest attempts to ensure that "bad history" is not written—then it is time to look carefully at
their work and register a complaint. If, on the other
hand, biographers can manage to create triumphs, however small, over our culture's natural animosity toward
the mixing of art and life, critics must move with the

same quickness which they use to celebrate fictional successes to recognize biographical accomplishments.

Generally, though, in this type of literary biography, as James Clifford observes about his first type, "few risks are taken." Facts are stated. Seldom do we even find the rudimentary experimentation with form that appears in Jay Martin's *Nathanael West: The Art of His Life* (1970), which begins not with its subject's birth, but with his death. Seldom do we encounter the major imaginative gamble that is itself a significant attempt to grasp a larger kind of truth than facts can usually hope to yield. Sometimes a biographer, almost apologizing as he writes, will venture a timid speculation. Martin, for instance, does so in the very last paragraph of his book, daring to enter West's mind at the instant before the author's death and to record his thoughts. And Mark Schorer, in *Sinclair Lewis: An American Life* (1961) (a typical "definitive" *omnium gatherum*, but one which, extraordinarily, possesses no documentation apparatus), uses a similar technique. He begins his conjectural penultimate chapter in this way: "Thus he was spared the necessity of any final contemplation of his fall. But suppose that, through the next ten days, his whereabouts in effect unknown, he had rested there in full and lucid consciousness — what, then, would he have known?"; he continues with small guide passages like ". . . what could we expect him to see?" and "Dying, would he have wondered, could he have, whether his work would live?"; and he ends, after a dream survey of Lewis's accomplishments, with this question: "Could he have consoled himself with this knowledge, had it been his, and he aware?"[6] But basically, unfortunately, "few risks are taken."

The problems involved in worshipping the historical fact made self-important and the possibilities available through the use of careful "contrivances": these are the chief motifs which I will next explore in my predominantly structural analysis of a specific Monument of the Famous Writer.

I

Ostensibly, Joseph Blotner's *Faulkner: A Biography* is a most representative example of this type of literary biography. It is enormous; it is filled with external facts; it is heavily documented; it appears to be primarily concerned with preserving what might now be called the public records of a Major American Writer. And, like Baker, Schorer, Thompson, and many other modern American literary biographers, Blotner is the "official" chronicler of his subject by virtue of his receiving full cooperation from Faulkner's family in the project. At the same time, however, the biography is more than somewhat unusual among the lives of modern American novelists.

Many of the biographers mentioned in the preceding pages never (or barely) knew their subjects personally; consequently, the very real distances between subjects and biographers in these cases were formidable at the outset. Joseph Blotner did not know William Faulkner via a long and intensive correspondence in the manner in which Lawrance Thompson knew Frost, but Blotner was a close personal friend (indeed, a "spiritual son"[7]) of his subject during the last five years of Faulkner's life. And Blotner—unlike Thomas Wolfe's friend and agent, Elizabeth Nowell, who utilizes the third person in referring to herself in her "official" biography of the author[8]—chooses quite deliberately to use first person narrative in relating at least the events of these five years, thereby making his own autobiography an integral part of the biography of Faulkner. Coming late into his subject's life and showing great enthusiasm for making up lost time, Blotner might be termed the New Boswell—or, to avoid that cliché, at any rate a kind of lesser, real-life Jeffrey Cartwright. Surely to the extent that it is a paean to its subject and his work, Blotner's biography might almost have been the primary model for

Steven Millhauser's loving parody of the whole genre. *Faulkner* is an attempt at supreme objectivity; it is also that most subjective of vehicles, the memoir. The biography's uniqueness lies, perhaps, in its endeavor to reconcile the tension between these opposites.

The reviewers have both damned and praised Blotner's biography. Surveying twelve representative major reviews of *Faulkner* in both popular and scholarly sources, I find four of these highly favorable, four highly unfavorable, and four mixed in their applause for and dissatisfaction with the volumes (although the members of this last group are possibly more favorable than not).[9] Those who praise it the most do so mainly because of their admiration for the quantity of new material which it provides about Faulkner, because of their visions of its possible usefulness to critics, and because of their respect for Blotner's scholarly achievement. Thus Carlos Baker quite predictably christens it "one of the great biographies of the present century" (p. 440). Those who reject it do so not primarily upon the basis of evaluations of what Blotner has provided; rather, their judgments depend most heavily upon what Blotner has *not* provided. Jonathan Yardley in the *New York Times Book Review*, for example, faults Blotner for denying us "what the biographer, because of his intimate relationship with his subject, should be uniquely equipped to offer: analysis, interpretation, speculation" (p. 1).

As the reviewers suggest, *Faulkner*, in its major function as a repository, a sepulcher, for reliable but inert data about the Famous Writer, is certainly a miracle of tireless accumulation. Its authenticated details will undoubtedly be of great use to scholars as "good history." Particular facts may sometimes be difficult to isolate among the multitudes: its simple index—"simple" as compared, say, with the complicated, cross-referenced one in Thompson's *Robert Frost*—is neither complete nor completely reliable. Blotner's two volumes, however, do not constitute a "good biography," a "true" one in aesthetic terms—although in some respects they

possibly come closer to being a "good story" than even
the most sympathetic of Blotner's reviewers have
noticed. Blotner has definitely shirked part of his very
real and personal duty by refusing, in many cases, to
provide responsible interpretation even where it is
necessary to achieve his own chosen design. But we
must in every case examine the biography "as it is" (in
light of what Blotner intended it to be) before we indict
it sweepingly for what it might have been. Finally,
though, both the factual weaknesses and the interpretative, speculative strengths which *Faulkner* does possess
are most evidently displayed in its shape. The form
through which Blotner attempts to re-create a literary
life is often antithetical to the spirit of Faulkner's life as
a man and his work as an artist; but what might be
called Blotner's best-delineated factual tension creates,
nevertheless, the most provocative "interpretative" matrix which begins to nurture his book as a work of art.

II

In future years scholars will undoubtedly come to
question or refute at least some of the data which Blotner
presented in 1974 as historically authentic. Certainly
this is as it should be. However, if one were to accept,
quite categorically, Blotner's research as "true" in the
historical sense, then one would be free to investigate
more fully the manifestations of "truth" in an aesthetic
sense. In the following analysis, I have indeed taken the
authenticity of Blotner's presented materials for granted;
aside from the one reviewer who cites (without furnish-
ing even one example) "a disturbingly high incidence of
errors in copying" of documents (Adams, p. 393), no one
has given me reason at this point to doubt their integrity.
With this assumption, then, I may ask: What artistic
truth may be found in Joseph Blotner's *Faulkner: A*

Biography? Necessarily, the place to begin is Blotner's own stated purposes as a biographer.

"It is private life that makes the greatest biographies," A. O. J. Cockshut contends.[10] Yet, literary biography demands that the dimension of the subject's work somehow be added to this premise. Thus, in the foreword to his book, Blotner states his own solution to the problem: "This is meant to be a biography of William Faulkner's works as well as of their creator; since each element of them was in some sense a product of his total life experience, I have tried to present the life as fully as possible" (p. vii). Just as Blotner mentions first the works and then the life here, so his emphasis seems finally to be more upon the work than the "private life"—but upon the work as "a product of the total life experience." We might say, therefore, that Blotner's intended focus is really upon the *author* of the public's curiosity, the Famous Writer.

Blotner's decision to perform his collecting of personal details "as fully as possible" automatically provided him, as it were, a large form for his book. And this fact, of course, is the source of much of the controversy about it, as with others of its type. While voicing his approval of Blotner's academic endeavors, Floyd C. Watkins raises the question of audience and the book's size: "The large amount of what one might call layman readers of Faulkner will need a different work, more selective and less documented, one, indeed, which Blotner himself might write" (p. 527). Watkins's comment represents that faction of biographical criticism which says, "Get all the facts in a book first; provisions may be made at any later date for cutting and shaping this raw material so that it will be readable." Faced with this approach, of course, one is prompted to inquire whether it might not, in fact, be wise to issue this initial, purposely scholarly book in the form of a log. In the following remark, Robert Craft shows that he takes the opposite attitude toward this aspect of the genre: "The totally documented biography, reconstructed from all the recorded trivia of the daily life, has become one of the most effective means of obliterating its subject's personality. Shortcuts result in slanted views, but may be preferable to unselective and less biased ones, for which, in any case, the future will always have room."[11]

Craft's approach would certainly seem appropriate for a first full-length biography of William Faulkner by a man who knew him extremely well in his last years. For any future scholar could dig up the facts of Faulkner's life; this good friend, though, would possess the valuable (if "biased") knowledge of personal memory which might illuminate Faulkner's personality and his genius. Of course, one would need to guard against making the resulting book merely an excuse for autobiography. Furthermore, the risks involved would require courage and strong artistic self-confidence in the biographer. But it is not my aim at this point to say what Blotner's purpose-created method should have been— especially since this biographer has managed, in many cases before it was too late, to collect the memories of others who were close to Faulkner, as well as recorded facts. Such a service is valuable. With this observation, however, must come an evaluation of how well Blotner has delineated rather than obliterated, within the boundaries of his chosen goals, that basic element which Cockshut terms "the plain lines of interpretation" of personality.[12]

One of Blotner's most enthusiastic reviewers, Terry Heller, calls *Faulkner* "a kind of achievement in humane biography" (p. 355) and seems thoroughly satisfied with the "picture of Faulkner that emerges" from Blotner's details. Here is a key paragraph from Heller's essay:

> In her book on Faulkner's novels Olga Vickery says his fiction is unique in part because while his characterizations are various and full, he preserves the mystery of character "by ordering his material to provide a maximum of concentration, illumination, and implication." These words

> may accurately describe Blotner's presentation of
> Faulkner. He does not know why Faulkner wrote,
> drank, loved to fly, or why he so often chose to
> live quite dangerously. Blotner sometimes specu-
> lates, frequently quotes friends' opinions, but
> rarely asserts. (p. 356)

In the first place, Vickery's words regarding Faulkner do
not apply to Blotner's "presentation of Faulkner" at all.
Aside from the natural "ordering" of chronology, very
little "ordering" has been used in *Faulkner* to show the
man. What David Levin writes concerning our need to
break down one of the "misconceptions" about the criticism of history may be especially appropriate in considering Blotner's reasons for failing to order his
biography. Levin believes that we must overcome "a
surprisingly naive version of what Yvor Winters has
called the fallacy of imitative form." "Many historians
fail to distinguish," he says, "between a book in which
action rises to climax and then subsides, and historical
reality that conforms to such a chart of action. The distinction must be made."[13] *Faulkner*'s length alone does
not make it a weak life-writing. As I shall illustrate,
Blotner has not wielded the necessary intricate control
of his myriad details to present a strong, steady image of
William Faulkner—to give his book, in fact, the needed
form or dramatic organization. William Faulkner was
indeed a very complex man; but if, as one might argue,
Blotner is attempting to mirror that complexity in the
chaos of personal facts which he tosses, according to
clock time, like handfuls of buckshot at his readers, then
he is certainly confusing the art or craft or science of
biography with life itself.

Furthermore, while Heller is right to claim it is
commendable that Blotner "rarely asserts" in trying to
show us the Faulkner that he knew (and even more so,
the Faulkner for whom he searches in the past with the
knowledge of the man he knew), Blotner's speculating
"sometimes" about Faulkner the man in this biography
is not enough. To adapt a statement made by Richard

Todd about yet another new life of Emily Dickinson, "one of the frustrations of reading [*Faulkner*] is the sense that [Blotner] has earned the right to say much more than he has said"[14]—in spite of the size of his biography.

A successful biographer may choose to articulate his vision of his subject in two basic ways: first, he may ostensibly "let the facts speak for themselves" while very carefully juxtaposing these facts in a manner which guides the reader to share his vision; or second, he may use the devices of overt interpretation of presented facts and conjecture to make his point. Joseph Blotner is not a successful biographer of the man William Faulkner because he has actually chosen neither of these methods. In most cases, he has indeed tried to let the facts speak for themselves, but finally the facts as he has served them say very little. He has indeed used interpretation and conjecture "sometimes," but he has not used them often enough to be effective over the expanses of his big book. In short, it is virtually impossible to discern major, imaginative thematic patterns among the private details—beyond such stock motifs as the need for money, the author's reaction to his plight as an author in a materialistic world.

And what of Blotner's desire to write a biography of the works? It is unfortunate that Blotner often feels it necessary to furnish his readers with extended plot summaries of Faulkner's works, although such summaries may be quite worthwhile for the lay reader who will not consult available critical studies (for example, Blotner's summary of *The Sound and the Fury*, pp. 574 ff). But, while Heller's claim that the "summary accounts of Faulkner's composition" are "fascinating" (p. 356) may be somewhat inflated, surely the biographer is more successful in this aspect of his book. Here the order that Blotner manages to create is not merely chronological; Blotner shows the internal continuity in Faulkner's writing by his persistent notice of the abundant connections in theme, character, and technique among Faulkner's works, moving freely backwards and forwards in time. Each work-to-work connection he makes adds to his major statement regarding the organic unity of the *oeuvre*, and this statement both substantiates and adds to the theses of such vintage Faulkner critics as George Marion O'Donnell and Malcolm Cowley. One concentrated example should suffice to demonstrate the constant (perhaps sometimes excessive) comparison technique Blotner utilizes in his composition summaries. In this paragraph he is discussing the forming of *Absalom, Absalom!*:

> All the other major characters were seen in relation to Sutpen. His wife Ellen was acquiescent and—*like* the aviators of *Pylon*—ephemeral as a butterfly. Her mating and breeding cycle completed, she would soon vanish, looking a little *like* Mrs. Compson with "bafflement in the dark uncomprehending eyes." (86) Her two children were growing beyond her. Judith had passed through the state that *suggested* Drusilla Hawk and Tochie Oldham: "the hoyden who could— and did—outrun and outclimb, and ride and fight both with and beside her brother." (67) This relationship, *like* that of "two cadets in a crack regiment" (80), was, "the town knew . . . closer than the traditional loyalty of brother and sister even. . . ." (79) Faulkner had treated this kind of closeness *before*, in "Adolescence" and in *Mosquitoes. Later* it would take on overtones *suggesting* the incestuous feelings Quentin declared in *The Sound and the Fury*. No longer a hoyden, Judith waited for maturity *like* Eula Varner, "parasitic and potent and serene." (67) (p. 897; my italics)

In this way, then, Blotner provides ultimately a fully articulated, unified description of and attitude toward the work—which, after all, he treats as one might treat a person—that he does not furnish for the man.

Thus, Blotner has solved for himself one major

problem of literary biography. "Though I hope this study will provide some critical insights as well as biographical ones," he writes in his foreword, "its main business is not primarily critical in the restricted sense. There are several excellent studies devoted exclusively to criticism. In treating the works I have tried to use a developmental approach" (p. vii). By announcing his abdication from all critical responsibility save that of "linking [each work] to other elements in both the canon and the life," Blotner has utilized Clifford's "interwoven" technique, but with severe limitations. Despite this, however, he does manage to communicate some critical judgments on the works that go beyond tracing their "development." In this passage from his treatment of *A Fable*, for example, the reader is made well aware of Blotner's strong feelings about the work's low value in the canon:

> Starting as a film property, it had undergone an evolution—in Faulkner's terminology—from synopsis to fable to allegory, from poetic analogy to novel. And in the end it had become for Faulkner a massive vehicle for a courageous but costly summary statement of his view of the human condition. In a final irony [besides the obvious irony involving Hollywood's lack of interest in the published novel], which he may have been unwilling to recognize, it had probably had the same effect as the scores of screenplays written in the same place where the novel had originated. It had deprived him of the time and energy that might have gone into more characteristically Faulknerian fiction. There was, of course, one difference between the two situations: he had no alternative to the earlier work as a screenwriter, but it had been only himself who had driven him to complete the struggle to finish *A Fable*. (pp. 1502–3)

Not even the use of the word "courageous" lightens the accusation that Blotner makes in these lines.

Still, even in this particular kind of critical passage, Blotner is also trying to connect the literature and the life. Jonathan Yardley has attacked Blotner's purposes here, pointing out that Faulkner's "fiction is rarely autobiographical, and the mundane facts of his life shed no particular light on it—as often they do in the cases of Hemingway and Fitzgerald and Wolfe" (p. 1). Yardley, of course, fails to stress enough that "autobiographical" in terms of Faulkner's writing must mean not only what the author himself experienced directly and put into his work, but also (and more importantly) what he saw and heard and was told—and, as in the case of Quentin Compson in *The Sound and the Fury* and *Absalom, Absalom!*, what he heard and did *not* heed, what he did *not* know, what he did *not* do. As Blotner himself writes in his pre-defense of the first hundred or so pages of the biography, "I think one can learn not only from what [Faulkner] used but also from what he discarded" (p. vii). Yardley offers as one bit of evidence for his assertion the fact that "Hollywood appears nowhere in his work—with the entirely irrelevant exception that the plot he used for 'A Fable' began as a film idea" (p. 2). In fact, the Hollywood story is actually "autobiographically" important precisely because of the effect which it did *not* have on William Faulkner's fiction, as the Blotner passage quoted above clearly shows. If *A Fable* is indeed Faulkner's "Hollywood novel," the fact that it does in no way deal with Hollywood as subject speaks reams about the solid Faulkner personality itself (as opposed, say, to the Fitzgerald who was both attracted and repulsed enough by his experiences in Hollywood to be driven to reexamine his own world view in Hollywood's physical terms in *The Last Tycoon*). Ironically, then, one of the clearest images in terms of theme we get of Faulkner the man in *Faulkner* is that which sometimes seeps out of Blotner's rather self-conscious "criticism" of the works.

It is in Blotner's interesting account of Faulkner's sojourns in Hollywood, moreover, that the biographer does seem to freeze for one of the few times a moment of "character in action." Blotner relates how Faulkner, on one of his return trips to the movie capital, accepted an invitation to stay once again in the home of his friend A. I. Bezzerides. The biographer remarks upon Faulkner's usually reserved, motionless manner, and adds: "Busy with his own immediate concerns one day, Bezzerides looked up startled to see Faulkner leap from the couch across the room to catch Peter Bezzerides as he toppled from his highchair. This was the kind of energy and passion, Bezzerides thought, from which the stories came." Man in motion: complete action from a totally inert starting position. The exact nature of this starting position fascinates Blotner, who, through Bezzerides, later sees Faulkner sitting, staring into nothingness, exhibiting an "extreme" of the "nature of the obsession to write": "And this was what was hard on Faulkner's family: he wasn't a father or a husband or a companion first, he was a writer. The house could burn down and Bill would write. What it was difficult for wives to understand was this separation of the life and the work" (pp. 1183–84).

In spite of the complicated statement of "interacting" purposes which opens his biography, Joseph Blotner is thus fully and practically aware of this schism and of William Faulkner's own realization of it. Early in the first volume he quotes a letter in which an awed Faulkner expresses his amazement that "the most beautiful short story in the world" could have just been imagined by "that ugly ratty-looking face" that the author examines in the mirror (p. 463). Much later Blotner reveals one of Faulkner's most touching letters to his youthful student/friend/lover Joan Williams, in which the great man says that "now I realize for the first time what an amazing gift I had" and asks, "I wonder if you have ever had that thought about the work and the country man whom you know as Bill Faulkner—what little connection there seems to be between them" (p. 1457). And Blotner reiterates his point near the end of the biography: "[Faulkner] had always had this curious attitude toward his finished work, as though it were something completely outside himself, and he showed it particularly with [*The Reivers*]" (p. 1817). Confronting facts about Faulkner's apparent self-knowledge, Blotner perhaps inevitably aimed to make a monument of his subject. If he could truly penetrate neither the calm of the obsessive artist nor the real source of passion in the "leaping" man, perhaps he felt he had no other choice.

So the connections that Blotner draws between the autobiography and the art are generally quiet ones, studiedly inexplicit. Before William Faulkner has even been born in his biography, we hear of such peripheral figures as Robert B. Shegog (p. 72), G. R. Hightower (p. 82), and later, J. B. Bundren (p. 144), "twins—called Uncle Buck and Uncle Billy" (pp. 176–77), James Kimble Vardaman (p. 129), an idiot named Edwin, "who could be seen playing in fair weather through the high fence" (p. 94), and "one bear in particular, called Old Reel Foot" (p. 177). And we hear the name "Yocanapatafa" breathed in passing (p. 73). But no mention is made of the possible later place of these elements in the literature. The reader makes the acquaintance of a rising young redneck named Lee Russell early in the book (p. 81), but Blotner never draws a direct line from this man to Flem Snopes—although, of course, it is easy for the reader to make this connection with the information given. Young William Faulkner, we are told, once sat with his Uncle John and watched "a string of calico ponies wired together with barbed wire" (p. 341). But Blotner does not specify that the event was the inspiration for a work of literature until almost two hundred pages later when he is discussing *Father Abraham*, where the pony story first found words. Blotner gives the reader a detailed account of what may have been the germ for *Sanctuary* (a girl who was born in a village called Cobbtown tells Faulkner in a nightclub about a sadistic gangster nicknamed "Popeye") on page 492, and he notes that Faulkner "would continue to dwell on the girl's story and its possibilities for fiction"; but he does not link it with the novel until page 604, where he summarizes the composition of *Sanctuary*. Rarely does Blotner make an early overt connection like the obvious one he draws between the real Colonel Falkner and the fictional Colonel Sartoris (p. 50). Sympathetic reviewers of *Faulkner* have praised Blotner for using these "subtle" techniques.[15]

When Faulkner has an experience or is told about one, Blotner, according to his chronological schedule, merely states the facts; when Faulkner reaches the time when he uses (or discards) this material, Blotner usually causes the reader to remember it. And when, sometimes, Faulkner makes immediate use of an incident, Blotner immediately comments. Such is the case in 1931, for example, when Faulkner hears a story told by an acquaintance, Robert Abercrombie Lovett, and then proceeds to write down his own version of it in the story "Turn About." Blotner comments, "The things Faulkner did with Lovett's story indicated his growing craftsmanship," and he uses much detail from the story in demonstrating how Faulkner carried out his announced task of "sublimating the actual into the apocryphal" (pp. 735, 526–27).

But Joseph Blotner's accomplishment of his self-chosen task of directly connecting the biography with the bibliography has actually been lessened by the power of Faulkner's own comments on the subject and the complete elusiveness of what we might call the imaginative negative aspects of Faulkner's operations. In an aside, Blotner notes Faulkner's friend Bob Farley's statement, "The reason why Bill's characters are so real is because they were real" (p. 428). But he records Faulkner's own shrewdly amusing statement about his characters in *Flags in the Dust*: "Created, I say, because they are composed partly from what they were in actual life and partly from what they should have been and were not: thus I improved on God who, dramatic though He be, has no sense, no feeling for, theatre" (p. 532).

Blotner's book would have been even more enormous if he had really attempted to compare the finished literary characters ("what they should have been and were not") with the people discovered in Blotner's historical research ("what they were in actual life"). And even the most diligent Lowes among us would soon despair of trying to find every real little girl in muddy drawers who provided a spark for William Faulkner's genius.

Blotner merely seems content, therefore, to make his book as long as it is by sprinkling in, at every turn, such details as this: "To help with the painting he hired Joe Peacock. (Joe's sister, Dewey Dell Peacock, had been a classmate of Estelle's in grammar school)" (p. 657). "So this is where Faulkner got the first name for Dewey Dell Bundren!" the reader is commanded to exclaim to himself. "So Faulkner rarely even invented names!" he should logically conclude. But the reader must also ask himself if, finally, getting this information is worth the trouble—Blotner's and his own. For learning it tells us no more than finding out that V. K. Suratt (later V. K. Ratliff) was created long before Faulkner knew that a man named Hugh Miller Suratt existed in Lafayette County (p. 1010). Whether he borrowed someone's name or made up a name himself, Faulkner seems always to have believed what John Updike expresses in this declaration: "Once I've coined a name . . . I feel utterly hidden behind the mask, and what I remember and what I imagine become indistinguishable. I feel no obligation to the remembered past; what I create on paper must, and for me does, soar free of whatever the facts were."[16]

Beyond the tenuous relationships which Blotner attempts to draw in his text between the life and the works, there exists his more courageous effort in this area: his placing of snippets from the works at the opening of each of his seventy-six chapters. Again, here is the biographer's statement of purpose: "The epigraphs are meant to underline the way in which elements of the life got into the writing, not necessarily that the events of a particular chapter were transmuted into those particular passages (though this was sometimes the case)" (p. vii). Ostensibly, Blotner is here trying to obtain a kind of deliberate associative continuity which he seldom allows himself in the text. And apparently his source of encouragement may be found in a passage of *Faulkner* which begins with the sentence, "It was habitual with him to see the present against the past," which perhaps explains Blotner's sound rationale for giving us his long, but intriguing, narrative about the Falkner family before William's birth.[17] Blotner continues in this passage to tell about Faulkner's plan, in 1955, for "a collection of his hunting stories": "But they would not simply collect them with some sort of brief introduction; Faulkner would link them together with what he would later call 'interrupted catalysts' . . . [which], taken from other works, . . . fused with the stories as they both provided historical perspective and emphasized the elegiac note" (p. 1522). But these are in fact the real accommodations of Blotner's epigraphs: they suggest larger attempts at "historical perspective" than they finally provide, and "the elegiac note" which they strike is strangely isolating, rather than broadening, in its effect. As Ilse Dusoir Lind observes, the connections of Blotner's epigraphs "heighten the emphasis upon the local, parochial, and immediate as the sources of Faulkner's work. They stress the retrospective, or Proustian aspect. At the same time this emphasis tends to diminish exploration of the life of Faulkner's muse insofar as it was nourished by external sources, intellectual and esthetic" (p. 563).

Lind subsequently excuses this weakness in Blotner's epigraphs because, she says, we cannot really "expect that Mr. Blotner, in his function as biographer, will solve" the "great Faulkner mystery—the means by which his work manages to seem contemporary and universal at the same time that it is backward-looking and local." But Blotner has chosen a most indirect, delicate, timidly suggestive technique for making his strongest, most direct, parachronological connections. And Lind's objection is more important, I think, than she makes it appear. One has only to compare Blotner's use of epigraphs with that of Lawrance Thompson in *Robert Frost* to see where Blotner has fallen short in realizing the opportunities in this device. Thompson's epigraphs give a broader view of the connections between Frost's two worlds simply because the biographer has not taken them only from the poems; and they likewise provide thematic motifs for the biography's text. In truth, Blotner's epigraphs function more as "interruptions" than as "catalysts."

We may thus conclude that Blotner's biography of the works is relatively successful within the scope of his stated purposes, whereas the success of his attempts to discover the sources of that work in the life is severely restrained by the complexities of Faulkner's own writing methods and living modes. It is necessary to examine more closely now the "shape" of Blotner's biography. For within this shape lie not only Blotner's palpable artistic failure in establishing and sustaining the "plain lines of interpretation" of Faulkner's personality, but also his tenuous success (whether by accident or by subtle design) in almost making *Faulkner* a "good story."

III

At the end of the introductory statement of intentions in his biography, Joseph Blotner declares that he believes William Faulkner was "America's greatest writer of prose fiction." And he adds, "The narrative will perhaps reveal more clearly how he seemed to me as a man" (p. viii). Blotner may use the word "perhaps" here because of his modesty as a biographer—or, more likely, he may use it because he senses that he has, in fact, failed to articulate clearly enough his vision of Faulkner as a man. His biography has certainly delivered the new

personal facts about Faulkner that critics had so
patiently awaited since long before Faulkner's death,[18]
but overall it provides very little interpretation of the
man. Consequently, the burden of interpretation is
shifted, rightly or wrongly, to the reader, and the architectonics of the biography do not make this task an
easy one.

In his great life of Carlyle, James Anthony Froude
"succeeds as a biographer because he is firm in his strategy and flexible in his tactics. The main lines of interpretation are never obscured by the rush of facts; but
exceptional and surprising facts are never suppressed or
misrepresented because they might blur the picture's
clear outline."[19] In many respects, Blotner also seems
uninterested in censorship (either for his own purposes
or to spare the subject's family, except in one instance to
be identified later in this chapter). In contrast to Froude,
it is Blotner's tactics which are firm: he piles up the details, minute by minute; his strategy, however, is hardly
discernible. "Any good story can be told in one
sentence, I mean, the line, the why of it," Faulkner once
wrote in a letter (p. 1406). Blotner copies this statement
but does not cope with its meaning in relation to how he
might have applied its sense to his own book. Perhaps
Blotner's greatest fault as a biographer is that he seems
unable to make up his own mind about what is most
significant in the personality of the man he seeks to
portray.

Beyond this apparent indecision, much of Blotner's problem involves his use of time. Blotner quotes
his subject's most pointed comment on time: "I agree
pretty much with Bergson's theory of the fluidity of
time. There is only the present moment, in which I include both the past and the future, and that is eternity.
In my opinion time can be shaped quite a bit by the artist; after all, man is never time's slave" (p. 1441). But
again Blotner does not heed the statement—nor does he
dare to adapt to the art of biography Faulkner's comment
(quoted above) about how, as an artist, he "improved on

God." Blotner clearly fears any creativity in biography. As Michael Holroyd, Strachey's biographer, has written, "Nonfiction is regarded by many critics [and by many biographers as well, he might have added] as noncreative. They confuse invention with creation. . . . This is about as sensible as saying that a portrait or landscape painter must be noncreative, and an abstract painter creative—as if it were the subject that conferred creativity on an artist."[20] So Blotner has rarely attempted to "shape" time. He is, in *Faulkner*, in every sense "time's slave."

The biography is neatly divided into twelve books which bear such titles as "Fiction, Farming, and Films (1935–1942)." This categorization begins to give the work the illusion of a superficial order, but the device is not carried far enough to be of much real value in helping the reader to discover an organic unity in the book. For the titles of the various chapters in these divisions are simply the dates of the events described therein. And while the dates at the top of each page will possibly aid the scholar in locating particular facts, they also serve as constant reminders of the biographer's rigid adherence to the conventions of clock time. These dates help to obscure the reader's own sense of the time—past, present, future—flowing within the life of Blotner's William Faulkner, which is thus fragmented, diffused, isolated within its many contradictory elements in this rather unpatterned re-creation.

Curiously, it is often the patterns which Faulkner himself saw (and in some cases, created deliberately) in his own life that give Blotner's biography much of the small unity it has. Let us look at one example. No doubt the most obvious reason that Blotner's two volumes are divided in exactly the way they are is that, for printing convenience, the publisher has put half of all the pages into the first one and the other half into the second. But this is nevertheless a lucky split. It is particularly appropriate because the primary event which bridges the two volumes forms what Faulkner himself realized was a major intersection in his life: his brother Dean's death in an airplane crash. Early in the biography, Blotner reports that William aided Dean in obtaining an airplane and learning to fly, and he worked closely with him in air shows. At the time of the crash, William was too busy writing to help in a show. As a character in this biography, Faulkner possesses an acute sense of guilt about this occurrence which drives him to take the immediate responsibility for the future care of Dean's widow, Louise, and her expected child. And the novelist consciously makes the carrying out of this responsibility an elaborate ritual in the center of his life. Thus, well into the second volume, when Dean's daughter (also named Dean) is married, Faulkner conducts a kind of rite of completion, and Blotner faithfully acknowledges it. Soon after Dean's Faulkner-financed wedding, Faulkner makes sure that the flowers from the church are put on his brother's grave: "With the flowers he had told his brother he had seen his daughter through childhood and adolescence, through college and her year in Switzerland to graduation, and now from maidenhood to marriage. He had fulfilled the vow he had made almost exactly twenty-three years before by the wreckage of the Waco in the pasture outside Thaxton" (p. 1703). But Faulkner's vivid sense of personal dramatic organization actually carries the ritual further than this—and, for once, Blotner's dogged practice of saving every action until its proper point in time definitely serves him well.

Early in volume one, Blotner spotlights an old Oxford tale about an unfortunate young girl, Judith Shegog, who died during the Civil War while trying to elope with her Yankee lover (p. 138). Later, when Faulkner is settled in his own home, Blotner relates to the reader the stories which the novelist tells his family at Halloween about how Judith Shegog had taken up ghostly residence in Rowan Oak (p. 660). Because Blotner himself lays out Faulkner's story of ghostly noises and appearances at Rowan Oak with such a straight face, the reader is left at this point with the slightest feeling of suspense—

something which Blotner rarely evokes.[21] But finally, late in volume two, Blotner picks up this suspense. When Faulkner is riding to Dean's wedding in 1958 with Dean and Vicki (Estelle's granddaughter), he shocks the girls by abruptly referring to this old tale: "'I made up the story of Judith for your mother and Buddy when we moved into Rowan Oak,' he told Vicki. 'The house needed a ghost.' Just then they reached St. Peter's, and a few minutes later, at four o'clock, he gave the bride away" (p. 1702). It is, of course, Faulkner's own superb dramatic timing that makes this scene an artistic success in the biography. A traditional story from Faulkner's prehistory, Faulkner's personal family Halloween adaptation of it, Dean's spectacular aerial death and funeral, young Dean's wedding—all these ghostly rites and exorcisms become perfectly merged in the demonstrated capacities for "lying" and for carefully carrying out promises within the "present" sweep of Faulkner's personality; and the two volumes of Blotner's biography are thereby momentarily drawn together by a force that is much stronger than the isolating push of clock time.

Perhaps one additional illustration should be made here of how the biographical subject has actually awarded outright to his biographer the most telling motifs for giving the work its real skeletal form and, consequently, for beginning to give the reader a small feeling of what Faulkner was like as a man. In this case, we may be concerned again with Faulkner's talent for "lying"—his talent, in fact, for using his ability to "improve on God" not merely in writing his fiction but also in trying to live his life.[22]

"It is always useful, before considering in detail what a man really was, to consider his myth," writes Cockshut.[23] The comprehensive myth of Faulkner has become so large that to follow adequately Cockshut's suggestion in his case would be an immense task for the biographer. Generally, in his book, Blotner has wisely chosen to deal with merely those parts of the myth which Faulkner seems to have created himself. Blotner's process of identifying and exposing Faulkner's "lies," of course, is part of his own commitment to telling the "facts." And he has been diligent in his crusade. Nevertheless, his presentation of these Faulkner-instigated myths, these un-Faulkners, are themselves usually more interesting to the reader than his diffuse attempts to recite "how it really was." In dramatic terms, the facts are pale beside these sparkling fictions.

Apparently, Blotner has not deliberately intended to stress these myths. Terry Heller observes that "a more practical popular biography could well be built around anecdotes" involving them (p. 355). But it appears that indeed this very scholarly impractical biography before us *has* been built around these fictions. The myths that Faulkner made of himself link together throughout the biography to create its major structural motif system; they give the biography both verbal and psychological coherence. Although the impulse to use these myths biographically may be said to have originated with Faulkner himself, Blotner has been shrewd (or perhaps merely intuitively right) in utilizing what was not to illuminate what was. But further, we must note that this organic motif system is occasionally responsible for elicting some of the few useful questions and interpretations which Blotner offers his reader.

One of the earliest myths which Faulkner creates for himself in Blotner's biography is that of the dandy. Billy Faulkner becomes well-known for his "sartorial splendor" (p. 180); near the end of his life Faulkner loves the dressiness of formal riding attire on and off the meadows of Virginia; in between, of course, he affects the ill-dressed pose of a Mississippi farmer (p. 1415). But his poses are not always so external, and sometimes they extend to his writing. Early in his first volume, Blotner observes the melancholy of Faulkner's youthful poetry and asks, "Was it a pose, or simply a late adolescent malaise from which he would soon recover? Or was it just a fairly common literary posture he had assumed?" And from these questions he proceeds to explore briefly, but in one of his finest speculative passages, the "factors which were forming [Faulkner's] psychological attitudes and responses to life" (pp. 186–88).

Over the long haul of the biography, one reason that our attention is not allowed to wander more than it does is that we wait to view the process which Faulkner, according to Blotner, carries out in discarding old personae and adopting new ones. We see the dandy's feelings of betrayal in love, his apparent death wish, his changing of the spelling of his name—and of his neat uniform—with his entry into the RAF (p. 210); we hear the stories of supposed plane crashes and metal plates in the head (pp. 232, 369, 556); we watch his feigned British mannerisms give way slightly to "the new persona of a bohemian poet" upon his return to civilian life (p. 236); we encounter the university personality of "Count No 'Count" (p. 264). And with Blotner as guide, we are able to observe how Faulkner can sometimes mix several personae. For example, upon Faulkner's visit to New York City and Elizabeth Prall (Sherwood Anderson's later wife), the novelist "had this time combined the elements of more than one persona: the wounded hero, the struggling artist, and the Southerner from the plantation" (p. 325; also pp. 410, 427, 451). Blotner quotes from a Cummings-esque poem that Faulkner wrote during his year in Paris; its last stanza begins with the line, "Or what'll I be today?" (p. 454). He tells about Faulkner's purely fictitious claim to having shot an Oxford doctor after the death of his infant daughter Alabama (pp. 682–83). And the masks and variations proliferate until we reach Blotner's pages which bear the masthead "1932." Here, three years after his *annus mirabilis*, Faulkner can still lie (he claims, for example, that he has never read *Ulysses*), but he also begins a brand new role of The Silent One in relation to his earlier personae (p. 759).

One reason for his silence involves urgent requests from national magazines to print biographical material about him. Finally, in 1946 when Malcolm

Cowley pushes to tell in print of Faulkner's war exploits, "The chickens of his fancy were coming home to roost. The persona of the maimed hero had been one thing when he was an obscure aspirant in New Orleans. Now, with a body of work behind him, it was a different matter; nothing that he did or said or implied should cast a reflection on that work" (pp. 1202–3). And by 1950 Faulkner can write to one of his critics, "'Am proud to have belonged to RAF even obscurely. But had no combat service or wound.'" Blotner adds, "He had not told Cowley this much when he had protested the biographical material for the Viking Portable edition. Even less now did he need or enjoy the fictions which he had propagated twenty-five years before. From now on, William Faulkner would not only refrain from using this particular persona, he would try to eradicate it" (p. 1305). Thus we see that Faulkner's mendacity is again intricately related, finally, to his sense of responsibility; in this case it simply involves his work rather than his family.

But Faulkner still continues to create new myths, and Blotner continues to record them. Faulkner becomes briefly the immensely ingenious actor (p. 1439), and he takes "refuge in a disingenious manner which was part of his most useful and habitual persona" (p. 1402) when meeting "literary" men like Thornton Wilder. In fact, his own affectation of "anti-literary-ness" is articulated best by Faulkner at one point on his trip to Japan in the double role as diplomat-visitor: "I am not a true 'literary' man, being a countryman who simply likes books, not authors nor the establishment of writing and criticising and judging books" (p. 1540). This statement gives flesh to yet other personae, the farmer and the hunter.

Let us look at three of Blotner's passages which are decades and several hundred pages apart:

> Some of his fellow townsmen might think Greenfield Farm was a plaything Faulkner used for posing as a farmer, and it was true that farming, like flying, was an avocation for him. Yet, like flying, it was an avocation which not only

satisfied a deep need but provided experience
which was translated directly into fiction. (p.
1091; "1942")

Though some might scoff when he styled himself a farmer—and this was clearly as much of a
persona as the maimed war hero and the bohemian poet—it was a genuine avocation at which
he periodically worked hard. Like the three
Falkners before him he owned a productive farm,
and he had now worked his longer than any but
the Old Colonel, and much more closely than the
old man had done. . . . [H]e apparently gained
from it not only diversion but a kind of strength.
(p. 1395; "1951")

And what would they think now, could they see
him, those who had called him Count No 'Count?
Some in Charlottesville, aesthetes and intellectu-
als, sneered at his country associations and his
pleasure in the hunt—an affectation unworthy of
a great writer, they said. What they did not realize
was that he had adopted still another persona to
follow those of the wounded war veteran, the
bohemian artist, and the working farmer, and this
one gave him as much satisfaction as any of the
others had. (p. 1772; "1960")

Within this series of statements scattered throughout the
second half of his biography, Blotner has managed to
utilize the persona motif—from young aerial hero to
sage hunter—to unify the entire biography. Further, he
has enhanced the importance which Faulkner himself attached to poses by showing how remarkably close to the
novelist's true personality Faulkner's postures finally
came to be. Passages like these connect volume one to
volume two, persona to personality, and (minimally) life
to work. And, unfortunately, they also demonstrate,
when set in a row as I have placed them here, why
Faulkner has such a fat form. Random repetition can
produce boredom as well as cohesion.

That Blotner has, indeed, sometimes had the good sense to recognize in Faulkner's self-created roles and rituals possibilities for shaping his biography is commendable. Most of the artistic credit here, however, must certainly go to Faulkner himself. Such moments of cohesiveness for which Blotner is exclusively responsible are extremely rare in the book. And, as I have suggested earlier, we must expect more of a biographer simply because he is not limited to the subject's perspective—because he alone should be able to see the whole life. The "counterfeit" Faulkners are vivid with Blotner's handling. We may even begin to convince ourselves that Faulkner's early facility for lying was his *élan vital* (Cousin Sallie Murray Williams remembers, "It got so that when Billy told you something, you never knew if it was the truth or just something he'd made up" [p. 128]). But finally the "real" Faulkner does not come alive over the expanses of the biography for at least two major reasons—one involving Blotner's adamant refusal to "improve on God" by culling and ordering the superabundant facts he found, the other concerning mysterious gaps in the biography's architecture where Blotner has failed, ironically, to present enough facts.

The first type of weakness in form stems directly from the fact that, as Malcolm Cowley states it, Blotner has not used synecdoche: "A part taking the place of the whole. One incident carefully selected then presented in detail, with implications that make it stand for many similar incidents . . ." (p. 1). Blotner has crammed accumulated fact-blocks into his monument, letting them fall where they will in layer after layer, but he has not stopped his labors often or long enough to examine either the need for many of these details or the quality of the cement he is using.[24] It would be possible to compile gigantic catalogs of the passages in *Faulkner* which are prolix and of the points where transitions between passages are weak or nonexistent. By using synecdoche myself, perhaps I can demonstrate Blotner's failure to use it and can identify some of the cracks in his narrative.

On page 547, for example, Blotner ends a paragraph that treats both Faulkner's writing and his golfing with a statement from Tom Clark, the greenskeeper on the Oxford course where Faulkner played; the last sentences of the statement (and of the paragraph) are: "'Time seemed not to mean anything to him. He appeared to live independent of the tyranny of the clock.'" In making his transition to the next paragraph—which begins, "There was a tyranny more oppressive that many of his countrymen would feel that spring of 1927"—the biographer presents us with a good example of what I sometimes call the Fort Worth Principle (First Man: "My grandmother just got run over by a Mack truck in Fort Worth." Second Man: "In *Fort Worth!*"). Blotner chooses to quote Clark's very telling observation fully, but he does not choose to discuss its major idea. Instead, he seizes upon the least important element in its final phrase and then whirls his biographical perspective outward to advance to another application for Clark's fortuitous word "tyranny"—an application which permits him to use the transparent newspaper summary technique that the reader has learned to expect at frequent intervals in the biography. Here is the rest of Blotner's paragraph:

> It began to loom in early April as the waters started to rise after the heavy spring rains. The Mississippi had always overflowed its banks— levees were built, of course, and there was periodic agitation for federal flood control, as when Calhoun, Lincoln, and others had declared something must be done—but the river still rose and sent its waters out over the fields of the Delta. The flood of 1912 had destroyed forty million dollars' worth of property. Five years later the first Federal Flood Control Act became law. In 1922 flooding began in the Mississippi Valley in March and continued into June. Now, in 1927, by April 15 masses of water were sweeping down the river from Cairo to the sea. In four days' time twelve

were dead and 25,000 were homeless. Thousands
of men struggled to shore up the levees at New
Orleans against the sweep of the pounding brown
waves. A week later the flood had spread over
9,000 square miles and typhoid serum was being
rushed in to stem an epidemic. It looked as
though they would have to blow up the levee at
Poydras to save New Orleans, and people were already fleeing the land that would be inundated.
On April 30, at a cost of two million dollars, mud
and water shot skyward with a tremendous roar
as they dynamited the levee. (On the same day, in
New York, William Faulkner's second novel,
Mosquitoes, was published.)

In this passage, Blotner is obviously continuing his efforts to establish an environmental and historical feeling
for Faulkner's South. But why must he do it at such
great length? It scarcely seems worthwhile to be re-
quired to wade through all these details (now mud
rather than even mute, imposing stone?) which Faulkner, timeless on his golf course in northern Mississippi,
hardly seems aware of himself. Earlier in the biography,
when Faulkner has gone to live in New Orleans in 1925,
we have been given a disruptive three-page history of
the city (pp. 386–88); even if the inclusion of that passage can be justified because of the way it places Faulkner within a keenly-realized milieu, we cannot say that
this long paragraph is a necessary continuation of it. Nor
do all these facts seem obligatory for making Blotner's
little parenthetical link between the New Orleans of the
flood and the New Orleans of *Mosquitoes*. The
Mississippi River is timeless—is this idea the real connection between the paragraphs? Actually, Blotner
moves into yet another paragraph and yet another page,
providing twenty-nine more detail-filled lines about a
flood in which the reader may easily drown while trying
desperately to retain a vision of William Faulkner.

Ostensibly, Blotner's favorite device for delineat-
ing character is the anecdote, and he has surely dis-

covered some interesting ones. Unhappily, though, he includes too many anecdotes from those told him by people who knew Faulkner, and very frequently one will be so truncated or directionless (for example, look on p. 336, say, or p. 1805), that the reader can only groan and wait for the next one. Further, Blotner is often not content to give us his better anecdotes just once; for some reason, he insists upon repeating them. For instance, Blotner seems unable to permit the William Faulkner of his biography to make one of his frequent visits to Aubrey Seay's Mansion restaurant in Oxford without repeating once more the story of how the author will not eat unless the juke box is unplugged (see pp. 1220, 1698, 1713, 1724). Faulkner's sassy aphoristic story about how he wrote himself into *Sanctuary* ("I was the corncob") must be given twice (pp. 739, 777). Faulkner's explanation of how he could stand to work in Hollywood (he kept telling himself, "They're gonna pay me Saturday") is likewise related twice (pp. 960, 1265).

When first told, anecdotes such as these certainly dramatize much about Faulkner's personality; but when Blotner repeats them, he begins to blunt their serviceability while enlarging the size of his monument. That Faulkner wrote to Joan Williams, " . . . haven't I been telling you something: that between grief and nothing, I will take grief?" (p. 1431); that the novelist said the same thing to another young woman, Jean Stein, two years later; that "Harry Wilbourne had said the same thing in almost exactly the same way sixteen years before, in *The Wild Palms*" (p. 1520); that Blotner has pointed out all these repetitions—these facts are perhaps noteworthy for what they suggest to us about Faulkner's mingling of art and life, and about how he *used* these young women (albeit tenderly) to fulfill what appears actually to have been a strangely impersonal need within his life. But only once in a great while does notice of such historical repetition really seem effective in Blotner's book.

The second type of structural weakness in *Faulk-*

ner—Blotner's not allowing the reader enough facts—
may best be seen in the treatment of the various women
who were apparently closest to Faulkner in his personal
life. Among these major characters, of course, we may
include Faulkner's women friends, Jean Stein and Joan
Williams (and also Meta Carpenter, although she is
merely mentioned in this biography); his daughter Jill;
and his wife, Estelle.

Virtually all reviewers have noted that we owe
much to Blotner for printing, for the first time, the story
of Faulkner's womanizing—implying, of course, that
knowing this fact will ultimately (even if very indirectly)
add to our knowledge and appreciation of the works;
just exactly *how* useful this information is remains to be
seen.[25] If we consider Jean Stein and Joan Williams
primarily as literary characters in this biography,
though, we must conclude again that Blotner has failed.
For we do not learn enough about either of these two
young women or about their relationships with Faulkner
to satisfy fully either our simple curiosity or our need to
know their real influence on the literary character
William Faulkner.

The sketchier of the two stories, of course, is
Jean's. Her affair (if such it may be called: we never learn
for sure) with Faulkner is given short shrift; we only
start to feel her attraction as a woman. In dramatic terms,
her primary role in the life story appears to involve her
being introduced and waiting when it comes time for
Faulkner to manipulate his *Paris Review* interview (p.
1594). On the same page of the biography where we see
Faulkner pen his real goodbye to Joan (p. 1484), we first
meet Jean. Intermittently, Jean catches our attention up
to page 1628—and then she abruptly drops out of view
permanently, except for a one-sentence reference almost
two hundred pages later (p. 1824), where we are told
that she is now married. Perhaps the shortness and the
intensity of Faulkner's close relationship with Jean are
the very qualities which might make it biographically

important. If so, Blotner spoils his point by neglecting to signal the end of the affair.

While Blotner gives us more facts about the Joan Williams–William Faulkner affair, he handles those facts very uneasily from the beginning. But within Blotner's own discreetness, luckily, seems to be buried a sense of tension which begins to approximate that in the love relationship itself (e.g., pp. 1313, 1373–74). Only near the end of this affair—after the point in clock time when Blotner would normally have given us this information—does the biographer become explicit: "His ardor had finally made them lovers, and though only briefly, it had been enough to add hope to desire in him while it evoked all Joan's impulses for disengagement and flight" (p. 1431). Certainly the most damaging gap in the Joan section of the biography is that which Blotner creates by not quoting from any of the letters Joan wrote to her famous lover.[26] Blotner interviewed Joan extensively many years after she wrote the letters, and he summarizes some of them; but basically the biography is dramatically one-sided in this respect—and this fact supports my contention that the focus of Blotner's work is not the man, certainly not the artist, but the Famous Author. Within his own framework, then, Blotner has cheated that gossip culture which he has perhaps compromised himself to serve.

Faulkner's own sometimes cruel treatment of Jill (at one point he reminds her, "Nobody remembers Shakespeare's children" [p. 1204]) hardly seems to justify the small amount of space she is allotted here as the daughter of the man Faulkner, not as the daughter of Faulkner the Famous Writer. Yet, in spite of this slight, Blotner does manage, within some of his few anecdotes about Jill, to suggest a depth of character in the child, and, concomitantly, in the parent. The reader is most impressed by the strong protective impulse in Faulkner for his daughter (he insists upon having an Easter egg hunt for her when she is fourteen) and the equally strong urge in Jill to achieve "mediocrity" ("she went to the dime store and came home with cheap pink rayon underwear in preference to wearing the edged and embroidered things in her drawer" [p. 1228]). And Blotner, apparently with the surety which repeated interviews with Jill have given him, even allows himself at one point the luxury of adopting an almost impressionistic mode of expression in reconstructing Jill's memories of childhood (pp. 1065–66). Therefore, one must conclude that Blotner begins to draw Jill satisfactorily—in spite of his standard operating procedures.

But one of the greatest weaknesses in the biography involves the blank spaces which Blotner leaves in his portrait of Estelle Faulkner. Because the reader never adequately comes to know the wife, he likewise can never hope to know well the husband via Joseph Blotner's vision of him. "Tell the truth and shame the devil!" This is the command that Estelle gave to Blotner when he began to research his biography.[27] Seemingly, Blotner has indeed been extraordinarily frank in exposing all details, both favorable and unfavorable, directly about Faulkner himself; one cannot in good conscience accuse him of censorship in this respect. Yet one also cannot help but feel that Blotner has not fully carried out Estelle's instructions to "tell the truth." He has not failed to give us the bare facts about the marriage relationship, but he has not tried hard enough to tell us what they mean. In creating the art of *Absalom, Absalom!*—the story and its method of getting told—Faulkner "sees that the essence of *what* happened is often *why*."[28] Blotner has not been able to see that this idea stands just as true in writing biographies as in writing novels. Finally, from reading *Faulkner*, one gets the impression that Blotner has sacrificed a very definite personal theory about the basic nature of the William–Estelle relationship to—what? Good taste? His artistry suffers.

The psychological truth that resides in any whole character in a good work of literature is missing in

Blotner's Estelle simply because of a lack of facts. If Blotner has quoted none of Joan's letters, he has quoted or summarized very few of Estelle's. When he does use an excerpt, it is extremely illuminating of the relationship, but in its isolation it mainly serves to arouse the reader's curiosity. The first letter by Estelle which is quoted, for example, appears late, in the 1943 section. Blotner tells us that "there was often discord in their correspondence, some of it arising from financial matters and some from other causes. . . . One of her own anxieties would become persistent" (p. 1148); and then he reproduces a few select lines of Estelle's letter of 4 August to her husband in Hollywood:

> "Your letter sounded so cheerful that it made us all feel good. I've a notion that Mr. Hawks must have his old secretary back and that once again you're finding California worth while—Don't misunderstand this, and write back that I begrudge you pleasure—I truly do not . . . Suppose I've lived so long now with the knowledge that it has become a familiar and doesn't frighten me as it did."

What "knowledge," exactly? About Faulkner's womanizing? Blotner's ellipsis intrigues the reader who wants to know more about the personality of the very human woman who can pen this subtle exclamation of hurt and resignation.

In addition, the reader may be somewhat mystified by Estelle's reference to the "old secretary" of "Mr. Hawks." In fact, her name was Meta Carpenter, and she was, according to her memoirs, *A Loving Gentleman* (published two years after Blotner's biography), indeed a very close friend of Faulkner: she was his Hollywood mistress. Although Blotner does mention this woman very briefly—and confusingly—in eight other passages in his text and twice in his notes (sometimes using her married names, Doherty and Rebner; e.g., pp. 776 and

1130), he never even attempts to make her a character in his biography. One may wonder silently whether Blotner really knew about this liaison. (Meta Carpenter writes in her book, under a photograph which includes Faulkner and herself, "In a 1975 [sic] biography of Faulkner, I am identified in the same picture as—was it one of Estelle's little jokes?—someone named Mrs. Ernest Pascal."[29]) But undoubtedly these confusing references serve mainly to tease us into asking why this biographer has not, in this case also, pursued his facts more diligently (see especially p. 947).

The reader learns very little about Estelle's psychological make-up. She is a pretty cardboard woman, moving from the affluent security of her Oxford family into an arranged marriage to a man she does not love who carries her to the Orient; returning with her two children; divorcing; finally marrying Faulkner, helping him make his home, bearing his two children. And, consequently, the reader does not really learn enough about an important part of Faulkner's own personality. Does Faulkner's obsession with privacy (e.g., pp. 102, 1261, 1276) extend, damagingly, into his relations with Estelle? Blotner gives us the minimal facts about Estelle's attempt at suicide by drowning during the summer after her wedding to Faulkner—and makes utterly no comment about its significance in her husband's life and work. Astoundingly, he merely tells us that "in a few days she was better" (p. 630). At a later point, Blotner describes a scene in which Estelle becomes enraged at her husband and, from the window of their car, scatters the manuscript pages of *Light in August* over the Mississippi countryside (p. 765). Why? Blotner never tells us—nor does he seem to care why.

It is this general indifference, I believe, that makes him pass over one element that, if utilized properly, could have provided another strong motif for giving his biography better form. I refer to the obscure hurt that Faulkner must have felt when the young Estelle followed her family's bidding in marrying Cornell Franklin instead of Faulkner. At that early point in the biography, Blotner remarks, "It was a deeply traumatic experience for him. As his brother later put it, 'his world went to pieces.' Mixed with his feeling of loss was a reaction of bitterness toward Estelle" (p. 195). If this loss was so "traumatic" for Faulkner, must not this "bitterness" have permeated their later life together? Does it begin to explain Estelle's suicide attempt? To see how Blotner has failed to carry through with the obvious lines of interpretation he has set up, we have only to compare another biographer's use of a similar situation in an artist's life for providing structure for his book. Lawrance Thompson sounds a major chord in *Robert Frost* when he writes at the beginning of his second volume, "Grimly continuing his courtship until he overcame Elinor White's reluctance, [Frost] carried into their marriage the conviction that his beloved must be punished for having hurt him so dreadfully."[30] Do the differences in the novelist's personality prevent him from later demanding the penance which the poet expected from his wife? (And further, of course, one might ask: Do essential differences between the genres novel and poetry define the varying ways in which such tensions get into the artist's work?)

At one point, Blotner apparently does try to explain the tension in the Faulkner marriage (pp. 939–40). This brief passage immediately follows his telling about an ad which Faulkner places in a local paper disavowing any responsibility for Estelle's debts. But as good as it is, this explanation does not satisfy the reader because at no place in it does the biographer tell us one fact about Estelle's own personal, human reaction to her husband's ad.

Regarding matters of writing and drinking, might Estelle have potentially been Faulkner's Zelda? Blotner, of course, does not pose this question either. He does tell us much about Faulkner's drinking—and very little

about Estelle's. Although he relates in his text the fact
that Estelle wrote, with Faulkner's encouragement, a
novel, *White Beeches*, Blotner forces us to refer to a note
to learn that she burnt it after one rejection notice (see p.
541 and notes, p. 79). Was it another fit of overwhelming
rage, was it a strong sense of her own weak identity or
talent, or was it a powerful devotion to her husband and
his genius that forced her to this act? A much greater
regard for the conflict between such a potentially explo-
sive character as Estelle and his protagonist might have
given Blotner much material for shaping his book. As it
stands, not even the few "confrontations" between Estelle and Joan in the visible psyche of Faulkner (e.g., pp.
1326–27) carry much force as emotional templates for
the biography.

Perhaps one can excuse the weaknesses in psychological perception and in drama here, but finally one
cannot excuse Blotner's shoddy literal handling of the
woman whom Faulkner chose to be his wife. Even if one
argues that Estelle is, after all, not really the central subject of the biography, I still suggest that she deserves a
better fate—and I think the putative authors of *Orlando*
and *Edwin Mullhouse* would agree. Late in the biography, while Faulkner is playing diplomat in Venezuela,
Estelle is seen at the University of Mississippi Medical
Center in Jackson, about to have one of her kidneys re-
moved (p. 1782). Blotner almost has her placed on the
operating table—and then he leaves her suspended, not
mentioning her again until five pages and over a month
later, where, mysteriously, the reader finds her coming
off the road with her husband, arriving back in Charlottesville! Multiplied as they are, such non sequitur
movements help not only to warp the major shape of this
monument, but also to chip its surface with hieroglyphic
lines that, ironically, most closely resemble some of
those celebrated illustrations in *Tristram Shandy*.

IV

In the last book of *Faulkner*, "A New Life," Blotner becomes one of his own major characters. And here he defines for the reader his closeness to his central subject. We even hear Faulkner himself call Blotner his "spiritual son." Blotner tells us at one point that he was "garrulous" around Faulkner (p. 1171)—and he demonstrates this trait in print through his abundant anecdotes about their friendship: no minor fact or anecdote seems, in Blotner's scheme, too small to discard.[31] For example, in this biography Blotner is close to Faulkner because the great man will tag along to a track meet which Blotner is judging and make sophomoric remarks (p. 1656); Blotner is close to Faulkner because Faulkner can be talked into going to an amateur play in which Blotner's wife is acting (p. 1664). And so on. Describing a day-long trip with "The Chief" (as Blotner calls Faulkner), the biographer can sigh, "As we drove home that night I reflected that Mr. Faulkner and I had spent a total of fifteen hours in each other's company that day between dawn and darkness, and neither of us seemed the worse for it" (p. 1672).

Blotner even helps with Faulkner's writing: he provides a personal war story which Faulkner adapts for a section of *The Mansion* (p. 1711), and he concocts a "counterfeit Faulkner" speech for his mentor to revise slightly and use (p. 1820). In this last instance, Blotner not only reveals his true friendship with Faulkner, but also shows that he, in contrast to those many friends who betrayed Faulkner for money in the past, is virtually a saint. When Faulkner returns a copy of the speech to its original author, the novelist remarks, "Maybe you can make some money out of it sometime." Blotner's miraculously reported reply (in a book that will, perhaps, make him some money) is "Oh, no, I had not thought of that. It was only to help out a friend." In *Faulkner*, then, the biographer in a sense has become his own hagiographer.

Yet, as I have indicated, the uniqueness of this literary biography arises primarily from Blotner's bold attempt to reconcile memoir with objective report. Ilse Dusoir Lind (who suggests that "three observably different biographical modes can actually be found within [*Faulkner*]: the memoir, the official biography, and the modern scientific biography") believes that Blotner has succeeded:

> By including himself towards the last as one of the characters in the story of Faulkner, Mr. Blotner modestly defines the meaning of objectivity in his work to be what a single academic scholar, searching for truth by gathering verifiable evidence, can assemble and order. Reading the biography with this understanding enables us to appreciate his data. The ponderousness of the work is ponderousness with a purpose, and the pedantry which is the less appealing side of its scholarly-academic method proves—in the final analysis—to be a trifling annoyance. (pp. 562–63)

Perhaps Lind is right. But if so, is this definition of objectivity the only reason for Blotner's irritating "I" in "A New Life?" For in literary terms, his inclusion of himself as a major character cannot be justified. "Mr. Blotner" is really no character at all; we learn that he is good and "garrulous" (though we see that his garrulity seldom extends to analysis)—but we are not given here the one big element on which "good books" thrive: tension—in this case, any real conflict between him and the protagonist of the book.[32] Though, like Boswell, Blotner is very near and dear to his subject, unlike Boswell, he does not possess the eighteenth-century biographer's strength of character or his desire to create (or re-create) "natural" drama. Before examining other ramifications of this ostensible weakness, I must pose another question in response to Lind's *apologia pro* Blotner: Is not what Lind terms "the spirit in which Mr. Blotner has gathered his data" in fact antagonistic to the spirit of William Faulkner and his work?

". . . I dont care much for facts, am not much interested in them, you cant stand a fact up, you've got to prop it up, and when you move to one side a little and look at it from that angle, it's not thick enough to cast a shadow in that direction" (p. 1205). This is "The Chief" talking. Blotner has heard the statement well enough to repeat it as one of the facts in his biography, but, strangely, he has not really understood its meaning. And over and over in his book Blotner demonstrates his basic insensitivity to this significant Faulkner attitude. In discussing how to resolve the problems regarding factual changes in his Snopes trilogy as it evolved over the many years of its composition, Faulkner writes: "What I am trying to say is, the essential truth of these people and their doings, is the thing; the facts are not too important. If we know the discrepancy, maybe, if to change the present to fit the past injures the present, we will not come right out and state the contravention, we will try to, you might say, de-clutch the past somehow" (p. 1721). Blotner responds to the comment, totally disregarding the idea of the importance of "essential truth": "this would not be much help to a reader wondering which account of an event was the *correct* one."[33]

At various points in *Faulkner*, Blotner does in fact seem to be approaching a consideration of Faulkner's polarities, but he always retreats to his fact finding. He explains, for example, that Faulkner agreed with Ellen Glasgow's statement about "the relation between historical and fictional truth" (p. 711), but he does not tell us what Glasgow said. He remarks twice that Faulkner and Robert Penn Warren once talked about "the distinction between the fact of a thing and the truth of a thing" (p. 1426), but he does not repeat or summarize their conclusions. And Blotner himself creates still more terms with which to identify the dichotomy. Describing Faulkner's class sessions at the University of Virginia, he notes that "though a class was often hearing invention rather than fact, he would still tell a great deal that was objectively rather than just poetically true" (p. 1644). But the reader is assured by his manner that Blotner himself has no patience with "poetic truth" in literary biography.[34]

This is not to suggest that Blotner should have deliberately created "lies" in quite the same way Faulkner himself did in both fiction and life. However, Blotner's relentless quest for facts has perhaps kept him from finding important truths which, had they been carefully expressed, would not have detracted from the historical, utilitarian authenticity of his book and might have added immeasurably to its aesthetic value. This relates directly, of course, to Blotner's ultimate failure to provide enough responsible conjecture—even when sometimes he himself leads the reader to its brink. A typical instance occurs when Blotner is telling about Faulkner's practice of giving erroneous accounts of the composition of *Sanctuary*. Blotner writes, "A complicated psychological process evidently lay behind the early formulation and consistent repetition of these answers. . . . What kind of truth, then, even if it was symbolic rather than literal, resided in those curiously persistent and self-condemnatory answers?" (p. 605; for similar examples, see pp. 570, 978). He takes it no further. He does not even attempt to answer his own good question. On a very few random occasions, of course, Blotner does explain or speculate at some length; the best of such passages involve Faulkner's hatred of television, his "recklessness," his desire to write for the stage, and his love of alcohol.[35] But it is unfortunate that Blotner has not used these passages more systematically in presenting either a good "static" character like Boswell's Johnson or a "developing" character of the sort that Ellmann demands from the modern literary biographer.

In an interview published several months after the appearance of his biography, Blotner complained that one of the major problems he faced in his work involved "the fallibility of human recall." "People, with all the good will in the world," he said, "will attempt to reconstruct the past for you. But it's difficult." His duty, he maintained, was to stress "verifiable facts as opposed to recall." And he also spoke of how he rejected for his own purposes "a method which gives an overview of life as if rendered by God with no doubts and the motivation perfectly clear and the sequence of events absolutely straightforwardly laid out."[36] Ultimately, these statements must be viewed as rather ironic. For if Blotner, because of his close friendship with Faulkner, is most suited to gather the facts for us, he is, by the same logic, most qualified to bring us a more intelligent, well-founded, and—yes—God-like interpretation.

Recently, Marshall Waingrow has spotlighted and examined Dr. Johnson's "argument in *defence* of conjecture":

> ". . . by conjecture only can one man judge of another's motives or sentiments." Motives and sentiments, in contradistinction to facts, are what must make up the "colouring," the "philosophy" of ["real authentick"] history [Waingrow refers to Johnson's comment in the *Life*, 18 April 1775]; and despite the risks in searching for them, the alternative is to default entirely. "If a man could say nothing against [or for] a character but what he can prove, history [and biography as well] could not be written; for a great deal is known of men of which proof cannot be brought."

Waingrow concludes that Johnson's "thesis about conjecture may *not* be an overstatement, but rather a true statement subject to various applications":

> That is, one may only be able to judge another man's motives or sentiments by conjecture, but the better one knows the man the more likely the conjecture is to be right. . . . The biographer must ultimately ask himself, what motivates people to act as they do, and he will answer himself by

examining his own mind. However exceptional
his subject may be, he will be understood only
against a background of general human nature.[37]

After reading Faulkner's own remarks about facts versus
truth (as, thankfully, some of them are reported by his
biographer), we must say that the novelist was at least
familiar with the spirit of Dr. Johnson's theory. Joseph
Blotner apparently is not.

As I have suggested, the I-Joseph Blotner who is
the narrative voice of the last two hundred pages of this
biography is a weak character as we see him moving
within the story he is telling directly about William
Faulkner. Remarkably, however, in another way the
author reveals himself as very strong-willed indeed. This
involves his handling of Phil Stone, the final major character in the biography.

Viewed as a literary character, Phil Stone himself
is marvelous and mysterious. The sustained tension that
we should have been able to perceive more readily in the
Faulkner-Estelle relationship is virtually tangible in that
between Faulkner and Stone—in part because we are
given more detailed information about this second relationship. Phil Stone, then, is really the one major character close to Faulkner whose actions and statements
may be observed at frequent intervals throughout most
of the biography. Stone grows up just ahead of Faulkner,
and he is present at the novelist's funeral; Stone is
Faulkner's earliest literary mentor and his final financial
problem. The displayed vicissitudes of what might be
called their love-hate relationship provide *Faulkner* with
an intriguing gestalt. But this tension-created configuration becomes even more intriguing when the figure of
Blotner as biographer is added to those of Faulkner and
Stone as characters.

In his 1940 section, Blotner discusses the financial
sacrifice (cashing a life insurance policy) which Faulkner makes to aid Phil Stone in his mortgage difficulties.
Here the biographer notes, "The vectors of the Stone-

Faulkner relationship, having begun a turn some time before, were now fully reversed" (p. 1020). Although this point is not the center of William Faulkner's physical, chronological life, it is near the middle of *Faulkner*, and, more importantly, it occurs at the very center of Faulkner's creative life. It is, in fact, the heart of the matrix which forms a sturdy (if rather baroque) "X" in the center portion of this biography. As the line of Stone's influence upon the novelist has fallen, that of Faulkner's position of authority over Stone has risen—and so the relationship continues for the rest of Faulkner's life, and for the remainder of *Faulkner*. As far as the reader knows, Stone never repays his loan, and Faulkner grows less and less interested in the sometimes "curious" critical comments of his erstwhile friend (see p. 1181). Even though Stone subsequently makes "poignant" remarks about Faulkner's winning the Nobel prize (p. 1344) and Faulkner makes fruitless social visits to Stone's office, the lines of the relationship move always further apart. And Blotner utilizes the first-person singular to move swiftly into the resulting chasm between the two in "A New Life."[38]

Of course, if the widely separated lines of this central "X" move on one side into this later section of the biography (within which Blotner is a character), they also move on the other side into the earliest section (where, strangely, Blotner seems most comfortable as a biographer). In these opening pages of *Faulkner*, for example, we find the native Falkners casually contrasted to the "New Man" Stones, who have migrated to Mississippi from other, more northern, more cosmopolitan states (p. 162). Local boy Faulkner needs to be led to the world, and the descendant of these Stones is the one for the job. Although Blotner is caught, inert as a character, within his final two-hundred-page memoir, ironically, his overwhelming (and, in terms of the juxtaposition he uses, interpretative) control as a biographer is felt throughout his first hundred or so pages. In his writing about the prehistory of Faulkner, Blotner can perhaps most legitimately exercise his passion for facts. For in any attempt to reconstruct the more distant past, the expectations of the reader for conjecture may naturally be lessened, while the good impression or flourish made by presentation of laboriously-discovered facts — in old family documents, books, newspapers, and so forth — may be heightened. And one other point about this opening section is significant: here Blotner does not need to struggle with anyone for the "possession" of William Faulkner.

Blotner is certainly not like the would-be literary biographer in a story by Joyce Carol Oates who becomes emotionally involved with the widow of his potential subject;[39] but evidence in the later sections of *Faulkner* does suggest that Blotner has experienced strong feelings of jealousy — or, at least, fierce competition — toward his subject's *early* best friend. And finally it is the labyrinthine turns which this tension causes in the biography that obscure the more explicit, neater "X" matrix which I have described. It is part of Blotner's job to state the facts about both the lights and the shadows of Phil Stone's connections with Faulkner, and he has done it well. Too well, perhaps, in terms of the shadows. For some of the facts about Stone which Blotner includes also constitute a kind of revenge and, simultaneously, of course, a perhaps unintentional glorification of Blotner's own role as *later* best friend to the Famous Writer.

But possibly this feeling of competition is only natural. After all, both Stone and Blotner are "creators" of William Faulkner. Blotner gives us a clue to his own feeling of ownership in the title of his last book. Apparently the reader is supposed to infer that, at least in part, it was Blotner who gave Faulkner this "new life," for this section coincides exactly with the five years when Blotner was Faulkner's friend. If this suggestion of "design" is reading too much into Blotner's motives, we can say at the very least that this biography is his deliberate attempt to re-create Faulkner. Blotner leaves few doubts about Stone's attitude toward Faulkner. He quotes

Stone's early statement, "This poet is my personal property" (p. 373), and adds, "Doubtless he meant to strike a jocular note, but the words suggested a very real and deep proprietary feeling." Earlier, Blotner describes in detail the literary education which Stone said he gave Faulkner—and, predictably, Blotner minimizes Stone's influence, ridiculing especially Stone's supposed lessons in punctuation (pp. 169–70). Like Blotner, Stone is a biographer of Faulkner—like Blotner, a biographer of sorts. Blotner almost gleefully reports the failure of Stone's abortive biographical effort (which, generally unlike *Faulkner*, moved by "mixing praise and blame"), and generously dismisses it in this sentence: "The pupil had outstripped the teacher, and though the teacher had loyally predicted his success, he could not always recognize it when it came, nor could he concede that his friend's aesthetic judgments could be superior, finally, to his own" (pp. 840–41).

When Blotner is in the process of establishing his own credentials as Faulkner's friend, he may eagerly equate what he experiences with "the kind of friendship Phil Stone" knew with Faulkner (p. 1752), but most often the later biographer sets up a negative view of Stone and his relations with Faulkner. When Stone is first introduced, for instance, Blotner seems to protest too much by stating twice within four sentences that "Stone was a complicated person" (p. 162). Stone is compared to "Mr. Compson" because of the manner in which "he had been selling off parcel after parcel of the Stone land" to pay his debts, and Blotner makes Stone's sale of early Faulkner manuscripts in his possession seem positively disgraceful (p. 1720).

The one term which Blotner applies, almost like a Homeric epithet, to Stone throughout the last third of the biography is, oddly, one that he applies to himself: Stone is "more garrulous than ever" (p. 1285), "more garrulous now than ever" (p. 1335), like Gavin Stevens in his "garrulity" (p. 1612); with Blotner in Faulkner's funeral procession (both men serve as pallbearers—but

Blotner seems to take special pride in the fact that his own hand is the last to release the casket), Stone continues "his habitual garrulousness," "chattered incessantly," "chattered on" (p. 1844). In his first volume, Blotner tags Stone as "a talker and observer rather than a doer" (p. 903). Perhaps this is Blotner's most unkind cut of all, for the reader, presented with the statement, is obliged to connect it with Faulkner's own statements— both in his fiction, through Addie Bundren, for example, and in his conversation and correspondence (see pp. 521, 1743)—about his distrust of language and the curse of the human voice. The final sound of Stone's droning voice in the stillness of Faulkner's burial is perhaps enough to damn him forever in the reader's mind. By comparison, "garrulous" Blotner seems as silent, and wise, as his subject. Finally, though, maybe both Stone and Blotner are indeed real-life equivalents, in their Faulkner dealings, with the fictional Gavin Stevens—a character that the subject of this biography obviously loved, however mistaken or quixotic Stevens may be.

Beyond this, Blotner possesses numerous other kinds of artillery. Under the pretense of connecting literature with life at one point in the notes, for example, he explains needlessly that it was Stone who once admitted that he had a favorite whore named Everbe Corinthia (notes, p. 214). In a bitter comment, Blotner informs us that, seriously, "there was probably some part of Stone's psyche that did wish [Faulkner] had not won the [Nobel prize]" (p. 1736). Through his remarks upon interviews with Stone's wife, Emily Whitehurst Stone, Blotner makes Stone seem a liar second only to Faulkner himself (notes, p. 43). And he takes uncharacteristic care to include Emily's extraneous personal statements about her husband's "psychic realities," which hardly seem appropriate or useful in a biography of someone else. "'Phil Stone was burned out,' she said. 'His life was over when I married him, but I didn't know it'" (p. 903). Is this detail included to explain Faulkner's great patience with Stone? If so, how would Faulkner himself have known about it, or others like it? One must conclude that such facts are present in *Faulkner* purely for the strange manner in which they help to discredit Stone as a human being—and as a kind of competitor for Blotner. The situation begins to turn somewhat absurd when a biographer who religiously avoids much psychological analysis of his major subject pauses to ask questions about a lesser character's Freudian slips—as Blotner does in this passage regarding an early letter Stone writes to a publishing company: "' . . . and I shall probably have to handle most of the business matters connected with [Faulkner's] part of the publication of this check.' (He had actually dictated—or his secretary had typed—'check' for 'book.' Was it an insignificant error, or some sort of slip?)" (p. 358).

Finally, can the conflict between Blotner and Stone for the "possession" of Faulkner be seen implicitly in the fact that Stone is curiously absent from the documentation of *Faulkner*? Although Stone's writings are credited, there are no references to interviews that Blotner might have had with the man. Was Stone dead by the time Blotner decided to attempt the biography? If so, were Blotner's earlier, "garrulous" conversations (at the funeral, for instance) not "authenticated" enough to be of use? The reader is not told the answers to these questions, nor is any acknowledgment made of Stone's help in any capacity.

But the tensions which the reader may discern between Stone and Faulkner—and, consequently, between Stone and Blotner—make this Mississippi lawyer the real "stone" in a Monument of the Famous Writer. It is the structure which Stone provides that begins to make *Faulkner* most intriguing as a work in itself. Even if Blotner has failed in making a "true" biography, he has succeeded (perhaps by lucky compulsion) in giving his work a provocative embryonic design—both in terms of its shape and texture and in terms of his own attitude toward his materials.

_____V_____

If recognition of individuality—in each subject, in each biographer, in each life story—is most important in the criticism of biography, then it may seem grossly unfair for me to place certain modern American literary biographies in the category "Monument of the Famous Writer"; and, further, to propose that a close examination of one biography from this group, Blotner's *Faulkner*, is sufficient for a consideration of all of them. Yet, within the spatial confines of this study, the preceding observations about *Faulkner* may indeed suggest many of the strengths, possibilities, and weaknesses within what I have identified as a particular type of literary biography. Finally, after all analysis, in all monuments, as in *Faulkner*, this fact remains: the "pure" fact remains supreme. And all is not ripeness; much, as Steiner complains, is inflation.

At the end of *Voyager*, John Unterecker offers his reader an eloquent apology for the weaknesses of his biography of Hart Crane. His statement might serve as a kind of explanation for the ultimate failure of all literary biographies, but especially for those of this type:

> Even if we locate his last letter, even if we wring the memories of all living acquaintances until they are dry, can we hope to discover the "true" Hart Crane? I think not. For the truth of Hart Carne—the truth of any man—lies neither in the events of his life nor in the memories of his friends nor even in his art, if he happens to be—as Hart Crane was—a great artist. Truth is so subtle that it hovers in the flicker of an eyelash, so swiftly changing that it is transformed while a breath of air whispers through the lungs.[40]

chapter three

Portrait of the Author as a Man or Woman

In 1974, John Leonard, writing in the year's-end edition of his *New York Times Book Review,* summed up the past year as "a good, but not a great, year for literary biography"; listed some notable volumes (including Sybille Bedford's *Aldous Huxley*); and then made this striking statement: " . . . the writers writing about the writers often seemed better than the writers being written about."[1] Although Leonard's phrasing is catchy and his view of the implicit competition between biographer and subject is quite valid, one cannot, unhappily perhaps, apply his evaluation to literary biography in general. For, in fact, few modern literary biographers seem to recognize the need for "style" as well as "content" in their work.

Another *Times* writer, Hilton Kramer, in a more recent issue, echoes Lytton Strachey almost sixty years after the *Eminent Victorians* preface and reminds us that neither general readers nor critics appear to be disturbed:

> The art, or at least the enterprise, of literary biography—the writing of the lives of writers—flourishes so prodigiously these days that it comes as something of a surprise to realize how little critical attention is normally paid to this particular form. Indeed, we tend not to think of it as a form at all. The usual thing is to devour biographies for their content, and to complain . . . only when

> their shapelessness or prolixity actively inhibits
> easy access to the content. . . . It is the subject of a
> biography that commands attention, not the art or
> craft or thought that has gone into the writing of
> it. . . . As a subject for criticism—which is to say,
> for thought—literary biography remains a largely
> unexplored territory.[2]

Further, Kramer shows his great concern about those
literary biographies, such as Quentin Bell's *Virginia
Woolf*, which fail to cope with what I have called the
special demand of the genre: "the fact is, a literary biography can never be complete without an account of the
subject's writings."[3]

Even more recently in the *New York Times*,
Richard Locke, noting that "biographies of writers show
up in great quantity on lists of the best books of the year
and tend to appear on the cover of the *Book Review* with
more frequency than any other genre," has called for a
more vigorous interaction between biography and criticism—"a balance between anecdote and analysis . . . between explication, judgment, history and moral argument."[4] But by supplying not only critics (Harold Bloom
and Richard Poirier, for example) but also biographers
(Ellmann, Edel, Walter Jackson Bate in his newest capacity as author of *Samuel Johnson*) as exemplars of this
interaction, Locke seems to make the unsatisfactory suggestion that we need not distinguish between these
genres at all.

Of course, many years ago Virginia Woolf showed
the true complexity of the critic vs. biographer debate by
considering, in addition, the common reader's response.
Certainly her bias regarding biography was evident
when in her delightful, but sometimes rather precious,
essay "How Should One Read a Book?" she observed
that "facts are a very inferior form of fiction" and
suggested that we should "enjoy . . . the purer truth of
fiction."[5] But within the brief comments about biography
which this essay contains, Woolf does ask some important questions. When we read autobiographies and biog-

raphies of authors, she says, "sometimes we may pull out a play or a poem that they have written and see whether it reads differently in the presence of the author." Then she muses: "How far . . . is a book influenced by its writer's life—how far is it safe to let the man interpret the writer? How far shall we resist or give way to the sympathies and antipathies that the man himself rouses in us—so sensitive are words, so receptive of the character of the author?" For Woolf, then, a primary function of literary biography may be to send the reader back to the subject's art; and in going back to that art, each reader should ideally become his own critic: "These are questions that press upon us when we read lives and letters, and we must answer them for ourselves, for nothing can be more fatal than to be guided by the preferences of others in a matter so personal."[6]

This element of possible danger which bothers Woolf in examining persuasive information about an author's life alongside his or her works could conceivably disturb the contemporary reader even more. For the media constantly make available to us materials that put us "in the presence of the author."

Many of these materials are visual. For instance, the success of such recent author-specialist photographers as Jill Krementz, Nancy Crampton, and Thomas Victor attests to the reading audience's desire to capture personal images of both popular and esoteric writers. The "critical" impact of such still images cannot be overestimated—but the addition of motion must certainly establish an even greater influence. James Dickey defines this influence well when he describes how he

> happened to see an old, grainy film print, about fifteen seconds long, of F. Scott Fitzgerald and Hemingway sitting and talking at a table in the South of France. Of course, there was no sound to it, but there they were. I couldn't have been more amazed if it had been Chaucer, or Ben Jonson and Shakespeare at the Mermaid Tavern. And I realized that it's a great thing to be able to have a

video tape and make a visual presentation of
writers reading from their works. My God, suppose we had something like that of Keats reading
the "Ode to a Nightingale"? Wouldn't that be
stupendous? You'd crawl on your knees a
hundred miles to see that if you were really interested in Keats—and who isn't?[7]

Public relations manipulators have learned, of course, to
take full advantage of such hunger, such enthusiasm, by
adding the "sound to it" on "The Today Show," "The
Tonight Show," "The Dick Cavett Show"—and every
other interview program, large or small, within television's ubiquitous range. As supercilious as most of these
television programs prove to be, we cannot really dis-
miss their ultimate connection to the literature from
which they are generated.

After many years of fighting such a conclusion,
Wilfrid Sheed, novelist and critic, admits that "gossip is
the very stuff of literature, the *materia prima* of which
both books and their authors are made. . . . Literature is
the one subject in the world one cannot be priggish
about." Sheed's comments appear in his introduction to
*Writers at Work: The Paris Review Interviews, Fourth
Series*, which, he maintains, constitutes "sixteen . . . self
portraits of the artist of a kind scholars are lucky to piece
together, much less satisfactorily, from diaries and letters." He gives evidence of his own enthusiasm for such
image-making: "Speaking for my frivolous self, I would
trade half of 'Childe Harold' for such an interview with
Byron and all of 'Adam Bede' for the same with George
Eliot."[8]

Although Sheed dismisses autobiography because
of its "rambling form" and says that most writer interviews are "not art at all, but a sort of cultural packag-
ing," he pleads a special case for the *Paris Review*
pieces, suggesting that several of them "may even rank
among their subjects' finer recent work."[9] But even in
these works (which balance somewhere between biog-

raphy and autobiography, apparently), a consideration of both the life and the work of the subjects is always involved. Such a dual involvement is inevitably precluded in the type of literary biography with which this chapter is concerned—precluded by virtue of the self-stated function of the biographer.

A second type of literary biographer is primarily interested in re-creating his subject in the role of private human being. To such a biographer, the fact that his subject was an author is of decidedly minor consequence, even though the subject's role as author may have first attracted his attention. Naturally, this type of biographer shares many interests and methods with the type discussed in the preceding chapter. But here the finished work is characteristically smaller, more intimate in both size and scope. Because of the biographer's chosen purpose, then, this second category of literary biography is not the monument of a writer, famous or otherwise; it attempts, rather, to be the portrait of a man or woman. At its extremes, it may be an intimate, yet static record of the physical person, or it may be a dynamic study of personality. In every case, however, this type of biographer's work is best when it pulls these extremes together, when its creator does not fail to recall Henry James's dictum that "action is character." And, of course, such a biographer's greatest challenge is not contained within the often painstaking search for historical facts. More readily, it is present in the always difficult struggle with language.

Thus, the portrait type is fundamentally inadequate from its inception, since its writer refuses to combine the role of critic with his primary role of biographer. Any small success which he does achieve must be engendered in his own art: in the shape which he finds in and makes of his materials and (even more significantly in this type, perhaps) in the way he shows his own sensitivity to how "sensitive are words."

While even the summarizing of the external details of a man's life requires a definite skill with the writ-

ten word, the adequate drawing of character demands a
style. This chapter, then, will examine "style" and its
significance in specific examples of this particular kind
of modern American literary biography. First, however,
there follows a brief discussion of the truth of style and
design.

————————— **I** —————————

In his journal entry of 28 February 1841, Henry
David Thoreau wrote, "Nothing goes by luck in composition. It allows of no tricks. The best you can write will
be the best you are. Every sentence is the result of a long
probation. The author's character is read from title-page
to end."[10] This is still another way to say that "style is
the man," and it is perhaps fortunate that few reputable
literary biographers attempt to make specific, literal applications of this theory—that is, attempt to locate a
particular author's personality solely in his prose style.
Critics such as William Gass expect biographers to
posit the whole significance of a writer in the language
he uses. Therefore, in his review of Blotner's biography,
Gass pens these stylish sentences: "Faulkner's life was
nothing until it found its way into Faulkner's language.
Faulkner's language was largely unintrigued by Faulkner's life."[11] Gass's is, of course, a very provocative approach to literary biography; it is not, however, always
the most suitable approach. On rare occasions, the design which such a method creates may seem to be not
only aesthetically pleasing and psychologically apt, but
also quite practical (although not necessarily in the
sense of useful). Take, for example, Caroline Spurgeon's
portrait of Shakespeare, which is drawn via an analysis
of the author's images, since few other historical, con-

crete materials are extant.[12] But with most authors, such an approach is dangerous.[13]

It is most unfortunate, however, that modern biographers in general seem so naïve regarding the possibilities for deliberately using their own prose styles for re-creating the personalities or physical styles of their subjects. David Levin relates how he had

> often wondered how much thought modern historians give to the question of what methods they might use to make the printed word reveal a character. At a panel discussion on biography before a group of graduate students in history a few years ago, every historian present denied awareness of having learned anything about the techniques of portraying character from twentieth-century writers of fiction, and each one introduced his denial with a disclaimer emphasizing the difference between fictitious character and biographical character.[14]

Surely, few modern American biographers may be termed "stylists"—even in the broadest sense of that word. Ostensibly, this is a matter of choice: perhaps, we may conjecture, they are not stylists because they do not want to call attention to their own artifice. Their main concern is with the informational value of their work; and thus, they satisfy their largest audience, which discerns the truth of "content" (what René Wellek and Austin Warren call "materials"—"aesthetically indifferent elements"[15]) but not that of "form," "style," or "design."

But, in specifically literary biography, there may be another reason involved. Because the literary biographer is forced to work in the very same medium in which his subject has achieved his success, there is from the outset a natural element of competition at work. "The writers writing about the writers," to use John Leonard's phrase, are necessarily testing lives, both their subjects' and their own, through language.

For numerous reasons, therefore, the biographer's

purpose must be to find the right style—one which will
do him credit in his competition with his subject and,
simultaneously, one which is truly appropriate in treating his subject. Or, to quote part of Leon Edel's pronouncement in the first issue of the new "interdisciplinary quarterly" *Biography*, "Biography is not art when it
. . . sets the jewelled words of a great style in the prosaic
utterances of the *fonctionnaire*. This is like setting
diamonds in brass."[16] Other theorists might argue, of
course, that biographers would, indeed, show good taste
in choosing a "brass" style. But such good taste would
approach that which so many critics, and biographers
themselves, invoke when they fear to use the so-called
"fictional" techniques advocated by Levin—and by Steven Millhauser in *Edwin Mullhouse*.[17]

Weaknesses in even a "diamond" style, while ob-
servable in all types within the genre, may be particularly noticeable in the portrait type, where space is often
more limited than in other types—whether the "portrait" involves full-length physicality or personality vi-
gnette. The smaller size draws the critical reader's attention away from the analysis of structure and around
to an analysis of style.

The world has survived myriad attempts to define
"style." According to these definitions, considerations in
the study of style (or, to the extent that it serves the purposes of literature, "stylistics") may begin with a "thorough grounding in general linguistics"[18] and branch
outward in many directions. Thus, recently, George T.
Wright could proclaim that "style is poetry,"[19] and Huntington Brown could begin a volume of definition with
this sentence: "That which we take to be characteristic
in a work of art or class of works, we call its style."[20] In
his discussion of Boswell's *Johnson*, David L. Passler
"maintain[s] that *prose* style is a characteristic pattern of
choices in diction and syntax."[21] And Richard Poirier extends the scope of such a definition in *A World Elsewhere: The Place of Style in American Literature*: "As it
is used in this book," he advises, "the word style refers

to grammar, syntax, and tropes only by way of defining some more significant aspect of style: the sounds, identities, and presences shaped by these technical aspects of expression."[22]

So my own use of the term "style" in reference to literary biography covers the range of possible definitions. At points it deals in linguistic considerations on the level of, say, the biographer's sentence structure and variety, or his use of certain recurring images; but, more broadly, "style" also refers to the biographer's attitudes toward his subject and his reader—as these attitudes are manifested in the tool which is at his disposal: language.

Nicholas Phillipson, writing in a special *Times Literary Supplement* issue on biography, asserts:

> The treatment of personality remains essentially intuitive. In fine biographies . . . the particular adventures of the heroes are set out systematically and are closely documented. But the feeling we get for the working of their personalities develops by implication as the story unfolds. They are knights who travel through life with their visors raised. But their faces are still shaded by the armour they wear.[23]

This "implication" is thus suggested in these attitudes or (to follow I. A. Richards's example in using that most elusive of literary terms) tone. Finally, "effective style-study must lie somewhere between . . . hard-line linguistics and subjective criticism."[24]

Hence, "Style" is almost as difficult to define as "The Truth," even with all our "subjective criticism." But perhaps we should at least consider Northrop Frye's definition of "stylist" in his comments on Gibbon in *The Well-Tempered Critic:*

> Gibbon is writing not direct prose but consciously rhetorical prose; or, as we say, he is a "stylist." The stylizing of his sentences indicates a more self-conscious bid for literary fame. He expects to be read for entertainment, in the genuine sense, as

well as instruction, and he expects this quality to
keep him alive after his work as a historian has
been superseded.[25]

Of course, by this definition (the phrase "consciously
rhetorical prose" notwithstanding), virtually all fiction
writers could be termed stylists. The rubric could be
applied to such ostensibly diverse American writers, for
example, as F. Scott Fitzgerald and Theodore Dreiser—
no matter that Fitzgerald's desire to "entertain" and his
bid for literary immortality are presented mainly in his
phrase-making ability and Dreiser's in his talent for
providing "action."

In fact, Frye's distinctions between stylist and
nonstylist are most useful, it would seem, in discussing
nonfiction writers. He does, after all, contrast Gibbon
with Charles Darwin in his example—not two fiction
writers. Frye identifies a "meditative quality" in Gibbon's prose:

> . . . a quality of wisdom and insight rather than
> merely of learning, and one which may range in
> the mood of its expression from solemnity to
> irony. This meditative quality manifests itself in
> prose sentences with a distinctive roll in them
> which is unmistakably metrical. If we stop a
> sentence of Darwin's in the middle, we feel
> chiefly that certain words are needed to complete
> the sense; if we stop a sentence of Gibbon's in the
> middle, we feel that there is also a rhythmical
> space to be filled up, as we should if we inter-
> rupted the reading of verse.[26]

Yet this "distinctive roll" is definitely not found in many
modern American literary biographies, and its absence is
the *first* most obvious weakness in such recent works as
Virginia Carr's *The Lonely Hunter: A Biography of Carson McCullers* and Matthew Bruccoli's *The O'Hara Concern: A Biography of John O'Hara.*[27]

Biographers seem to fear "consciously rhetorical
prose" as much as modern fiction writers seem to revel

in it. To state this idea in another way—and to apply a term coined by Tony Tanner in his *City of Words*—the work of modern literary biographers is seldom "foregrounded": that is, they seldom "use . . . language in such a way that it draws attention to itself—often by its originality." Tanner explains that "obviously the term is of widespread applicability in discussing literature. One could say that some writing . . . seems to have a minimum of foreground, the language inviting no lingering at the surface but directing us instantly back to its referents"[28]—directing us instantly back, naturally, to "meaning."

Indeed, biographies must have meaning, we are told. And when applied in a study of literary biography, the controversial critic Susan Sontag's rallying cry takes on a much more precise meaning of its own. "What haunts all contemporary use of the notion of style is the putative opposition between form and content," Sontag maintains. Further, she asks, "How is one to exorcise the feeling that 'style,' which functions like the notion of form, subverts content?" Sontag rightly sees that

> the ambivalence toward style is . . . rooted in . . . a passion . . . of an entire culture . . . to protect and defend values traditionally conceived of as lying "outside" art, namely, truth and morality, but which remain in perpetual danger of being compromised by art. Behind the ambivalence toward style is, ultimately, the historic Western confusion about the relation between art and morality, the esthetic and the ethical.[29]

Similarly, before turning to analyses of Andrew Turnbull's *Scott Fitzgerald* and W. A. Swanberg's *Dreiser*, I must ask: How is one to exorcise the feeling of both biographers and critics that style, or any part of "design," constitutes a "design" against the historical, factual integrity of a literary biography?

Admittedly, this is a most difficult question to answer—doubly and ironically so in light of my investigation, which concludes that both Turnbull and Swanberg, in the biographies which I have chosen as representative of their type, do, in a sense, use "style" to "subvert" their books' intended content. For even though both Turnbull and Swanberg attempt purposefully to avoid outright evaluations of their subjects' writing and to focus, instead, upon their authors as men, each biographer has produced—contrary to his conscious efforts, apparently—a very "literary" biography. And even if neither Turnbull nor Swanberg can be labelled a stylist in the terms of Frye's full definition, the literary nature of each of these biographies may clearly be found in its style.

II

At first glance, a more obvious example of the portrait type would seem to be a more recent and more famous literary biography: Carlos Baker's *Ernest Hemingway: A Life Story* (1969). In his foreword Baker states that he is writing neither a "definitive" nor a "thesis" biography. He also insists that he is not writing "what is commonly called a 'critical biography,' in which the biographer seeks to explore, analyze, and evaluate the full range of his subject's literary output simultaneously with the record of his life." This last point seems strange when one notices that in his previous paragraph Baker has said, "Although most of [Hemingway's] adventures make their way sooner or later into his work, it is his writing, rather than his career as a man of action, which justifies a biography."[30] Baker's indication that his reader should consult the biographer's earlier critical work, *Hemingway: The Writer as Artist*, does little to alleviate the reader's suspicion that Baker's self-chosen purpose has weakened his endeavors from their inception.[31]

Taken alone, then, is *Ernest Hemingway* a portrait type of literary biography? In fact, it is not. For Baker has not only left Hemingway's writing out of the biography; he has, according to several critics of the work, also omitted the man. William Seward, an academic who knew Hemingway, charges that he doesn't "get any feel of the man" in Baker's biography, and adds, "The facts are there but the personality is missing."[32] In the preface to Gregory Hemingway's *Papa: A Personal Memoir*, Norman Mailer, biographer as well as fiction writer, agrees. Baker, Mailer writes, "felt his literary mission was not so much to present the man as to cover every year of Hemingway's existence in the recollections of his friends."[33] And Irving Howe believes that "if [Baker's] 'Ernest' were to appear as a character in a story by Hemingway we'd immediately believe in his reality, for behind the character there'd be the authority of his creator. But Mr. Baker fails to provide a convincing portrait of the man who might have *written* the story in which 'Ernest' appears."[34] Hence, Baker's book in some ways more closely resembles the monument type of literary biography. In fact, several critics, including Mailer and William White, invoke the oft-used term "monumental" to describe Baker's book.[35]

In *Modern Fiction Studies*, Peter Lisca writes that "Baker seems to have seized upon Hemingway's 'iceberg' theory of writing and turned it upside-down, so that the great mass visible now above the surface is made to intimate the reality beneath. Unfortunately, in this process the 'dignity of movement' suffers."[36] Lisca's and Howe's comments seem to suggest that in a manner Baker has attempted to emulate, perhaps even compete with, his subject in matters of style. Hemingway's prose style—which is "very nearly Basic English: concrete nouns, common adjectives, inactive verbs"[37]—is justly famous. But, as Richard Ellmann has made clear, Baker's particular type of imitation is unwise: "Hemingway's style is easily overwhelming, and it affects the biographer's, until one longs for a Henry James suspended sentence instead of this play-by-play chronicle. Not that Hemingway's style can be easily assimilated: Mr. Baker doesn't always sense its difficulties."[38] Vance Bourjaily likewise refers to Baker's "deliberately flat prose."[39]

Thus, Baker's imitation is neither well-done nor enough. Many years ago in "Observations on the Style of Ernest Hemingway," Harry Levin asked "what is personality, when it manifests itself in art, if not style?" And, in addition, Levin observed that "no critique of Hemingway . . . can speak for long of the style without speaking of the man."[40] Surely the inverse is also true: no biography of Hemingway can speak for long of the man without speaking of the man's style. By omitting critical treatment of Hemingway's work, Baker surely has not shown well enough the immensely significant connections which critics like William Gass would press us to discern between Hemingway's life and his language—and the new "life" which that language created. So Carlos Baker's Ernest Hemingway seems to be a hybrid type of literary biography.

This chapter treats, instead, two works which are more representative of the portrait type of modern American literary biography. Further, Andrew Turnbull's Scott Fitzgerald (1962) and W. A. Swanberg's Dreiser (1965) illustrate somewhat the antipodes of this type. First, although both biographers intend to exclude criticism, Turnbull (whose book is relatively brief) aims to treat his subject's "personality," while Swanberg (whose book is over half again as long) wants to provide his reader with nothing less than "the whole man." Second, the subjects of these two biographies, who both possess the talent for recognizing and portraying very different kinds of intriguing vulgarity in American life, are authors whom critics have customarily termed "stylist" and "anti-stylist." And third, Scott Fitzgerald and Dreiser constitute works whose authors reveal strikingly different attitudes about the subjects and the readers of their respective portraits.

"Biographers," James Atlas has observed, "naturally tend to become devoted to their subjects (if they don't end up loathing them), and one of the problems before them is to conceal their inevitable bias."[41] Andrew Turnbull's unconcealed bias is overwhelmingly toward the positive qualities of Fitzgerald, and in this respect, his work may be linked to Blotner's *Faulkner*. Turnbull's "style" is the mirror which reflects Fitzgerald's own romantic self-image. Balancing such adulation here is Swanberg's cautious "loathing" for Dreiser. Apparent hatred of this kind is not uncommon in modern American literary biography. Mary Hemingway, Malcolm Cowley, Truman Capote, and Reynolds Price, among others, have charged (usually without truly specific explanations) that Baker is "subtly hostile" to his subject.[42] Atlas, in repeating a similar charge made by Edmund Wilson against Mark Schorer in *Sinclair Lewis: An American Life*, posits at least part of the problem in Schorer's prose style: "His bantering disapproval, the precious exclamatory rejoinders, a tone of sarcasm intended to demonstrate intimacy with his subject— these are tactics that serve only to subvert the importance of his enterprise."[43] Swanberg's "subtle hostility" is also evident in his style in *Dreiser*.[44]

III

According to F. Scott Fitzgerald, "there never was . . . a good biography of a good novelist."[45] Since Fitzgerald's early death, several biographers of various types have attempted to produce such a biography of the "good novelist" Fitzgerald.[46] When Andrew Turnbull's *Scott Fitzgerald: A Biography* appeared, reviewers were generally enthusiastic. For example, one suggested that "in many ways this book might serve as a model for a certain type of biography," and another stated outright that "here, unmistakably, is first-rate biography which displaces every work before it, including the earnest and admirable pioneering effort of Arthur Mizener."[47] Undoubtedly, this volume at least contains Turnbull's best work, superior by most accounts to that in his later *Thomas Wolfe* (1967). Turnbull's purposes in this Fitzgerald biography are explicitly set forth in the author's "A Note on Method and Sources" at the end of his volume. "When I began the research for this book," Turnbull commences, " . . . I knew my focus would be Fitzgerald's personality. Since the revival of interest in him, there had been extensive criticism and exegesis of his work, but the man remained elusive, as he had been in life. My desire was to get back to the sources."[48]

And this goal seems to be supported in the biography itself when near the end of its text Turnbull states his thesis (if such it may be called) and, incidentally, epitomizes his characteristic method for "criticizing" Fitzgerald's creative work: "Whether *The Last Tycoon* would have been his best novel we cannot know, but does it matter? The important thing was Fitzgerald's belief in his work and in himself . . . against great odds . . . and after long apostasy. *The quality of a life can be more impressive than art*" (p. 320; emphasis added). This last sentence is an extraordinary statement—but one that is consistent with (indeed, a corollary of) Turnbull's commitment to "personality."

Like Blotner's *Faulkner*, Turnbull's *Scott Fitzgerald* is both biography and memoir; and in attempting to portray the personality of his romantic-author subject, Turnbull is indulging a most romantic biographical impulse. For like Jeffrey Cartwright in *Edwin Mullhouse*, the biographer here is an eleven-year-old boy. More precisely, Turnbull is writing this book to recapture and expand upon the image of the man Fitzgerald as Turnbull knew him when the biographer was aged eleven and the author of *The Great Gatsby* was living on a Turnbull-family rental property outside Baltimore. Like Joseph Blotner (and, metaphorically, even Jeffrey Cartwright), Turnbull is virtually the last person to move away from his subject's graveside after the funeral. Unlike Jeffrey (and James Boswell), however, Turnbull is merely an awed observer, not in any real way a manipulator, of his friend and subject. And in contrast to Blotner's memoir, Turnbull's is full of telling details and understated intimacy. But in spite of Turnbull's ostensible aim, *Scott Fitzgerald* is a very literary biography—if not an entirely successful one. It is a memorable book because of its story, its attitudes, its phrases—but it is the subject, primarily, that makes it so. Turnbull's work has style, but beyond the selection of its materials, it is mainly Fitzgerald's own style.

In *The Great Gatsby,* Fitzgerald defines personality as "an unbroken series of successful gestures."[49] Although Turnbull never mentions this phrase, it is quite possible that he is attempting to re-create a personality through a most sympathetic rendering of, to adapt Fitzgerald's expression, a broken series of unsuccessful gestures. At one point in his biography, Turnbull notes how Fitzgerald believed that although "Zelda wasn't a natural story teller in the sense he was," it didn't matter; for "'anyhow the form of so many modern novels is less a progression than a series of impressions, as you know—rather like the slowly-turned pages of an album'" (p. 206). The structure of Turnbull's book depends heavily upon a series of "successful" impressions of his subject—and of persons who were closely associated with Fitzgerald. And, indeed, this series does resemble a kind of picture album which the reader thumbs through slowly, savoring the carefully-lined portraits of such figures as Max Perkins (p. 118), Hemingway (p. 159), Harold Ober (p. 262), Budd Schulberg (p. 296), and Irving Thalberg (p. 306). Among all these vivid but static impressions are many small, detailed portraits of Fitzgerald himself—like the one from which this observation is taken: "Fitzgerald would be sitting there with a cigarette clenched in the fingers of his gesticulating hand, with the deep inhales oozing out of his fine-cut nostrils (he belonged to that class of smoker that seems to eat the cigarette rather than smoke it)" (p. 218). Like Fitzgerald, Turnbull certainly has "an unfailing eye and heart for the *little* things that make up our existence, the little things that are really of such vast importance—the whole story for most of us" (p. 221).

The larger portrait which the book draws of Fitzgerald, though, is not as dynamic as some of these vignettes. The character "Scott" does not grow, does not evolve in the course of the book. Instead, from the outset, Turnbull presents the reader with a fully-formed man—in fact, a man who is an author most of all—and then proceeds to show his many sides, most of them quite positive as they are viewed through the filter of a distinctly romantic, literary, sympathetic consciousness. Ironically, Turnbull's decision to create this stasis is one of his few original contributions to the style of his book. To help establish it, he sometimes utilizes the device of anticipation. For example, in reviewing Fitzgerald's early notebooks, Turnbull begins a sentence with the phrase, "Showing the future novelist's eye for detail" (p. 19). And, later, he composes this sentence: "The great event of his autumn, though he couldn't know it at the time, was . . . his meeting with Father Sigourney Fay" (p. 39). Although such critics of biography as André Maurois and Paul Murray Kendall abhor all anticipation in the genre (and certainly these examples should cause most readers to pause at least briefly to consider the narrative point of view being used), one must admit that at least at these points the biographer is presenting his own controlling image of Fitzgerald. In most other respects, Turnbull does not exert such power.[50]

In addition, Turnbull seems eager for his reader to share this image. Throughout his biography, apparently trying to achieve a style which is as informal and familiar as his title, he relies again and again on the second person point of view, almost as if to reassure himself that the reader will indeed agree with his conclusions.[51] He might not have worried so much about this point, however, because in fact most of the style that he does achieve depends on the "literary" view which Fitzgerald formed of himself—the view which he recorded in his novels and short stories, the one which Fitzgerald's readers accept enthusiastically, easily, completely. For Turnbull continually uses the literature—*its* attitudes, *its* own phrasing—to portray its author. As noted in a previous chapter, equating of the literature and the life is always controversial and often unwise; but in this particular portrait biography, the technique compels one to extend the application of the common term "uncritical" to even wider connotations. Turnbull has chosen not to criticize Fitzgerald's creative work; yet, paradoxically, he freely uses it—sometimes in a manner confusing to the reader—to locate the man.

Early in his biography, Turnbull observes that Fitzgerald "liked to dramatize the incongruities of his background in a manner more literary than accurate" (p. 127). However accurate Turnbull's own "dramatizations" are here, they are certainly literary, for by using the literature of Fitzgerald, Turnbull takes on a subtle power beyond his own art. Even his smallest references to Fitzgerald's characters and episodes make the biographer's job considerably easier—if not more historically "true."

Turnbull, it appears, usually accepts the content of Fitzgerald's fiction as fact; in the process, he appropriates the style of the fiction. It is possible, of course, that Turnbull is also trying to assume Fitzgerald's *method* for appropriating another's content for his own use. This possibility is suggested when Turnbull, after quoting an "irritated" Sara Murphy's letter to Fitzgerald, remarks upon how Fitzgerald utilized the facts of another's life. "He didn't run home and write it all down like a newspaperman," Turnbull says, "Rather he courted a mood, a vision, a state of mind and feeling that would enable him to pluck his impressions out of the air, like an artist" (p. 185). But there is a difference. Turnbull himself does not work "like an artist." In taking Fitzgerald's method of borrowing content, he does not, at the same time, create, as Fitzgerald himself did, his own style for treating it.

Only once in his book does Turnbull even begin to use caution in his literature/life connections. At that point, he writes:

> In a sense, The Beautiful and Damned was a re-pudiation of the Younger Generation thesis that had brought him to power. . . . Gloria and An-thony, however, were not literal renderings of Scott and Zelda. "Gloria was a much more trivial and vulgar person than your mother," Fitzgerald wrote his daughter in after years. . . . "We had a much better time than Anthony and Gloria had."

But in the next paragraph, Turnbull sweeps away this prudent tone:

> Still, an imagined kinship remained. The Beautiful and Damned was a projection of what Fitzgerald had come to consider the decayed part of their lives, and his amazing prescience, as we read the book today, gives a touch of heartache to its brassy prose. (p. 131)

Otherwise, Turnbull makes, quite explicitly, the expected links between fictional characters and historical persons; he *does* make it his "critical" business to identify the living models for the fiction.

Thus Rosemary Hoyt *is* the young actress Lois Moran (p. 170), Tom Buchanan is Tommy Hitchcock (p. 172), Abe North is at least part of Charles MacArthur (strangely, Turnbull never really draws the expected lines between Ring Lardner and Abe North) (p. 165), and Sheilah Graham, whom Mizener left out of the first version of The Far Side of Paradise, is the love interest of The Last Tycoon (p. 288). Thomas Parke d'Invilliers in This Side of Paradise, we are told, is John Peale Bishop

(p. 52); and Isabelle in that novel, naturally, is Ginevra King, Fitzgerald's early sweetheart (p. 54), who apparently served Fitzgerald more than once as a model: "Thus Gatsby's love for Daisy was Fitzgerald's love for Zelda—and before her, Ginevra—decked out in Keatsian prose" (p. 150).

Turnbull, therefore, evokes Fitzgerald's style through references to his characters. But Turnbull is sometimes even more direct. Sometimes he quotes the romantic fiction to sustain his own romantic biographical images. Consider, for example, this instance in which he is describing Scott and Zelda:

> ...as Fitzgerald wrote in *The Beautiful and Damned*, "of the things they possessed in common, the greatest of all was their almost uncanny pull at each other's hearts." (p. 111)

Scott, Zelda, Anthony, Gloria—all of them are "they." Or note the end phrasing of this passage regarding *Tender Is the Night:*

> Beneath the Murphys' facade (for the Divers' way of life, their *style* was that of the Murphys) Fitzgerald had explored his relations with Zelda. He felt she had swallowed him up, or more precisely, that he had allowed himself to be swallowed. Zelda, like Nicole, was ill-fated when he met her, but Diver-Fitzgerald had "chosen Ophelia, chosen the sweet poison and drunk it." (p. 241)

In each such case, Fitzgerald's own words (or perhaps Shakespeare's) create the real shadings of character.

Turnbull's "linking" seems more oblique (if not truly more subtle) when he uses his question technique:

> Who can say how much of his longing for Ginevra went into Gatsby's timeless and untouchable love for Daisy Fay? (p. 72)

> Who can say but that Fitzgerald's jealousy [over Zelda's affair with Jozan] sharpened the edge of

Gatsby's and gave weight to Tom Buchanan's
bullish determination to regain his wife? (p. 146)

The obvious answer for each of these sample questions
is that "You the Reader" can say—now that you have
read Turnbull.

Often the biographer absolves himself from all
necessity of describing whole episodes in his subject's
life. He does this simply by mentioning an appropriate
matching episode in the fiction, as when he notes that
Fitzgerald "went on a drunk that lasted several weeks
and gave him one of the most vivid episodes in *This
Side of Paradise*" (p. 96). No need to be more specific
about Fitzgerald's own binge, for every reader of the
novel remembers instantly the fictional one—and remembers as well its style.

In his most vivid snapshot of Fitzgerald himself,
Turnbull relies on a reference to Dick Diver to set the
mood (p. 218). At various other points in the biography,
Turnbull tells us that Jay Gatsby (and, of course, the protagonist of "Absolution" as well) is "Fitzgerald's alter
ego" (p. 28); that "Fitzgerald came to La Paix [the place
he rented from the Turnbulls] as Tom Buchanan came
East in *The Great Gatsby*—'in a fashion that rather took
your breath away'" (p. 210); that Fitzgerald is "like Joel
Coles" in "Crazy Sunday" (p. 202); and that Fitzgerald is
"like Bill McChesney, the cocky young producer in 'Two
Wrongs,'" and "like [Charlie] Wales" in "Babylon Revis-
ited" (p. 205)—these last two stories being "poignant
with [Fitzgerald's] own disintegration." And we must
note that Turnbull turns (not surprisingly, considering
the biographer's retrospective point of view) most often
and at greatest lengths to Fitzgerald's younger pro-
tagonists. For example, the biographer borrows a paragraph from *This Side of Paradise* to help describe one of
the young Fitzgerald's "euphoric" moods (p. 41); quotes
a long Fitzgerald paragraph about Basil Duke Lee to
characterize Fitzgerald's "'first faint sex attraction'" (pp.
29–30); and lifts three long paragraphs in Nick Carra-

way's nostalgic voice to illustrate how "going home for Christmas" made the schoolboy Fitzgerald feel "that oneness with the continent which he was to describe so hauntingly in *The Great Gatsby*" (p. 49).

One need not question the cleverness that Turnbull demonstrates in discovering passages in the fiction which fit (or, maybe, grew from) moments in the life — although again one might stress the irony of this exercise in a book that purports to treat the man, not the literature. But in at least two instances in the biography, both of which seemingly involve the equation of Zelda with the narrative persona of her fiction, Turnbull's quotation technique confuses the reader.

In the first case, Turnbull quotes a paragraph and comments, "Thus Zelda would recall the *mise en scène* of her love affair . . . with a French naval flyer named Edouard Josanne."[52] But the reader does not know the source of the paragraph. He should probably assume that it is from Zelda's novel *Save Me the Waltz*, but he cannot be sure, for on the same page on which it begins, Turnbull refers to letters which Zelda wrote to Max Perkins. Is Zelda really describing a place in her own history or one in the story of her fictional heroine and a character she called Jacques?

In the second case, Turnbull says outright in one paragraph that Zelda's "inner torment [regarding her life with Fitzgerald] is described in the novel *Save Me the Waltz*, where the asceticism of the dance becomes a sort of penance for Alabama Knight" (p. 191). But in the next paragraph he again quotes from a source which the reader cannot identify. Again the reader must ask himself, "Is this from letters, from an essay — or from the fiction?"

Without the crutch of Fitzgerald's — and sometimes even Zelda's — style, Turnbull's own style can often be as weak as his analysis of Fitzgerald's drinking problems: "He drank vindictively, as if he were trying to punish someone — himself, his mother, Zelda, Sheilah, the world — who knows?" (p. 299). Or it can be as sentimental, and inappropriate, as his attempts at "fine" writing. Fitzgerald, he says, "could epitomize *in a casual phrase* the beauty of our acres—the dark shadows of the pines *athwart* the moonlit lawns, the scent of honeysuckle and the thorny lemon tree, the winking fireflies, the mist rising from the pond *whence* came *the gutteral* [sic] *diatribe* of the bull frogs" (p. 227; emphasis added).

In those paragraphs of the biography in which Turnbull apparently tries deliberately to use repetition in his sentence structure à la Hemingway, the result is sometimes a disastrous machine-gun, anti-Fitzgerald style that has most of its short sentences beginning with "he" (e.g., the penultimate paragraph on p. 60). Turnbull's apparently unintended repetition of phrases can, at times, be somewhat irritating. Within the space of about two pages, for instance, he writes these four sentences:

> College players were an inch or two shorter and proportionately lighter *than they are now.*

> Princeton . . . was smaller and sleepier *than it is today.*

> Among Fitzgerald's contemporaries there was more hero worship *than there is now.*

> In those days the contrasts between East and West, between city and country, between prep school and high school were more marked *than they are now.* (pp. 44–46; my italics)

Perhaps I need isolate only one other phrase—"the few times [Fitzgerald] had criticized Wolfe . . . he had *felt badly* afterwards" (p. 310)—to suggest the solecisms which Turnbull is capable of producing. Turnbull refers to "the gay chic of [Fitzgerald's] style" (p. 225), penning a phrase which one critic has described as "quite unpardonable." The critic has further indicated that "the term 'gracious'—most overworked of words—should have been edited out of the book."[53]

Although *Scott Fitzgerald* is certainly not a book filled with metaphors, Turnbull does occasionally attempt to use figurative language. With sentences like these he is usually fairly safe:

> His head became a kaleidoscope of marvelous shapes and colors as inspiration drove him on he knew not how. (p. 97)

> Comparing [Hemingway] to Fitzgerald at this time would be like comparing a butterfly and a bull; the butterfly has beautiful colors on its wings, but the bull is there. (p. 188)

> Fitzgerald had the dangerous Athenian qualities of facility and grace as against Hemingway's Spartan virtues of ruggedness and perseverance. (p. 188)

But sometimes his slightly-extended similes can border on the humorous: "[Scott and Zelda] complemented each other like gin and vermouth in a martini, each making the other more powerful in their war with dullness and convention" (p. 142). And often Turnbull's figurative language is either simply unfortunate ("living with Zelda was like a poem" [p. 111]) or just downright perplexing (". . . Donahoe was the rock to which the more volatile Fitzgerald instinctively gravitated" [p. 37]). Most frequently it definitely supports the romantic tone of the biography as a whole. We may see such romanticism in this passage: "Sensitive as a young leaf, [Fitzgerald] trembled to all his surroundings. . . . [He] wrote [his fiction] almost like journalism with a dash of poetry added. Thus . . . his work and his play became hopelessly intertwined" (p. 116). The significance that this last sentence should have for any Fitzgerald biographer seems to have been lost on Turnbull, whose romanticism is most acute in the following lines:

> Let us remember Fitzgerald in his first glory. . . .
> A faun, with waving blond hair. . . . [h]e was living the American dream. . . . He and Zelda were a

> perfect pair, like a shepherd and shepherdess in a
> Meissen. You could hardly imagine one without
> the other, and you wanted to preserve them and
> protect them and hope their idyll would never
> end. (p. 107)

So these were the desires, the dreams, of a precocious,
romantic eleven-year-old boy (the "you" here is both the
boy and the reader), and *Scott Fitzgerald* is the book
which the grown-up Andrew Turnbull has created to
help make them come true.

Actually, the memoir section of this biography
does not commence until almost two-thirds of the way
through. Turnbull uses virtually no first-person-singular
references until he notes, "And so Fitzgerald entered the
sphere of my personal knowledge . . ." (p. 208). But, because of the changed tone of the biography, what has
come before seems almost a prelude to this sentence:
"My friendship with him . . . grew out of football" (p.
211); and "I can see him now . . ." (p. 213) embodies
Turnbull's biographical stance. He easily betrays his own
wonder at his literary subject—even at this distance.
"For . . . me . . . there was always something of the
magician in Fitzgerald" (p. 223), he says, emphasizing
that a major part of his friend's magic involved his
power over words (p. 217).

Conceivably, Turnbull's most effective stylistic
touch in his biography involves a metaphor which forms
organically out of the materials of his memoir section. It
equates a Poe-like Fitzgerald with the equally Poe-like
house, La Paix, which the novelist rented from the
Turnbull family: "And so he labored on amid the
water-stained walls and woodwork [Zelda had recently
set the house afire] in that hulk of a house, whose bleak-
ness matched the color of his soul" (p. 238). The
metaphor is even more subtle, perhaps, in this passage:
"It was a grim year for Fitzgerald. Dazed and wan, he
shuffled about the shut-in, *unwholesome* house in bath-
robe and pajamas, pondering his next move" (p. 246; my
emphasis). Here, Turnbull not only describes, but also

attempts, at least in a small way, to become an integral part of Fitzgerald's personality.

Family memories, romanticism, and literary influences—all of the elements thus far examined fall dramatically together, finally, in this Turnbull passage:

> When Fitzgerald came to La Paix his period of greatest acclaim was over. . . . My mother was grateful she knew Fitzgerald when she did, for he must have been more impressive then than at almost any other time—because more tragic, and therefore more profound. He said to her once with a wry sort of pride, "It is from the failure of life, and not its successes that we learn most," and he was counting himself among the failures. *He* was Dick Diver. (p. 239)

Indeed, Laura Guthrie, Fitzgerald's secretary, recorded in her journal that the novelist *did* say, "My characters are all Scott Fitzgerald" (quoted on p. 259). But, as James Clifford reminds us, "Today's life-writer must understand the meaning of the clues in his subject's inner life and reveal a side of his character that may have been hidden even from himself."[54] And by using Fitzgerald's admittedly autobiographical fiction so extensively to draw the author as a man, Turnbull has given us primarily Fitzgerald's fiction-filtered portrait of himself. Ultimately, the literary biographer here is not solidly in control of his work.

IV

In contrast to Turnbull in *Scott Fitzgerald*, W. A. Swanberg seems to wield a very tight control over his biographical subject in *Dreiser*. And Ellen Moers has charged that "Mr. Swanberg has made too little biographical use of Dreiser's fiction. . . ."[55] But in his re-

fusal to treat his subject's creative work, Swanberg's biographical purpose is similar to Turnbull's; and he proves
to be much more adamant in this respect than Turnbull.
In his "Author's Note and Acknowledgments," Swanberg begins, "This book is intended solely as biography,
not criticism. There have been many analyses of Dreiser's works, but no attempt to study the whole man."[56]
Further, like Turnbull's portrait, Swanberg's is quite static, with the author in this case also using the anticipation device often—so often in fact that he seems almost
to be competing with the *Beowulf* poet in his *wyrd* references. For example, when Swanberg introduces Helen
Richardson (Dreiser's long-suffering mistress and, late in
his life, his wife) into his story, he begins with this
sentence: "However, fate was preparing for him the most
protracted, searing and significant romantic attachment
of his life." Later he continues this method, in the process warping the reader's—and Helen's—perspective
considerably. About meeting Dreiser, Swanberg says,
Helen "was nervous . . . with reason, for she was letting
herself in for 26 years of . . . alternating ecstasy and torment" (pp. 241–42). Perhaps Dreiser's self-proclaimed
prescience was contagious.

One reviewer, Burke Wilkinson, has suggested
that Turnbull was using the "Titanic technique" to describe "the shipwrecked life of Scott Fitzgerald" (Wilkinson observed that the biography used "a mosaic
technique of research, interview and built-in disaster" in
much the same way that Walter Lord did in *A Night to
Remember*).[57] Dreiser, Swanberg tells us, just barely
missed being on the Titanic's ill-fated voyage (pp.
156–57). Whereas Turnbull tells his story, in a sense,
from the point of view of a child, Swanberg creates the
prevailing image of his subject primarily by referring to
Dreiser's childlike and often childish nature. Yet these
two literary biographies, beyond their both being portrait types, are very different.

Ellen Moers has also referred to Swanberg as
"Dreiser's first popular biographer," but it is not clear

what causes her to use the word "popular."[58] Perhaps
she chooses the term because Swanberg, unlike Turnbull
and most other biographers mentioned in this study, is
not ordinarily associated with university life, is not, to
use the popular term, an academic. His previous work
included a commercially successful biography of
William Randolph Hearst. Or perhaps Moers is referring
to the design of Swanberg's biography. However, the
book is certainly as carefully and as extensively documented as Turnbull's, and here Swanberg has quite in-
geniously divided his work into sections which, at their
best, almost constitute complete, synecdochic essays in
themselves.[59] So Moers is somewhat in error when she
further writes that Swanberg "has produced a mass of
new materials" and that he "*has left it all where it falls,*
not seeking to organize it into a political or moral ser-
mon, or even a literary analysis."[60]

   Yet, Swanberg's failure to produce—as a part of
his "whole man"—an analysis of Dreiser's literature
weakens his endeavors immeasurably. When the book
appeared, critics, while never agreeing on what should
be the purposes of literary biography, generally praised
Swanberg for collecting and sorting his multitudinous
materials and for "settl[ing] the factual biographical record."[61] And Granville Hicks wrote that "Swanberg is not
a hero worshipper."[62] In fact, this last observation is a
considerable understatement of the attitude which several other noted critics took toward the biography.
"Swanberg's covert distaste for his 'hero' becomes increasingly apparent," Daniel Aaron noted: ". . . in the
more than five hundred pages of this biography," Aaron
continued, "Dreiser's originality, feeling, and courage
figure less significantly than his less admirable qualities."[63] And Malcolm Cowley agreed:

> Sometimes it seems that Mr. Swanberg's method
> leads him to talk of little else but Dreiser's faults.
> In consulting the index of 32 pages, I found that
> one of the long sub-headings under "Dreiser,
> Theodore" is devoted to "His Traits, Habits, Ac-

tivities." Only one of the traits is given a eulogis-
tic name, "Artistic integrity," which, by the way, I
am inclined to question. It was not Dreiser, but
only his genius when it seized hold of him, that
had artistic integrity.[64]

It is this voice of Dreiser's genius that Cowley misses in
Swanberg's work.

Apparently Swanberg has taken his attitude
toward Dreiser from H. L. Mencken, Dreiser's sometime-
friend, whom he quotes at one point: "'Dreiser is a great
artist, but a very ignorant and credulous man. . . . [It is]
impossible for me to take him seriously—that is, as
man'" (p. 245). Unfortunately, though, Swanberg has
chosen to ignore altogether the "great artist." In his
"Author's Note," the biographer attempts to justify his
method; he proclaims, "Not even during his busiest
writing years was [Dreiser] exclusively a writer"
(p. 531).

The one image that sticks most securely in the
reader's mind after he has finished reading this biography captures Theodore Dreiser as a child. It is an
image that Swanberg has painstakingly created on his
canvas—both through his own broad, swift brush
strokes and through a kind of découpage technique that
utilizes the observations of those who knew Dreiser. Although this image certainly does not always belie an
overwhelming "covert distaste" for Dreiser (it sometimes
seems merely to be Swanberg's method of showing a
kind of cock-eyed affection for his subject), its cumula-
tive effect does indeed point to more serious stylistic
ramifications which ultimately support Aaron's and
Cowley's charges.

Throughout his biography, W. A. Swanberg imagines the object of his prose as a kind of overgrown child.
He refers to him, for example, as "this capricious child
of moods" (p. 300), or he captures him vividly in a moment (or several hours) of immensely childish talk or
behavior (e.g., pp. 372 and 385). He remarks that "at

times he took a juvenile pleasure in keeping his domestic status a close secret from his best friends" (p. 175); he observes that Dreiser "played with ideas as a child plays with blocks" (p. 402). For Swanberg, the novelist-as-manchild is "the boy who never really reached maturity and yet who exuded at times a charm and sympathy that is warmly remembered to this day" (p. 524). Dreiser's is the "attitude of the child discovering evil" (p. 420). The biographer points out that "the diary he kept [in 1916] was a revelation of the morose Dreiser temper and the troubled Dreiser mind—a mind that saw everything through the wondering eyes of a child" (p. 199).

"The historian who undertakes to write about Franklin D. Roosevelt creates Roosevelt's character through the words he chooses, including his selections of a certain kind of anecdote," writes David Levin.[65] Including his selections of a certain kind of image, we might add. Thus even more persuasive than these direct remarks from Swanberg are those which he collected from others to support his "thesis." According to Swanberg, Earl Browder, "the communist head man" who refused to admit Dreiser to the party, remembered that Dreiser "'did not seem quite an adult, which was a part of his charm'" (p. 393). Ralph Fabri, once conducting the novelist on a visit to the Westinghouse laboratories in New Jersey, "was astonished by his childlike wonder at scientific marvels, but thought he would be as impressed by an alchemist" (p. 436). And in her first adult meetings with her uncle, Dr. Vera Dreiser Scott "'had to keep reminding herself that this was the man who wrote *Sister Carrie* and the *Tragedy*. He was so childlike in many ways, and seemed to me so humble a person'" (p. 502). Perhaps Swanberg's portrait shows us, then, that Theodore Dreiser is one of our greatest geniuses, if Jeffrey Cartwright is correct in his definition of genius ("the retention of the capacity to be obsessed"—to retain the natural obsession which every child once possessed). For, in this biography, he remains a "child" to its very end.

But not every reference is as positive as those just identified. An uglier child emerges in Dreiser's close personal relationships: Helen Dreiser remarks in a letter, "He is a wonderful man but he is so self-centered. Nothing exists for him but his own sensations and his own interests" (p. 488). Metaphors make his much-maligned intelligence suffer even more acutely:

> To the intellectuals he was a lowbrow.
> Albert Boni thought him a terrible bore with a "schoolboy mentality."
>
> Ludwig Lewisohn wrote, "When Dreiser tries to think he writes like a child." (p. 233)

And his social and political relations become difficult: at a meeting in the *New Masses* offices, Dreiser, according to Joshua Kunitz, was drunk and "'behaved like a child'" (p. 427).

But more significant than any slighting connotations this figurative language has in itself is the broader effect it produces. If Dreiser the subject is the child, then according to Swanberg's logic, Swanberg the biographer must in a sense be the parent (the creator—in a double degree), and must, therefore, carry out his paternal duties. One of these duties, it would seem, is to sit in judgment of his child, who is repulsively secretive[66] and who practices "lying habitually" (p. 422).

Swanberg's point in his book might have been that great literature gets produced in spite of the little men who write it. In that case, it would have been sufficient to *present* the man, rather than to judge him. But here, in a book that supposedly omits the literature, we find the noncritic judging even that element. For instance, "*Tragic America* was a shambles. . . . [I]t was so bad that surely no publisher would have accepted it but for the name behind it" (p. 391). But certainly such references to the work are infrequent; usually when Swanberg does mention them (e.g., p. 219), he merely lists the titles sent out, giving no indication of how they came to be created.

Most of all, as Aaron and Cowley might have pointed out, the judgmental tone which Swanberg so often assumes demonstrates his impatience with Dreiser the man. The attitude may easily be discerned in these sample passages:

> Yet he *should* have been generous enough to forgive the Doubledays [their part in the early *Sister Carrie* publishing fiasco]. (p. 127; my italics)

> Having paid Louise Campbell a nominal sum for her work on [*An American Tragedy*], Dreiser *might* have sent her an extra check as her share of its success. (p. 308; my italics)

> After eleven years of supporting herself, [Jug, Dreiser's estranged wife] hardly deserved [Dreiser's note accusing her of being interested only in his money]. (p. 309)

Regardless of how much the reader may agree with Swanberg's judgments in these sentences, he must also agree that they *should* have no place in the just-the-facts, nonspeculative work which Swanberg has defined for himself.

Nevertheless, in spite of—and also because of—this negative tone, Swanberg's *Dreiser* is an intriguing book. And, in a sense, it succeeds in the type of imitation of its subject's prose style that Baker's *Ernest Hemingway* attempts and fails. Remarkably, it is within the confines of his attack through style that the biographer is most accomplished in a literary way.

Make no mistake: Swanberg forces his reader to be very irritated and impatient with the subject. But this elicited reader response approximates that which Dreiser himself provokes in much of· his fiction—and this response involves both content and style. As Saul Bellow has written, one must "often think the criticisms of Dreiser as a stylist at times betray a resistance to the feelings he causes readers to suffer."[67] Like the story of Clyde Griffiths, the story of Theodore Dreiser as it is told by Swanberg is gross, distasteful, inevitable—and immensely compelling. And while Swanberg does, at several points in his biography, confront directly the celebrated problem of Dreiser's slovenly style—his lifelong "incurable antipathy to the *mot juste*" (to borrow Mencken's phrase)[68]—Swanberg's greater, and subtler, confrontation with it may be located in the prose of his own book.

Just as we may say that content is almost palpable in biography, as it is not in so-called "foregrounded" fiction, so we may also say that it is almost palpable in Dreiser's fiction.[69] We might even maintain that Dreiser writes "biographies"—or, more precisely, given his philosophical and sociological bent, "histories"—whose reality exists in action rather than in the words which describe it. Richard Poirier expresses in this way his own satisfaction with Dreiser's performance: ". . . what I find admirable in Dreiser is that he does not in any way compromise himself by subscribing to a bourgeois faith in the reality of language."[70] Nor does Swanberg, in his own way in this other biography, need to "compromise" himself for language.

In *Homage to Theodore Dreiser*, Robert Penn Warren has defended Dreiser against charges that he is in no way a stylist. "Words," Warren maintains, "are not the only language of fiction. There is the language of the unfolding scenes, what Dreiser . . . called the 'procession and selection of events,' the language of the imagery of enactment, with all its primitive massiveness—the movie in our heads."[71] Further, in fiction, "the full meaning is embodied in the action. To be satisfied with a fiction, we demand this sense of meaning embodied in action, meaning of a depth and resonance far greater than the verbal language can ever literally declare. Insofar as this is true, the 'procession' of events is a language— what psychologists call the 'primary language.'"[72]

Dreiser's "biographer has to let the facts speak for themselves, just as Dreiser did in his novels."[73] Surely the "procession and selection of events" in Swanberg's biography, then, are the biographical equivalent of the "depth and resonance" of "action" which Warren imagines can compensate for the verbal stylistic weaknesses in Dreiser's fiction. In his "competition" with Dreiser, Swanberg is unquestionably the loser, for all of the "content" belongs to the Hoosier; and Swanberg's "journalistic" prose style is only slightly more refined than Dreiser's. But without intending to be "literary," Swanberg has produced a biography in the literary spirit of Theodore Dreiser himself.

V

Thus, the literary biographer who writes the portrait type triumphs, when he can succeed at all beyond the limitations of his own purposes, through the restrictive rightness of his own art—or artifice. Modern American literary biographers choose to produce this type less and less often, it seems. If the portrait type has a future at all, it probably exists as the product of the *"Savage* syndrome," in which the biographer selects his writer-subject not because he or she is a prolific major literary figure, but rather because of some extraliterary fame or notoriety in his or her personal life.[74] A recent example is John Leggett's dual biography, *Ross & Tom: Two American Tragedies*, whose author-subjects each committed suicide. But the type in this particular case has become, finally, another hybrid. For, since Ross Lockridge's total literary fame rests on the one-time immense popularity of his single novel, *Raintree County,* and Tom Heggen's on the similar success of *Mister Roberts*, the biographer of the "personalities" has been more readily able to bear the additional role of critic as well.[75]

chapter four

Vision of the Artist

A third type of literary biographer differs from the writer of the portrait type in his deliberately choosing to deal with both the subject's life and work in attempting to locate not just the man or woman, but, also, the artist. He differs from the monument-maker type in his attempting a deliberate and skillful utilization of the devices of structure and style to convey not a supposedly objective re-creation of his subject as a Famous Writer, but, rather, his own personal vision of a remarkable imagination. Such a life-writer, then, quite obviously aspires to be an artist in search of another artist—one who endeavors to infuse in his own work the radiance, harmony, and wholeness of true art.

The cacophony of critical reactions to one major example of this third type of literary biography, Leon Edel's five-volume *Henry James* (1953–72), illustrates well a very basic observation about the literary biographer's purpose with which this study began. In their disagreement about the merits of Edel's biography, commentators have demonstrated once again their considerable disagreement about the aim of literary biography as a genre and about the purposes of the criticism of literary biography. Many of the myriad reviews of the individual volumes of *Henry James* and of the few critical essays on the whole work take the biography to task not for what it does, but only for what it does *not* do. Few of them begin to evaluate the work in light of the stated purpose of its author. In an interview, the American playwright Edward Albee, reacting to criticism of his own work, has said, "You may dislike [an author's] intention enormously but your judgment of the artistic merit of the work must not be based on your view of what it's about. The work of art must be judged by how well it succeeds in its intention."[1] A critic must certainly use additional criteria for evaluation, but Albee is right to suggest that a consideration of how well an author has managed to serve his own chosen purpose is the place for the critic to *commence*.

If in the making of literary biographies, as in the making of all works of literature, form should follow function, critics of the Edel biography would do well to realize that the criticism of this type of writing should also follow function—should consider first the literary biographer's aim. They should not forget Henry James's own (pre-Albee) maxim, given in "The Art of Fiction": "We must grant the artist his subject, his idea, his *donnée*: our criticism is applied only to what he makes of it."[2] Applied to literary biography, James's sentence means not only that the biographer can choose his own subject, but also that he must be free to choose his own approach. Many scholars would object to this application of James's statement, which is about the criticism of fiction, to the criticism of nonfiction. Their objection is further indication of our culture's enormous hesitancy in making aesthetic judgments of historical materials.

Chapters Two and Three of this book register objections to the stated intentions of such representative literary biographers as Joseph Blotner, Andrew Turnbull, and W. A. Swanberg, whose diverse aims seem misconceived—or, at least, not broad enough. Nevertheless, these preceding chapters are attempts, first, to evaluate *Faulkner, Scott Fitzgerald*, and *Dreiser* according to "how well their authors succeed in their intentions." This chapter approaches Edel's biography of Henry James in the same spirit. Close examination of the combined volumes of *Henry James* reveals that unquestionably one may hurl many valid complaints at Edel's work and at some of his statements on the art of biography. Yet, at least in its eloquent and necessary balance of personal history and literary criticism, in its author's carefully articulated, controlled, and unified vision of both a human life and its literature, here is a literary biography worthy of considerable praise.

I

Those many contemporary reviewers who expressed an appreciation of Edel's biography seemed to like the work very much indeed. For example, at the time of the publication of the fifth volume, *The Master: 1901–1916*,[3] one reviewer labeled *Henry James* "the greatest biography of the century."[4] John Aldridge provided even broader praise, calling it "not only a major biography but one of the truly distinguished works of creative scholarship of our time, perhaps of all time."[5] However, other reviewers of the work were much less favorable in their reception—even those who felt that it was, finally, to be accepted as a major addition to James scholarship. Reasons given for unfavorable criticism—which often arose from a refusal to accept Edel's purpose—ranged from the trivial to the truly significant, but a handful of critics expressed their disinclination to accept Edel's biography at all. One must be fully aware of the difficulties of Edel's task to appreciate more fully, even with certain reservations, the value of his real accomplishment. Hence, what follows is a brief survey of eight characteristic charges which have been made against *Henry James*.

The first and most obvious criticism aimed at the biography involved its length. But Hilton Kramer has defended Edel on this count, writing that he considers "the

criticism of undue length wholly unfounded. There is
nothing trivial, nothing merely documentary, nothing
irrelevant" in the book; and he has further indicated his
own high opinion of the strength of the story line
throughout the five volumes: "this biography . . .
suggests that the fate of narrative as a viable mode of
literary discourse may have passed from the hands of the
novelists and the historians to those of the biographer."[6]

A second representative complaint, involving
documentation, is more justifiable. In Chapter Two, in
my examination of forms of documentation used by various specific literary biographers, I concluded that the
older, more traditional methods inevitably prove most
useful to the largest number of readers and users of literary biography. Unfortunately, Leon Edel seems to believe otherwise, and he has often been reproved for his
own documentation practice. In fact, Edel's method for
"footnoting" makes his apparatus as difficult to use as
Carlos Baker's in *Ernest Hemingway*. But with Edel,
one's search is finally even less rewarding than with
Baker. Even for the casual reader, Edel's documentation
is neither easy enough to use nor complete enough in
the information it provides. Edel's own basic attitude is
suggested in a comment he makes in the introduction to
the first volume of his edition of James's letters: "As for
footnotes, I have preferred to be simply informative,
with a strong feeling that if one carried footnotes to the
extreme one could end up writing a history of all civili-
zation."[7] In the life, Edel is not even "simply informative," and Rayburn S. Moore has complained, echoing
many other scholars, "Altogether it may be commendable to avoid 'sowing footnotes,' but in a work of five
volumes fuller and more thorough citation from the
author's prodigious research would have been of great
value to others working on James."[8] In this respect, then,
Edel, in writing his type of literary biography is no more
successful than Joseph Blotner in writing his type.

During the nineteen-year period when the volumes of *Henry James* were being published, a third, constant criticism from reviewers involved Edel's apparent refusal to make appropriate use of James scholarship by others. Most often, when Edel does utilize the ideas of others, he refers to critics as simply "critics" (e.g., IV, 213, 344; V, 205, 215). Edel seldom makes a bow to specific scholars, and when he does, he is even less likely to quote them directly, even very briefly. He does quote Edmund Wilson, a critic whose papers Edel has since edited, in *The Treacherous Years* (IV, 253). Once (in V, 223), when he quotes Stephen Spender, he fails in both the text and the notes to give his reader the place where Spender's remarks first appeared. Only with the greatest reluctance can one forgive Edel's choosing to ignore the work of other James scholars.

A fourth characteristic complaint about *Henry James* concerns its organization and form—a point to be considered at some length later in this chapter. But the fifth, and surely the most publicized, criticism deals with Edel's use of psychology to explain both the life and the literature of his subject. Robert L. Gale, for example, in his *Modern Fiction Studies* review of *The Treacherous Years*, accused Edel of "textual forcing," in passages "not isolated," in connecting life and work. The majority of readers of the biography critical in this way probably have reacted most swiftly to such instances involving psychological readings.[9] After the first critical whirlwind of reactions to the sibling-rivalry theme in *The Untried Years*, few truly new charges of this nature have been filed against Edel; but critics nevertheless continue to choose sides on the issue. Thus, in *Golden Codgers*, Richard Ellmann, Joyce's biographer, attacks Edel's celebrated psychological reading of the "Ledward-Bedward-Dedward-Deadward" passage from James's notebooks (I, 55), but the poet Stephen Spender offers a defense of the biographer (and subject) on rhythmic grounds.[10] And Mildred Hartsock declares, "When the biographer writes as the artist he is, he puts

James before us with vivid warmth; [but] when he writes as the amateur psychiatrist, he exacerbates with a constrictive glibness." Joyce Carol Oates, reviewing a new volume of essays on biographical theory and criticism in which Edel has an article, writes, "One does not shrink from Mr. Edel's method because his product is so thoughtful. But," she adds, "the 'psychological' method employed by less discerning biographers may give us very curious products indeed."[11] The controversy about this particular aspect of Henry James is likely to continue indefinitely.

A sixth common charge against the Edel biography is likewise a part of the debate about what should be the proper focus for biography in general. Edward Mendelson suggests a weakness in Edel—and in other biographers: "The tendency of modern biography, like the tendency of modern literary study, has been a progressive narrowing of focus, an ever-increasing concern with the interior organization of its subject, and a lessening of attention to its subject's relations with the world outside."[12] But the late Frederick J. Hoffman, like many other critics, praised Edel for stressing this very tendency: "The strongest impression left by [Henry James] is . . . of James as a fascinating exemplar of the American's intellectual self-dependence, of a continual spinning out of self-disciplinary, controlling forms and myth."[13] In this debate, the critics' own sociological interests appear, finally, more significant than their concern for evaluation of Edel's work.

But a seventh kind of criticism is easier to ignore. In it, the writer, under the pretext of attacking Edel's biography, is in fact attacking Henry James himself—or Leon Edel. One of the most vicious of these attacks was made in 1970 by Robert Garis. Reviewing The Treacherous Years, Garis charged that Edel refused to have "any interest in being a literary critic"; was confused, obtuse, "dishonest," and "naive"; was "relying on old notecards rather than on the actual re-reading of the text"; had a "simple incapacity to get the facts straight"; was "out of touch with the actualities of James's writing"; had written in "melodramatic journalese"; and had a "consistent lack of interest in James's language." Garis concluded that "Edel's biography is a waste of time."[14] Later assaults of this kind, after the appearance of *The Master*, included Philip Rahv's anti-James diatribe in the *New York Review of Books* and Mark L. Krupnick's "polemic" in *Novel*.[15] Such *ad hominem* attacks should perhaps not concern those seeking to evaluate literary biography. But it is at least interesting to note that, prior to their scathing criticisms of Edel's completed work, both Rahv and Krupnick had written basically favorable remarks about *part* of the project—or about their later victims.[16]

Finally, the eighth pejorative critical reaction is embodied in what is probably the most provocative essay ever written about Edel's biography: Quentin Anderson's "Leon Edel's 'Henry James,'" which is itself a kind of graceful compendium of all these criticisms I have listed. Although Anderson's most basic motive seems to be realistic appreciation of Edel's efforts, this critic refuses to use the term "biography" to describe the five volumes. According to Anderson, the man himself, his character, "the central figure has been spirited away, and the succession of his imaginative productions, letters and all, thrown up in a fountain of imaginative assertion, are standing in for that central figure." Further, he suggests, Edel has been too much influenced by his subject.[17] In his lengthy review of the first volume of the letters, Anderson also charges that Edel has "substituted James's imagination for his character. . . . Mr. Edel actually opens the door through which only an abstraction can come forth, that of the self-sustained and self-sufficient imagination."[18]

II

Anderson's complaint that the man is missing re-
calls one of the requirements for the literary biographer
which I stated in Chapter One: that he provide a sure
sense of the physical person and his or her human personality. Now, in the introduction to *The Treacherous
Years*, Edel writes that he is not interested in "the irrelevancies of daily life," and he further points out that
"it is the quest for [the secret of a man's life] that I regard
as the justifiable aim of literary biography. All the rest is
gossip and anecdotage" (IV, 17). These two rather limit-
ing statements should make anyone widely acquainted
with Edel's biographical writing somewhat uneasy.
Perhaps this uneasiness stems not merely from the
ridicule which a number of critics—not just Anderson—have made of the passage, but more solidly from
the knowledge that Edel has elsewhere stated his chief
concern, his major purpose, more clearly:

> I'm not trying to suggest that in writing biography
> I'm trying to . . . psychoanalyze the people—you
> can't do that. But at least I can look analytically at
> not only their work, but the work as a reflection of
> them, which is my great thesis. . . . I don't care
> whether you give me big archives or not. The
> work tells me a great deal about the writer, and it
> tells me a great deal not about the writer as flesh
> and blood, but the writer as an active imagina-
> tion. And when you're writing literary biography,
> that's really what you should be writing—the
> biography of an extraordinary imagination.[19]

In this declaration, Edel's "irrelevancies of daily life"
comment is put into perspective by his larger thesis: his
concern with "the work as a reflection of [authors]." But
in even intimating that he is rejecting "the writer as
flesh and blood," Edel at this point is, in fact, separating
his theory from his practice—and should be reproved as

critic of biography, not as biographer. Here, Edel, like
W. A. Swanberg and Andrew Turnbull, succeeds to a
degree in spite of his stated purpose.

If in his introductions and interviews Edel has
chosen to minimize the importance of the man in order
to spotlight his own more revolutionary ideas, he has
not failed to re-create also a man of "flesh and blood" —
in those parts of his biography that any portrait type of
biographer might envy. Not that Edel has gone so far as
to answer William Gass's facetious question, "What did
[James] do, one wonders, to punish his erections?" But
he has at least tried to provide the reader with the very
thing which Gass demands: "the history of his imagination."[20] And in the process, whether he wishes to accen-
tuate it or not, Edel has also provided us with a tangible
human character.

For example, as Edel presents him, the literary
character Henry James is a real human being that lived,
one who says goodbye to Minny Temple before his
travels — "a quiet, rather sedate young man, going on
twenty-six, of medium height, with a brownish beard,
receding hair, piercing eyes and shy manner. He spoke
in a well-modulated voice, without hesitancy (and without the stammer apocryphally attributed to him)" (I,
279). The beard which James shaves off at the end of the
century (IV, 355) is quite specifically real before it can be
symbolic, either in the life or in this biography.
Likewise, Edel's important philosophical and psychological examinations of James's last days detract not one
whit from the biographer's conveying an overwhelming
sense of heroic mortal struggle (V, 547 ff). So, too, does
Edel question the actions of a "flesh and blood" person
riding with spirit in Rome when he observes, "His letters convey a sense of well-being. Not a word about his
old backache, the 'obscure hurt' which had immobilized
him during the Civil War and which might have kept
him from the saddle" (II, 98).

In reporting external views of the man James, Edel
traces the lines of a very human personality. For in-

stance, in The Middle Years, he quotes from the early
London journal of the James friend and observer, E. S.
Nadal, and perceptively remarks that the writer "recognized the fundamental question preoccupying the
novelist at this time: the relationship of his art to the
world. 'He liked to have a look of success,' Nadal said"
(III, 308). Edel also gives us a finely amusing portrait of a
finicky James from the vantage point of visiting cousins:
"'He hangs poised for the right word while the wheels
of life go round. . . . We do nothing but thank our stars
that we are not Henry James'" (IV, 188). What more
vivid image of the man could one ask for?—unless, of
course, it is that implied by the spirit of James's "reply,"
provided on the next page by a clever Edel juxtaposition,
through a comment on their language. We get many
equally as entertaining and telling external views of
James, including those, for example, from his nephew
and a woman visitor from Boston at Lamb House, and a
close, sympathetic account of the dictating James from
his second typist, Miss Weld (V, 93).

Edel no doubt delights in the prospects of sounds
of astonishment from the reader who learns that the
aging James quite unself-consciously (or is it?) instructs
Hugh Walpole to call him "très cher maître or 'my very
dear Master'" (V, 403). (Incidentally, this little scene
may answer the many complaints from critics about how
often Edel himself uses the term "master" late in the
biography.) In The Master, Edel relates a charming Max
Beerbohm anecdote which illustrates "a case . . . of
[Beerbohm's] 'preferring the Master's work to the Master.'" In the same volume, he demonstrates James's very
real "generosity" for a fellow writer, the rather rough
Harold Frederick, and makes the reader see James's
being "sick beyond cure" over the coming war in his
tedious, Whitmanesque ministrations to wounded sol-
diers (V, 387, 512 ff).

That Edel has chosen, especially in his statements
about his art, to emphasize something more significant
to him than the daily facts worshipped by the monu-

ment-maker biographer does not really mean that he *has* left out a sense of Henry James's very earthly days. In his text, Edel gives the reader details of where, when, and by what instruments the man wrote (V, 126); of domestic worries (what is he to do about the tippling servants, the Smith couple, in his absence from De Vere Gardens, London?); and of personal desires (surely only James could have written, " . . . I must [deride me not] be somewhere I can, without disaster, bicycle") (IV, 157).

Perhaps there is no passage in the whole biography, though, which is more telling — of both Henry James as man and of the methods of Leon Edel as biographer — than this startling, amazing scene in *The Master* (in a section called "Images in a Diary"):

> He lost his dachshund Max and buried him in the small row of dog graves at one end of his garden. He decided he would have no more pets. One hot summer a chameleon turned up on his lawn as from nowhere; it blushed and flushed black and brown and blanched to pinkish gray ten times a minute. James found it to be an exquisite little pet. And one night in a rage against a too audible feline, he killed the creature on the lawn with a blow of his stick — and promptly was sick at the stomach.[21]

Edel lets his telling of the story speak for itself, proffering neither explanation nor analysis of any kind. Was the death an accident? Can one tell from Edel's presentation of it? The passage is so rich that most readers — even those who usually take Edel to task for his psychologizing — would ask for more. Ironically, though, in this passage at least, it is the "flesh and blood," not "an abstraction," that comes through most strongly.

III

Edel not only tells us that James the man "attached . . . much importance to his eyes" (I, 65), that he "invariably preferred to see rather than be seen" (I, 198), and that always "James invites us to look: and through sight we are asked to charge our other senses" (II, 55). He also makes us *see*, through his quoting "an American publishing lady, Elizabeth Jordan," Henry James's own human eyes and their "strange power" (V, 171). At one point in *The Conquest of London,* describing James's friends the Bootts and Frank Duveneck, Edel writes: "They were a strange group, the father, the daughter and the painter, and Henry was to watch the evolution of Lizzie's love affair with her bohemian teacher with the interested eyes of a friend — who was also a novelist" (II, 404). He shows us that he, Edel the biographer, is watching Henry James the novelist watching the real people who will turn up in both fiction and biography. It is the reader who has the last "look," but it is Edel, not James, who finally has total control of these five volumes.

Critics have often charged that throughout the whole project of producing *Henry James* the biographer has been manipulated by his subject. As early as 1963, with the issuance of the third volume, for instance, Stuart Hampshire viewed the biography as "a long-drawn-out match, a patient game of skill, played between the living biographer and his dead, but not defenceless, subject. It is still too early, with the fourth and fifth volumes still to come, to decide whether the defence will prove stronger than the attack."[22] According to Quentin Anderson, as I have indicated, "the defence" finally won; for, in the last words of his essay on the biography, he proclaims that Edel is "his deed's creature." And Alfred Kazin obviously agrees, calling the biographer "a loving recapitulation of the artist *as seen by himself.*"[23]

A. O. J. Cockshut has written of Froude's *Carlyle:*

"The greatness of this biography springs from a perfect aptness of author and subject that is almost, if not quite, unique. . . ."[24] It is this same "aptness" of Edel and James that Anderson and Kazin realize only in part. They see, perhaps, that Edel's purpose compliments the spirit and interests of James the man; but they fail to appreciate fully the extent to which Edel's own skill and temperament as an artist-biographer complement his subject's literary achievement. If the following statement is read out of the context of its author's mean-spirited "polemic," it comes closer to a just conclusion about *Henry James:* the biography is, Mark Krupnick writes, "an American *romance,* in which the *scholar* has merged himself with the *artist* and taken on his *omnipotence.*"[25] If interpreted in a way which Krupnick apparently does not intend—for he apparently means simply that Edel has identified himself too completely and self-servingly with James—these appropriated words (with apologies to Krupnick) can be used to state that in this work the scholar, though clearly capable of omissions and misguided emphasis, has nevertheless attained the creative power and also the position of the artist—has become the artist as surely as, say, Hawthorne—or James. I do not believe this judgment extravagant. In fact, the *Journal of Modern Literature* has observed: "*Henry James: The Master* shows a continued capacity for growth and understanding which matches the steady development of James himself." Also, William T. Stafford has written that the work "must be considered—in scope and in dedicatory zeal—a literary event of the first order, commensurate to nothing less, whatever the scholarly disagreements about methods or parts or indeed the quality of mind that produced it, than the indelible impact that the total oeuvre of Henry James has itself made on the imagination of the modern world."[26]

In an essay about the problems and satisfactions he encountered in writing *Henry James*, Edel has made it clear that he feels "any biographer must of necessity become . . . a peripatetic, obsessed literary pilgrim, a traveler with four eyes. His essential job is to see through the alien yet friendly vision of his subject, *while at the same time constantly seeing for himself.* The two ways of looking at the world ultimately become one, the four eyes become two." And he carefully adds, perhaps for the benefit of those commentators who have criticized him for slavishly "becoming" James: "A biographer cannot live inside the skin or vision of his subject and do a decent job of work. No good biographies have ever been written by biographers identified with their subjects. The biographer must remain participant as well as observer, travelling for his own joys."[27]

If we listened to one statement by James, we might find few joys for the subject: "'. . . the art of the biographer—devilish art!—is somehow practically thinning. It simplifies even while seeking to enrich— and even the Immortals are so helpless and passive in death'" (V, 162). Yet, in *Henry James,* we can sometimes view an amusing, mutually-aggrandizing interplay between the "attack" and the "defence" (as Hampshire calls them)—unless our chief motive is censure. Edel infrequently seems to coddle Henry James in the grave, as when, for example, he pictures a charitable gesture of the novelist and then quotes him: "'Let my biographer, however, recall the solid sacrifice I shall have made'" (V, 275). And James occasionally seems to praise Leon Edel *from* the grave: regarding James's last writing, "'These final and faded remarks,' he dictated, 'have some interest and some character—but this should be extracted by *a highly competent person* only—some such whom I don't presume to name, will furnish such last offices'" (V, 553–54; my italics). The end effect is, in a sense, roughly equal to the kind of playfulness one finds in the brilliant little parodic synthesis of James and Edel in Howard Moss's two-page "instant life" of James. Moss begins, "He took a dim view, if, indeed, a view, in all consciousness, could be considered one, when the very act of its perception was, by definition, barely discernible, of biography"; and ends, "He, Henry James,

write a biography? . . . The truth was he could not write
the book. He did not, to put the fact broadly and as simply as possible, know who Leon Edel was."[28]

Again, Edel's purpose and method in *Henry James*
reflect his full appreciation and understanding of his
subject, but the controlling point of view—the last
"look," before the reader's—is his. He is not, in fact,
manipulated; he merely takes full advantage of the practical realities and the aesthetic possibilities in his long
connection with James. It is, indeed, an *auspicious* fact
that Edel "found" James and could re-create him with
the mastery displayed in his final product—and with at
least the partial "cooperation" of James's own comprehensive attitudes toward biography.

IV

To be sure, in burning mounds of his personal papers, James expressed his "'utter and absolute abhor-
rence of any attempted biography'" of himself and lev-
elled "'a curse no less explicit than Shakespeare's own
on any such as try to move my bones'" (V, 142). As Edel
points out, "clearly James felt that the biographer, having no access to the consciousness of his subject in the
large omniscient way of the novelist, could do little with
a literary figure" (II, 17). In dealing with biography,
James, like his historian struggling in *The Sense of the
Past*, "'wanted evidence of a sort for which there had
never been documents enough, or for which documents
mainly, however multipled, would never *be* enough'"
(IV, 331; see also V, 147). However, he seems to have
admired "Sainte-Beuve's search in his biographical
studies for 'the seam as it were between the talent and
the soul'" (II, 396). And when he produced his autobiographical volumes, he rather astoundingly "wrote . . . in

the voice of his father and his brother. When he quoted from their letters he freely revised, as if their texts needed the same retouching given his own work in the New York Edition" (V, 456). Significantly, then, the "truth" which James finally sought before all others was an aesthetic truth.

In James's 1899 essay on George Sand, which Edel views as a kind of preparation for writing his biography of the sculptor William Wetmore Story, James provided us with a discussion of biography that, Edel says, is "nowhere more sustained" (V, 143). There James "suggested that perhaps the artist, the subject, should organize the game of biography on his own terms, rather than leave it to the terms of the biographer. . . . The thing was indeed to burn papers, keep the secrets, challenge the biographer to dig harder for his facts, demand of him a genuine effort of inquiry and research" (V, 144). This, of course, James did for Edel.[29] But the results of this "game" serve to commend Edel, not to condemn him. If James made his biographer work for the historical materials of his achievement, it is, nevertheless, the biographer who has finally done the work.

When James did his own work on the Story life, he let his "creative and organizing imagination play . . . around the impersonal and inanimate documents and sought constantly to 'novelize' them" (V, 157)—to use the techniques of structure and style to make biography effect the kind of enjoyable storytelling which we most often associate with novels. Edel's own best effort mirrors this impulse of James the biographer. In Edel's evaluation of the Story volumes, he says that they are "full of lessons for the modern biographer" (V, 159). In discussing "The Aspern Papers," he likewise suggests that this tale is "a moral fable for all historians and biographers" (III, 220). Conceivably, *Henry James* — as surely as the Story biography, "The Aspern Papers," *Orlando*, and *Edwin Mullhouse* — is also a kind of "fable" for biographers and critics.

At several points in *The Master*, Edel relays

statements from James which seem to justify the major focus of Edel's work. Henry James, for example, felt that "the artist was what he did—he was nothing else" (V, 141); that "Shakespeare, the man, did not exist. What existed was simply the Artist" (V, 148). Edel has written, "James was prepared to accept the art of biography only if it became 'a quest of imaginative experience.' In such circumstances it could be 'one of the greatest adventures of mankind'" (V, 149). James was "a hardy novelist and critic, one who had in him all the splendid egotism of art" (II, 18). It may certainly be a measure of Edel's own great egotism as an artist that he has followed James's phrase about "the greatest adventure of mankind" with this sentence: "This was Henry James's prophecy of the criticism of the future, and of the future of biography" (V, 149). Leon Edel has not become an artist himself because he has written a grand biography of James which fulfills the Master's prophecy. Rather, Edel has walked the tightrope between sycophancy and aptness, and, finally, his display throughout the project of a Master-like egotism has delivered him safely into the latter space.

The greatest truth in *Henry James* is, ultimately, the aesthetic truth of Edel's articulated vision of someone who lived and wrote literature. Regardless of the sources of or influences on the biography, the reader observes here primarily a creature of Edel's imagination. It is for this reason that Edel—unlike some biographers, egotistical in a completely different sense, in naming their handiwork—has not called his five volumes *THE Biography of Henry James*. Had Edel given his whole work a subtitle, it would surely have been *A Biography*—emphasizing that it was a literary re-creation, not a "definitive" reincarnation of an historical existence. This idea is at least suggested in one of Edel's comments about his finished work: "Someday, I'll revise the whole James biography and put it in one volume, adding new stuff. I don't pretend the Life is complete, but it is a total portrait."[30] In light of this statement (and

many scholars' charges of Edel's possessiveness notwithstanding), one might suggest that the biographer
more straightforwardly emphasize the ironically unpos-
sessive egotism of the work and call it *Leon Edel's Henry
James*—à la *Fellini's Satyricon*, or, better, because of
their factual, historical nature, *Fellini's Roma* or *Fellini's
Casanova*.

V

In his introduction to *The Master*, Edel, looking
back over his work, wrote, "This life of Henry James has
had an organic growth; it acquired in the process the
form proper to itself and the proportions suited to its
materials" (V, 20). Besides providing further evidence (if
such is needed) of his artistic self-confidence, this statement also validly, even if "egotistically," points to another kind of aptness to be noticed in this long work:
Henry James is apt not only in terms of its subject, but
also in regard to its formal design. The following pages,
therefore, return to a discussion of the fourth representative type of criticism identified early in this chapter—
that involving form and organization.

Geoffrey Hellman, in his *New Yorker* profile of
Edel, has summed up well the biographer's method:

> In his University of Toronto lectures [which be-
> came *Literary Biography*], Edel has advocated
> "the scenic method in literary biography." Typo-
> graphically, throughout the Life, he has highligh-
> ted this technique by breaking down the individ-
> ual volumes into titled "books," by breaking these
> down into short, numbered episodes, and by
> heading virtually every right-hand page with a
> separate title.[31]

And Millicent Bell, in a significant essay-review of the whole biography, has echoed several critics' characteristic assessment of this method:

> Edel has remembered James's injunction to novelists, "Dramatize, dramatize," and, novelistically, he has tried to make his presentations as frequently scenic as possible, and to bring down his curtains on climaxes of revelation. The result makes for liveliness, though eventually the production of climaxes and revelations seems forced and somewhat vulgar.[32]

Certainly it is true that the reader may become somewhat weary, after about the third volume, of Edel's insistence upon following through with his method. But this insistence may be very like that which we find in the late prose style of Henry James: if the insistence is indeed a weakness, it is, finally, to be patiently indulged for the rewards one may gather beyond it. If Edel were pretending to give us the "real life" consciousness of Henry James, the method would indeed be "vulgar"; but he is instead giving us *his* Henry James, so the insistently-completed design may at last even be endearing to some readers. One may take a *de gustibus* attitude about Edel's extensive use of the method, but one must also remember, as Bell suggests at the beginning of her statement, that it is right in treating James.

In *Aspects of the Novel*, E. M. Forster tells us that in a novel, "whereas the story appeals to our curiosity and the plot to our intelligence, the pattern appeals to our aesthetic sense, it causes us to see the book as a whole." Since the biographer's "plot" is limited by the historical facts he has gathered, it is his book's "pattern" over which he has complete control. Forster goes on to suggest that, in a book he is examining, "What is so good . . . is . . . the suitability of the pattern to the author's mood."[33] Since Edel's "mood" is essentially that of James, one may describe *Henry James* by using

the words which Edel has applied to *The Ambassadors:*
his biography "possesses . . . a felicitous symmetry of
form and content" (V, 70).[34] Selection and juxtaposition
constitute major virtues of the biography; we are getting
bits and pieces, even of facts—yet we get a strong sense
of the whole through the pattern they create.[35]

Early in *The Untried Years*, Edel tells his reader
that James "had a terrible need for order, for design, for
apprehending—and later communicating—the world
around him in an elaborately organized fashion" (I, 116),
and he cleverly explains this need by referring to the
conflicting views on "discipline and order" held by
Henry James, Sr., and William of Albany, Henry's grand-
father. While he continues to demonstrate this idea
throughout the rest of the biography, no passage in the
whole work seems to justify Edel's own method as much
as the following rich selection from *The Master* which
describes the aging Henry's return to America:

> James's inspection of Cambridge began, as might
> be expected, with Harvard, where he found him-
> self musing anew at the shape of the Yard and the
> fact that it was still not sufficiently enclosed. In
> the old days it had been wide open, and the stray
> horse or cow ambled through the campus as if the
> animal too had a claim on American education.
> To him, with his novelist's need for shape and
> form, the unenclosed gave an effect of extempori-
> zation and thinness. (V, 245)

Here, for once at least, the historical Henry James and
Edel's vision of Henry James seem almost to be con-
joined in a symbol of their mutual obsession. (And the
symbol is also remarkably, amusingly, similar to that
which Jeffrey Cartwright uses in *Edwin Mullhouse* when
he contemplates his dire fear, as a biographer, of "letting
the horse step completely out of its frame!"; see Chapter
One.)

Edel has written that "the single most difficult
part" of writing *Henry James* was in "making the reader
feel the passage of the years in the life of my subject" (V,

20). He obviously wanted to write, as Henry James did in "The Aspern Papers," "with the beautiful assurance of one who can make the clock take the rhythm of his tracing pen" (III, 222). But he has not succeeded—although this failure of purpose is not inevitably a weakness of the biography, as I shall demonstrate.

Edel's "retrospective" method (IV, 17) has been much discussed—both by critics and by Edel himself—so it is not necessary to illustrate it extensively here. Suffice it to say that the method works best when Edel uses it to link two or more themes or events that otherwise exist independently within James's busy world. In *The Master*, for example, in a section in which he has discussed, first, James's writing of plays, and, second, the preparation of the New York Edition, Edel neatly ties the various threads together in time with this concluding sentence: "At the moment when the last volume of James's New York Edition came off the press, late in 1909, Granville Barker was seeking a cast for *The Outcry*" (V, 378). Used in a larger way, of course, as Edel has explained, his rejection of strict chronology in a "retrospective" manner has permitted him to include materials which became available between the compositions of the succeeding volumes.

Just as significant, though, is a less well-discussed element of Edel's treatment of time. Like W. A. Swanberg and Andrew Turnbull, and unlike Joseph Blotner, Edel uses "anticipation" extensively through the five volumes (and does it, notably, much more often, it seems, than he shifts over to the historical present tense). Repeatedly, Edel uses phrases like "what he could not foresee" (I, 265), "what Henry could not know" (I, 322), "he could little guess" (II, 199), "he little knew" (II, 296), and "he did not know it then but" (III, 336). In *The Treacherous Years*, Edel writes, "*The Spoils of Poynton* marked a turning point in the fiction of Henry James, although the novelist, struggling on his terrace overlooking Rye, seems hardly to have been aware of this" (IV, 161). Near the end of that volume, the biographer tells us about the literary projects which "would account for the rest of the novelist's life" (IV, 338), stating that "the masterpieces he would write were already sketched in his notebooks" (IV, 354).³⁶ Even well into the fifth volume Edel continues to use the method, as in this passage: "The next four years would be years of great fertility in spite of his advancing years; and they would be Henry James's 'American years,' more American even than the years of his lost youth. The decade that remained to the Master would assert his recaptured self" (V, 316).

Quentin Anderson has noticed Edel's use of this device, writing that, although he finds "Edel's attempt [to give a sense of time passing] quite successful," "the life is made to answer to what it led to."³⁷ Anderson's second statement here is quite correct, but the use of the anticipation technique in fact *prevents* the reader from "feeling the passage of the years." More positively, though, what it does concurrently is reinforce for the reader of the whole biography a feeling of the instinctive "egotistic" control which Edel has over his text—if not over his introductions. (To paraphrase Lawrence, trust the biography, finally, not the biographer.)

Thus, the "lack of chronological stability" which David Passler has found in Boswell's *Johnson*, discussed briefly in Chapter One, may be found, and with some of the same "consequences," in Edel's *James*. The James we see, when we read the five volumes consecutively, is a static James, not truly an evolving one. Edel's image of James is sustained throughout; it does not change. By choosing *not* to tell his story from James's point of view, by *not* sticking to chronological order, by choosing a thematic or associative order, Edel finally makes all times one time—i.e., when Leon Edel is telling the reader his story of Henry James.

VI

Still, it is true that a kind of evolution has taken place, as Edel himself suggests in referring to the "organic growth" of his work. Recently, upon finishing his twelve-volume "novel," *A Dance to the Music of Time*, Anthony Powell was asked about the development of his work and its characters over its twenty-five years of production. He replied that he saw them "in terms of two moving staircases. . . . You are moving on one staircase, on another the books move. Really, I suppose there are three staircases, for life moves on at the same time."[38] At first impression, it would seem a good idea to attempt to analyze the varying methods in Edel's developing five volumes. But, in fact, the variance is more apparent than real; upon examination together, the five volumes reveal remarkably similar techniques and attitudes.

As I have already indicated, Edel's treatment of time is consistent throughout, and his use of particular structural units is sustained. Also, whether Edel always intended to or not, in an earlier volume he often prepared the reader for a motif, an idea, an assertion in a later one. This goes beyond those frequent anticipation passages noted previously and refers to something more subtle. For example, this statement in *The Untried Years*, upon being reread, seems to foreshadow the whole of *The Treacherous Years* and makes Edel's attitudes and theories in the later volume much more palatable than they might otherwise be to some readers who read the fourth book by itself:

> He was ill-equipped to stand editorial rebuff; he was temperamentally unsuited for the more strenuous competition of the literary marketplace. He made his literary debut in a fashion that was devoid of frustration and distinguished in every way. He was to gain self-assurance as he continued to be published and read; but *below the sur-*

> *face remained the fear of failure and of being*
> *considered a failure.* (I, 225; my italics)

Slightly later in volume one, we come upon this sentence: "Henry was as uncompetitive in affairs of the heart as in matters of literary import" (I, 234). The two ideas expressed here summarize and foreshadow attitudes about major areas of the remaining four volumes, in fact: the theatre and its relationship to James's life and work; love; and buried/compensated fear. Further, when we go back to The Untried Years after having read The Master, we may be amazed to find, in Edel's controversial pages about James's "dream of the Louvre" and "the Napoleonic style," the seeds of James's "Napoleonic" deathbed dictations.[39]

When The Master appeared in 1972, one reviewer wrote that "there is indeed an increasing hesitancy [to explore the psyche] throughout the five books which might imply a wavering uncertainty in the biographer." He continued:

> Just as James went back to his earlier writings and revised them for the New York Edition, Edel may someday be tempted to revise the earlier volumes so that the rather dogmatic tone of The Untried Years and its immediate sequels will reflect the liberalizing hindsight which completion of the biography has given him. But we hope he never does so, for there is an immediacy and directness about the five volumes when they are now read together which shows Edel himself maturing and growing wiser the more deeply and extensively he studied his subject.[40]

Noting well the ultimately favorable implication of these comments, I would suggest that Edel's willingness to use a basically psychological method in treating both the life and the works is not diminished after The Untried Years and "its immediate sequels" (meaning, I assume, volumes two and three). In fact, Edel's most provocative, least "hesitating" use of this method appears only when he reaches his fourth volume. For it has been Edel's potent thesis involving the psychology of James's plays, life, and fiction during his "treacherous years" which has sent critics scurrying most often to their battle stations to condemn or defend the biography as a whole.

Throughout the biography, Edel carefully develops themes separately and then intricately intertwines them. The famous vampire motif of James's fiction is linked to Minny Temple (the motif is perhaps summarized best in I, 331); the controversial Jacob-Esau rivalry between Henry and William in volume one[41] may be traced easily into volume four, where Edel tells us of Henry's buying Lamb House against his brother's advice (IV, 318ff), and beyond. Intimations of Henry's complex relationship with Constance Fenimore Woolson near the end of *The Conquest of London* rekindle in the reader memories of Minny—and also early link the Henry/Constance motif with that of Henry and William: "She was to try, during the ensuing decade . . . to write international stories, after the manner of the man to whom she became attached, and with whom she now felt herself, on some strange level, to be competing. Henry must have sensed this. It would have given her, in that case, something of the status of his brother" (II, 417). Of course, the Henry/Constance motif is, late in volume four, linked with that of James and the young sculptor Hendrik Andersen: Woolson, Edel writes, "had known what it was to have the object of her love fail her, fail to recognize the depth of her feeling. This James would in due course learn from Hendrik" (IV, 316). And near the end of volume five, when James is trying to write *The Ivory Tower*, he is "drawing upon the oldest material he possessed. . . . —tales of treachery and fraternal humiliation" (V, 505).

I offer these two passages as essences of the last two volumes:

> Step by step, James's imagination had found, had wrought, the healing substance of his art—the

strange, bewildering and ambiguous novels in
which somehow he had recovered his identity so
that he might be again a strong and functioning
artist. In this process he had opened himself
up—life aiding—to feeling and to love. (IV, 354)

. . .[I]n some strange way his writing of his late
novels was a reliving of his earlier life; as if in
middle age he had to re-examine, to try again, old
artistic experiences, and test them in his maturity.
In setting his ambassador in París he was rewrit-
ing his old story of The American who had gone
to Paris and sought the high world, the feudal
magnificence of Europe. But Newman was a
good-hearted parvenu: Strether was a middle-
aged romantic. And his story of a young woman
doomed to die seemed to be a reliving of his old
Portrait of a Lady which one might say had been
about a young American girl doomed to live. (V,
28)

They suggest in small how Edel thus confidently continues "exploring the psyche."[42]
    Surely any recognition of the remarkable oneness
of vision manifested in Henry James is intensified by our
knowledge of its being composed, on the three "moving
staircases," over five volumes and nineteen years.

VII

In the two passages just quoted from The
Treacherous Years and The Master, we may also see reminders of a final significant aspect of this biography as
a whole: the extensive marriage of biography and criticism.[43] James, Edel says, "shows himself, at every turn,
the novelist performing as critic" (II, 54); at every turn,
Edel shows himself the biographer performing as critic.

Repeatedly Edel gives us examples of how his far-ranging knowledge of all minutiae of the James canon can illuminate a detail in the life (e.g., V, 67); and as he switches from accounts of domestic details to analyses of stories, Edel most often makes his transitions pleasantly smooth (a good passage illustrating this movement is in IV, 159—64).

Edel's critical evaluations of individual James works sometimes seem to be based, naturally perhaps, upon the novelist's degree of artistic control. Compare, for example, his comments on *The Bostonians* and *The Princess Cassimassima* in volume three, pages 138 and 180. But the biographer does provide occasional instances of "social criticism"—as in his excellent, useful, and very favorable discussion of "Daisy Miller" (II, 302). In view of his many biographical finds, Edel is not to be faulted for seldom offering startlingly original critical insights, although he claims such a discovery in making a literary link between "The Turn of the Screw" and "Heart of Darkness" (V, 54).

His best critical contributions in *Henry James* are indeed a close function of his controlling overview as biographer. Thus, we are thankful for Edel's providing, in the context of the life, a discussion of the three versions of *The American* (II, 257, 453) and of the early and late versions, for example, of *The Portrait of a Lady* (V, 329). It is perhaps useful for the reader of James to see that "turned around, [*The Awkward Age*] was the very essence of 'Daisy Miller'" (II, 264), and that "Longstaff's Marriage" and "Maud-Evelyn," "separated by a quarter of a century, are corollary to one another; in reality they tell the same story" (I, 330). Undoubtedly, it is proper for James's biographer, of all people, to suggest that a self-interview which James did for the *New York Times* "belongs in the James canon" (V, 527).

Edel calls *The Golden Bowl* "the richest of all [James's] creations" (V, 211). At one point, the biographer-critic quotes from a scene in the novel—one in which Maggie watches a "game of bridge played by her

father and Mrs. Assingham with the two lovers"—and
then he observes:

> It is one of Henry James's great scenes, in its fine-
> toned "awareness," in the revealed sensibility of
> Maggie Verver, and in its open theatricality. *But
> its greatness perhaps resides in* that James has
> finally been able in a novel to bring into the open
> the deeply buried scenes of his childhood. . . .
> had finally found the combination that could un-
> lock the closed secrets of his life. (V, 216; my
> italics)

Such a critical judgment should not surprise the reader
who remembers the biographical/critical aim that Edel
emphasizes in his introductions to the various volumes:

> His work, in the end, becomes a kind of supreme
> biography. And this is the biography I have
> sought to read. (II, 18)

> Above all, Henry James issued an invitation to
> biographers to seek out the artist in "the invul-
> nerable granite" of his art. I have accepted this
> invitation: for this is where the artist should be
> sought. (III, 17)

> As always, his tales of this time, little fables of his
> own experience, tell us much more than his busy,
> anxious letters. (IV, 22)

> I have . . . been scolded by other biographers for
> regarding the works of the imagination as possi-
> ble "life" material—as if in literature imagination
> could belong to a disembodied mind. (V, 19)

Edel is everywhere noting "the reflections we catch in
the bright mirrors of the tales" (III, 236), "reading the
parallel columns of James's life and James's art" (V, 122).
However much one may object to this deliberate method,
one must still admire the likewise deliberate manner in
which Edel has translated this part of his theory into
practice.

In the biography itself, incidentally, Edel has quietly recalled precedents for his approach. Constance Fenimore Woolson, he tells us, "again and again, in her letters, under the guise of discussing and criticizing Henry's writings" criticized James himself (III, 88). In the last century, Edel says, James Herbert Morse, discussing *The Portrait* in *Century Magazine,* concluded: "'We cannot escape the conviction that [James] has at least so far written himself into his books that a shrewd critic could reconstruct him from them.' And [Morse] went on to be the shrewd critic" by drawing a portrait of James on the basis of his works (II, 428–29).

Outside the biography, where critics and biographers alike continue to disagree about the purposes and practice of literary biography, there are also proponents of Edel's method. Perhaps Richard Poirier, in discussing Frost, has best summarized this apparent support: ". . . the biographical material doesn't tell us as much about the man as the poetry does. By that I mean that the poetry doesn't necessarily come from the experiences of his life; rather the poetry and the life experiences emerge from the same configuration in him prior to his poems or to his experience."[44]

It is now Leon Edel who has gone on to be the "shrewder" critic by virtue of his long view of Henry James's completed life—and of the solid control he has shown in the completed *Life.*

VIII

In spite of Paul Murray Kendall's charge that Edel writes "superbiography," Edel is certainly not the only modern American literary biographer who has attempted to create "a vision of the artist." But it would perhaps be appropriate to call other American practitioners of this third type of literary biography "acolytes" of Edel. Two such followers are James R. Mellow and R. W. B. Lewis.

Mellow, in the acknowledgments of his *Charmed Circle: Gertrude Stein & Company*, straightforwardly admits that "it will be obvious to many readers that Edel's biography has been a model for my own."[45] In a review of the book, Strother Purdy, observing this statement, writes that Mellow "nevertheless spares us the combination of suffocating detail, intermittent excursions into heavy lay psychology, and aesthetic tone deafness that have come to highlight the Modern or Brobdingnagian School of Biography."[46] Is, then, the disciple outstripping the master? Hardly. Mellow's excursions into the world outside Gertrude Stein—the "& Company" of the title at least suggests that this is purposeful—serve not to enlarge the reader's comprehension of the character Gertrude Stein; rather, they tend to make him lose sight of her altogether at times in the book.

Coincidentally, if Edith Wharton is a "daughter" of Henry James, R. W. B. Lewis is a "son" of Leon Edel. And at first reading, Lewis's *Edith Wharton: A Biography* may, indeed, appear to surpass its apparent model. Its documentation apparatus is somewhat easier to use than Edel's. It is a fine physical portrait, as well as a vision of a creative imagination. Even the Lewis thesis is similar to Edel's—and Lewis's assertion that Wharton's fiction "opened up" after her affair with Morton Fullerton is most persuasive in the face of the preserved bit of "pornography" which Lewis displays in an appendix. But upon reexamining the biography, one may conclude with Edel himself in an *American Scholar* review of *Edith Wharton* that, like Mellow, Lewis "has too rigorously, and even mechanically, given us an excess of background. . . . The weakness of this biography . . . resides in Professor Lewis's failure to analyze Edith's psychosomatic medical history, and the psychology of her decaying marriage. . . . What is missing in this important life are the larger brush strokes . . . —the 'grand design' that a biographer must discover within the heaped-up papers of an archive."[47]

So, naturally, perhaps, of an acolyte, speaks the biographical master of The Master.

Afterword:

"Ultimately Fiction"

Through an analysis of specific works which represent three types of literary biography, this study has identified some of the crucial problems of the subgenre and has suggested further possibilities within it. The discussion here has treated literary biographies as vehicles for supplying information and ideas; but, more significantly, it has also stressed their potential value as aesthetic objects, and my title reflects this emphasis.

Bernard Malamud's novel *Dubin's Lives* has provided the first two words of this title. Malamud's fictional protagonist is a biographer who is writing a life of D. H. Lawrence; frequently, as in the following passage, William Dubin pauses in his own life to consider the intricate difficulties of his endeavor:

> There were a billion facts of Lawrence's short life and long work, of which Dubin might use a necessary few million. He would weave them together and say what they meant—that was the brave, the daring thing. . . . [But] no one, certainly no biographer, has the final word. Knowing, as they say, is itself a mystery; it weaves itself as you unweave it. And though the evidence pertains to Lawrence, the miner's son, how can it escape the taint, subjectivity, the existence of Dubin . . . through the contaminated words he chooses to put down as he eases his boy ever so gently into an imagined life? My life joining his with reser-

> vations? But the joining—the marriage?—has to
> be or you can't stay on the track of his past or
> whatever "truth" you're tracking. The past sucks
> up legend: one can't make clay of time's mud.
> There is no life that can be wholly recaptured.
> Which is to say that all biography is ultimately
> fiction. Therefore what else is new?[1]

The "taint" of "subjectivity" is indeed impossible for
any biographer to avoid. But my preceding chapters
have indicated the *positive* ramifications of acknowledg-
ing that "all biography is ultimately fiction"—have emphasized that more biographers should realize the
multilevel truth in this statement and then exploit it to
improve their art.

   "Ultimately Fiction," then, is meant, incidentally,
to suggest that the focus here is mainly upon the lives of
fiction writers. And perhaps it echoes, somewhat face-
tiously, the charges of those critics (often the relatives of
deceased writer-subjects) who characteristically see design of a sinister nature in the literary biographer's work.
More important, though, is the phrase's underlining of
the central ideas which this book tries to convey.

   Thus, *"Ultimately Fiction"* transmits the conviction that all biography should, in Edwin Mullhouse's
words, "aspire to the condition of fiction"—not in terms
of its relinquishing its demand for attainable historical
accuracy, but, rather, in its design: in the nature of its
form and style, in its *aesthetic* truth. The phrase locates
the essences of both the praiseworthy literary biographer's method and the literary subject's life. For the
major American novelists dealt with in this study did,
after all, ultimately transmute their own lives into either
the surface or the heart of their fiction. And the literary
biographers examined should have created literary characters who were finally "fictional"—both because the
biographers could never know their historical subjects
completely, as Malamud observes, and because they
have learned deliberately to utilize so-called fictional

techniques involving the creation of shape, texture, and character.

At first glance, Malamud's afterthought, "Therefore what else is new?" might seem to vitiate my argument. But, in fact, the sentence leads directly to this major point: When articulated, Dubin's discovery may indeed appear truistic. But too many biographers still fail to apply its "obvious" rightness to their own handiwork. And certainly too few critics of literary biography freely admit it.

For example, B. L. Reid, who is both a biographer and a critic, finally, weakly, acknowledges, in an essay called "Practical Biography," that "biography ought to be as well written as a novel"; but he immediately qualifies his statement by adding that "it should not try to be, or to feel like, a novel. Biography becomes a fine art when it performs superbly within the right limits of its own nature." And all of this comes only after he has earlier declared that "biography is not in its nature a fine art; it is a branch of history and Clio is its Muse. Its essence is fact and its shaper is time."[2] "Within the right limits of its own nature" suggests that Reid perceives biography as an inferior genre; in identifying the "shaper" of biography as "time," Reid is exposing his own confusion of historical reality with that which should be primarily literary. The best biography is shaped by that individual point of view—the biographer's—which alone may make it art.

In this new age of biography, the novelists may conceivably be the true heirs to Lytton Strachey's critical intelligence regarding biography. For instance, in an essay entitled "False Documents," E. L. Doctorow considers the essential natures of both fiction and "historical discourse." Ostensibly attempting to defend the novel's position of prominence in our society, this novelist writes that "a visitor from another planet could not by study of the techniques of discourse distinguish composed fiction from composed history"—and he clearly believes "there is no history except as it is composed." For Doctorow, and for other modern novelists, "history is a kind of fiction in which we live and hope to survive, and fiction is a kind of speculative history, perhaps a superhistory, by which the available data for the composition is seen to be greater and more various in its sources than the historian supposes." Doctorow is "thus led to the proposition that there is no fiction or nonfiction as we commonly understand the distinction: there is only narrative." He emphasizes his realization that this is "a novelist's proposition"; but I believe it is one which biographers also must at least consider.[3]

We may conclude, then, that both biography and fiction are *ultimately narrative*, and that the makers of both types of "composed" discourse should attempt the same graceful articulation of their respective purposes and vision. Biographical criticism frequently quotes Desmond MacCarthy's pronouncement that the biographer is "an artist who is on oath." Unquestionably, every biographer must be "on oath" not to deny or change the "truth" of historical facts. But the biographer *may* be an "artist" only if there is included in his or her biographical design another kind of truth as well. Finally, critics of literary biography should overcome American culture's habitual resistance to the mixing of life and art and should stress aesthetic—not merely historical—readings of specifically literary biographical works.

notes

Introduction

1 Robert Littell, "Truth Is Stranger," in *Biography As an Art: Selected Criticism, 1560–1960,* ed. James L. Clifford (New York: Oxford University Press, 1962), p. 125. Subsequent references to materials in *Biography As an Art* will be noted parenthetically, throughout this study, as "BA."

2 Ralph Waldo Emerson, *The Journals and Miscellaneous Notebooks of Ralph Waldo Emerson,* ed. William H. Gilman, et al. (Cambridge: Belknap Press of Harvard University Press). These quotations appear in the entries for 28 May 1839 (Volume VII, ed. A. W. Plumstead, Jr., and Harrison Hayford, 1969, p. 202); 27? October 1845 (Volume IX, ed. Ralph H. Orth and Alfred R. Ferguson, 1971, p. 314); and 13 January 1835 (Volume V, ed. Merton M. Sealts, 1965, p. 11).

3 See R. L. Samsell, "The Falsest of the Arts," in *Fitzgerald/Hemingway Annual 1971,* eds. Matthew J. Bruccoli and C. E. F. Clark, Jr. (Washington, D.C.: NCR/Microcard Editions, 1971), pp. 173–76.

4 Virginia Woolf, *Orlando: A Biography* (1928; rpt. New York: New American Library, 1960), p. 42.

5 Quentin Bell, *Virginia Woolf: A Biography* (New York: Harcourt, 1972), p. 340.

6 See Harold Nicolson, *The Development of English Biography* (1928; rpt. London: Hogarth Press, 1968), p. 70. Subsequent references to this book will be documented, throughout this study, within the text.

7 Paul Murray Kendall, *The Art of Biography* (New York: Norton, 1965), pp. 14–15. Further references to this book will be documented, throughout this study, within the text.

8 Leon Edel, "Biography and the Narrator," *New Republic,* 152 (6 March 1965), 25.

9 Leon Edel, *Literary Biography* (1959; rpt. Bloomington: Indiana University Press, 1973), p. 1. Subsequent references to this book will be documented, throughout this study, in the text; the symbol "LB" will be used.

10 Donald Greene, "The Uses of Autobiography in the

Eighteenth Century," in *Essays in Eighteenth-Century Biography*, ed. Philip B. Daghlian (Bloomington: Indiana University Press, 1968), p. 50. Subsequent quotations from the essays in this volume will be noted, thoughout this book, parenthetically as "EECB."

11 Roy Pascal, *Design and Truth in Autobiography* (London: Harvard University Press, 1960), p. 195.

12. L. P. Hartley, *The Go-Between* (London: Hamish Hamilton, 1953), p. 9.

13 Richard D. Altick, *Lives and Letters: A History of Literary Biography in England and America* (New York: Alfred A. Knopf, 1965), pp. 314–15. Further quotations from Altick's book will be noted, throughout this study, in the text.

14 There were numerous precedents for Adams's technique. Four early autobiographies that Kendall chooses for special mention and praise—those of Pope Pius II, Margery Kempe, and Jean de Bueil, along with that of Caesar—were also written in the third person. See Kendall, p. 63.

15 Leon Edel, *Henry James: The Untried Years: 1843–1870* (New York: Lippincott, 1953), p. 14.

16 Joseph W. Reed, Jr., *English Biography in the Early Nineteenth Century* (New Haven: Yale University Press, 1965), p. 155.

17 T. A. Dorsey, ed., *Latin Biography* (London: Routledge & Kegan Paul, 1967), p. xi.

18 William H. Davenport and Ben Siegel, eds., *Biography Past and Present* (New York: Charles Scribner's Sons, 1965), p. 3. Subsequent references to material in this book will be cited in the text as "Davenport."

19 Henry Seidel Canby, *Turn West, Turn East: Mark Twain and Henry James* (1951; rpt. New York: Houghton Mifflin, 1965), p. 294.

20 Plutarch, *Eight Great Lives* (The Dryden Translation, revised by Arthur Hugh Clough), ed. C. A. Robinson, Jr. (New York: Rinehart, 1960), p. 184. Twenty-two pairs of Plutarch's *Lives* are extant—plus four single biographies.

21 See the introduction in Vivian De Sola Pinto, ed., *English Biography in the Seventeenth Century* (London: George G. Harrap, 1951), pp. 11–46.

22 James Boswell, *Life of Johnson*, ed. R. W. Chapman (London: Oxford University Press, 1970), p. 121.

23 Ralph Rader (in EECB, p. 13) writes, "The pleasure

of Johnson's *Lives* is Johnson, not Pope or Addison [whereas that of Boswell's *Life* is the subject, Johnson, Rader maintains]. This shows how untrue is the usual statement that Boswell followed Johnson's biographical example. He followed it in its emphasis on character and on characterizing particularity, but he departed totally from the basic Johnsonian mode of presentation."

24 Few biographers have been permitted to work as closely with their subjects as Boswell; those who have, such as Albert Bigelow Paine (who thought of himself as Mark Twain's Boswell), have usually lacked Boswell's artistry (see Altick, p. 267). A promising avenue for study is the nature of the "simulated life-relationship" between the life writer and his subject (see Kendall, pp. 148ff). Ralph Rader says the relationship between Boswell and Johnson was "a magnificent literary symbiosis" (EECB, p. 37).

25 Boswell, p. 22.

26 EECB, pp. 93–94. See Clifford's further discussion in Chapter 9 of his *From Puzzles to Portraits: Problems of a Literary Biographer* (Chapel Hill: University of North Carolina Press, 1970), pp. 113–33.

27 Quoted in Thomas Elliott Berry, ed., *The Biographer's Craft* (New York: Odyssey Press, 1967), p. 61.

28 See Reed, p. 66, and Altick, pp. 184–86. Altick points out that Carlyle complained that Lockhart's *Scott* "collected all the materials for a fine biography, but was itself formless and far too long."

29 Nicolson, p. 129. See also A. O. J. Cockshut, *Truth to Life: The Art of Biography in the Nineteenth Century* (New York: Harcourt, 1974), pp. 144–74 (chapter nine), for a variation of this statement—especially regarding Froude's handling of Carlyle's sexual problems.

30 Lytton Strachey, *Eminent Victorians* (1918; rpt. New York: Capricorn Books, 1963), p. xii.

31 In "The Fairest Meed: Biography in America Before 1865," Diss. Columbia 1959, Stephen Jerome Haselton seems to concur with Kendall when he concludes that early American biographers often considered complex ideas but "made few of the methodological developments needed to present these ideas in a convincing manner" (*Dissertation Abstracts,* 20 [September 1959], 1014–15). But in "Biography in American Literature, 1800–1860," Diss. University of North Carolina

1958, James Wilson Webb concludes that "writers of the period were able to make biography a literary form that competed with the novel and other literary forms for readers. In their hands, biographical writing reached a pronounced level of intellectual maturity as literary art" (*Dissertation Abstracts,* 19 [March 1959], 2350).

32 See, e.g., Leon Howard, *Herman Melville: A Biography* (Berkeley: University of California Press, 1951), pp. vii-viii; Charles R. Anderson, *Melville in the South Seas* (New York: Columbia University Press, 1939), passim; and Lawrance Thompson, *Melville's Quarrel With God* (Princeton: Princeton University Press, 1952, p. 75.

33 William H. Gilman, *Melville's Early Life and Redburn* (New York: New York University Press, 1951), pp. 1–2. In 1935, Edward Hayes O'Neill, in *The History of American Biography, 1800–1935* (Philadelphia: University of Pennsylvania Press), praised Weaver's book and called it "as complete a record of Melville's life as we shall ever have" (p. 267); he likewise approved of the use of psychology made by such biographers as Albert Bigelow Paine and Carl Sandburg—but he vehemently denounced the use of "the derivative science, psychoanalysis" (p. 11).

34 See, e.g., John A. Garraty, *The Nature of Biography* (New York: Alfred A. Knopf, 1957), and Catherine Drinker Bowen, *Biography: The Craft and the Calling* (New York: Atlantic-Little, Brown, 1969). Paul Murray Kendall was a practicing biographer. Edgar Johnson, author of the historical narrative-survey *One Mighty Torrent: The Drama of Biography* (New York: Macmillan, 1955), is the biographer of Dickens. And in the 1973 foreword to his *Literary Biography,* a book which began as the Alexander Lectures at the University of Toronto in 1956, Leon Edel writes that "some day—if possible—I hope to expand this work into a full-fledged study. Even in its present modest form it can lay claim to being in the nature of a *poetics* of biography since it is concerned with the biographical finding and making that result in a work of art" (p. x).

35 Frank Brady, "The Strategies of Biography and Some Eighteenth-Century Examples," in *Literary Theory and Structure,* ed. Frank Brady, John Palmer, and Martin Price (New Haven: Yale University Press, 1973), pp. 245, 247. See also Cockshut, p. 11, for another eloquent statement of this problem. James Clifford's interviews with both English and American biographers regarding their work (as reported in Clifford's *From Puzzles to Portraits,* pp. 99–112) bear out dramatically Brady's accusation that biographers are "unaware" of the "formal aspects" of their art; Clifford says he "was curious as to whether practicing life-writers thought as much about form and the creative experience as did novelists and poets" (p. 100). Malcolm Cowley, in a review of the latest biography of Hart Crane ("Hart Crane: The Evidence in the Case," *Sewanee Review,* 78 [1970], 176), quotes a letter from John Unterecker in which the biographer admits quite candidly that "I know next to nothing about biography. . . ."

36 Leon Edel, *Henry James: The Master: 1901–1916* (New York: Lippincott, 1972), pp. 19–20.

37 See Michael Holroyd, *Lytton Strachey: The Years of Achievement, 1910–1932* (New York: Holt, Rinehart and Winston, 1968), pp. 285ff, for a discussion of Strachey's dislike of Florence Nightingale, for example. See also Edel, LB, p. 131; and Burton Bernstein's "authorized, if not approved" *Thurber* (New York: Ballantine Books, 1975)—especially its rather apologetic foreword.

38 For a brief definition of "form," see Notes for Chapter One, note 38.

39 W. H. Auden, *A Certain World: A Commonplace Book* (New York: Viking, 1970), p. vii.

40 Quoted in Altick, p. 402. John Livingston Lowes reinforces Amy Lowell's statement; he notes that some critics hold "the staunch conviction that to follow the evolution of a thing of beauty is to shatter its integrity and irretrievably to mar its charm. But there are those of us who cherish the invincible belief that the glory of poetry will gain, not lose, through a recognition of the fact that the imagination works its wonders through the exercise, in the main, of normal and intelligible powers" (*The Road to Xanadu: A Study in the Ways of the Imagination* [1927; rpt. Boston: Houghton Mifflin, 1955], p. 391). For a rather condescending attack on Lowes' book, see W. K. Wimsatt, Jr., and Monroe C. Beardsley, "The Intentional Fallacy," in W. K. Wimsatt, Jr., *The Verbal Icon* (Lexington: University of Kentucky Press, 1954), pp. 11–12.

41 Although James Dickey has published *Self-Interviews* (New York: Dell, 1970), ironically, he claims that he will never authorize a biography of himself (see p. 10).

42 The two biographies of Eugene O'Neill are Arthur and Barbara Gelb, *O'Neill* (Enlarged Edition with a New Epilogue) (New York: Harper & Row, 1973); and Louis Sheaffer, *O'Neill: Son and Playwright* (New York: Little, Brown, 1968) and *O'Neill: Son and Artist* (New York: Little, Brown, 1973). There are few other notable lives of modern American playwrights; indeed, Tennessee Williams's biography can most easily be approached through his *Memoirs* (New York: Doubleday, 1975).

Among the lives of modern poets, a major book is John Unterecker's *Voyager: A Life of Hart Crane* (New York: Farrar, Straus and Giroux, 1969)—especially because of the many new facts it provides about Crane. T. S. Eliot has, thus far, been treated only in memoirs by those who knew him (e.g., Robert Sencourt's *T. S. Eliot: A Memoir,* ed. Donald Adamson [New York: Dodd, Mead, 1971]) or in rather amateurish narratives (T. S. Matthew's *Great Tom: Notes Towards the Definition of T. S. Eliot* [New York: Harper & Row, 1974], e.g.). Although Eliot, like many modern authors, requested that no life be written, his wife Valerie has now announced that she will choose an official biographer in the future; see Matthews, p. xvii. At the time of Lawrance Thompson's death in April 1973, he had published only two volumes of his official biography of Robert Frost: *Robert Frost: The Early Years, 1874–1915* (New York: Holt, Rinehart and Winston, 1966) and *Robert Frost: The Years of Triumph, 1915–1938* (New York: Holt, Rinehart and Winston, 1970). Thompson's third and final volume, *Robert Frost: The Later Years, 1938–1963,* was completed by R. H. Winnick (New York: Holt, Rinehart and Winston, 1976). Other noteworthy biographies of poets include Noel Stock's *The Life of Ezra Pound* (New York: Discus/Avon, 1970) and James Atlas's *Delmore Schwartz: The Life of an American Poet* (New York: Discus/Avon, 1977).

43 Clifford, pp. 83–95. Clifford might have noted that Jay Leyda seems well aware that his compilation is less than fully "objective." Leyda says that his aim in making *The Melville Log: A Documentary Life of Herman Melville, 1819–1891* (New York: Harcourt, 1951) is "to give each reader the opportunity to be his own biographer of Herman Melville, by providing him with the largest possible quantity of materials to build his own approach to this complex figure" (I, p. xi). And of his later, similar project *The Years and Hours of Emily*

Dickinson (New Haven: Yale University Press, 1960), Leyda writes, "The reconstruction of her life that this book offers is not a substitute for biography; it presents the materials without attempting to build them into a comprehensive structure." Further, he warns "that a reconstruction employing documents of all degrees of relevance appears deceptively continuous and complete; it is neither" (I, p. xix). Leon Howard, in the preface to his *Herman Melville,* calls Leyda's compilation "a sort of cinematic experiment in biography" and his own book "a formal narrative biography" (p. vii). For an analysis of Leyda's *Log,* see Lavon Rasco's unpublished dissertation, "The Biographies of Herman Melville: A Study in Twentieth Century Biography" (Northwestern 1956) (*Dissertation Abstracts,* 17 [February 1957], 357).

44 Clifford, pp. 95–98.

45 The fact that, in setting up my types, I am using an element which involves the biographer's "choice" should not necessarily mean that I am committing the "intentional fallacy." For ultimately, in my analysis of individual literary biographies, "the evaluation of the work of art [in this case, a biography] remains public; the work is measured against something outside the author" (Wimsatt and Beardsley, p. 10).

46 For the purposes of this study, the type of biography which I would call "popular" (Clifford's "narrative" type) will, of course, be omitted. Another type, which might be viewed as a variation under my category "portrait," also will not be treated here, since it is principally concerned with the creative work. It is what Edel terms a "hybrid" of his own second type—the *"critical biography:* that is, a biography which seeks to delineate the subject in terms of the works and by a critical discussion of these is able to convey some picture of the creating mind or personality." Edel dismisses this type (and I concur with his judgment) with the suggestion that its force is usually "accidental" and that it is therefore inferior to his third type (see LB, pp. 127–28).

⚓ Chapter One

1 Louis Sheaffer, interviewed by William Glover, "Doubts Plagued Author of O'Neill Biography," *Indianapolis Star*, 28 July 1974, Sec. 8, p. 5.

2 Thomas Elliott Berry, ed., *The Biographer's Craft* (New York: Odyssey Press, Inc., 1967), p. 19.

3 Desmond MacCarthy's statement first appeared in his article, "Lytton Strachey as a Biographer," *Life and Letters*, 8 (March 1932), 90–102. See Altick, p. 301; Kendall, p. 15; and Leon Edel's review of Kendall, *New Republic*, 152 (6 March 1965), 25–27.

4 Virginia Woolf, "The Art of Biography" (1939), in *Biography Past and Present*, eds. William H. Davenport and Ben Siegel (New York: Charles Scribner's Sons, 1965), p. 170. Subsequent quotations from this book will be identified as "Davenport" in my text. See Thomas Haight Chalfant, "The Marriage of Granite and Rainbow: Virginia Woolf as Biographer," *Dissertation Abstracts International*, 32 (1971), 3298A (University of Wisconsin).

5 Leon Edel, *Literary Biography*, pp. 7–8. In an article which describes how he finished his *Henry James*, Edel writes: "The modern biographer, as I often say, must melt down his materials or be smothered by them" ("The Final Chord of the Quintet," *New York Times Book Review*, 6 February 1972, p. 2). See also LB, p. 31.

6 Frederick A. Pottle, "*The Life of Johnson*: Art and Authenticity," in *Twentieth Century Views of Boswell's* Life of Johnson, ed. J. L. Clifford (New York: Prentice-Hall, 1970), p. 72.

7 See Edward Hayes O'Neill, *A History of American Biography, 1800–1935* (Philadelphia: University of Pennsylvania Press, 1935), p. 184.

8 Kendall, *The Art of Biography*, p. 142. See Edel's review of this book (above, note 3) for a good argument against Kendall's statement.

9 See, e.g., John Dussinger, "Style and Intention in Johnson's *Life of Savage*," *Journal of English Literary History*, 37 (1970), 564–80; and Frank Brady, "The Strategies of Biography and Some Eighteenth-Century Examples," in *Literary Theory and Structure*, ed. Frank Brady, John Palmer, and

Martin Price (New Haven: Yale University Press, 1973), p. 251. Cyril Connolly includes the *Life of Savage* in his *Great English Short Novels* (New York: Dial Press, 1953).

10 The phrase is used in William T. Stafford, "On Movies and Literature: What They Can Do For (And Perhaps To) One Another," University of Tulsa Graduate Institute of Modern Letters Colloquium on the Current Critical Scene, Tulsa, Oklahoma, 8 July 1974, p. 18.

11 Aldous Huxley, *Point Counter Point* (1928; rpt. London: Chatto and Windus, 1963), p. 455.

12 William Hjortsberg, "*Edwin Mullhouse*," *New York Times Book Review*, 17 September 1972, p. 2. My view—and Hjortsberg's—should perhaps be contrasted with that of Joseph Kanon, who writes in the *Saturday Review* (30 September 1972, p. 78) that this level of the novel "—that of a commentary on, and remembrance of, childhood—is licked before it starts by the distance a satirical style imposes." Although I do not wish to pursue the point here, I maintain that often the two levels enrich, rather than cancel, each other.

Theorists of satire have not stressed enough, I think, this factor of truth in the genre. For example, when Gilbert Highet, in his *The Anatomy of Satire* (Princeton: Princeton University Press, 1962), only suggests it in his "final test for satire" ("a blend of amusement and contempt" in the author [p. 21]), Patricia Meyer Spacks has to expand the idea in her own summary of his theory: "The purpose of satire . . . is to combine jest and earnest, 'to tell the truth laughing.' The best satire contains the minimum of convention, a maximum of reality: satire constantly approaches truth-telling, but truth-telling formed and limited by special techniques" ("Some Reflections on Satire," in *Satire: Modern Essays in Criticism*, ed. Ronald Paulson [Englewood Cliffs, N.J.: Prentice-Hall, 1971], p. 361).

13 Northrop Frye, *Anatomy of Criticism: Four Essays* (Princeton: Princeton University Press, 1957), p. 224.

14 See Highet, p. 103.

15 Steven Millhauser, *Edwin Mullhouse: The Life and Death of An American Writer, 1943–1954, by Jeffrey Cartwright* (New York: Alfred A. Knopf, 1972), p. viii. Subsequent references to this volume will be cited in my text. Since 1978, *Edwin Mullhouse* has been available in an Avon/Bard paperback edition.

16 See, in addition to the reviews by Hjortsberg and

Kanon, "A Few Novels," *New Republic,* 16 September 1972, pp. 30–31; Walter Clemons, "Haunted Exile," *Newsweek,* 9 October 1972, p. 106; Martha Duffy, "That's All, Folks," *Time,* 25 September 1972, ST6; and the extraordinarily obtuse review by William H. Pritchard, "Long Novels and Short Stories," *Hudson Review,* 26 (Spring 1973), 233.

17 It might be noted that the device of the fictional biographer is better sustained, and therefore perhaps more successful, in *Edwin Mullhouse* than in *Orlando.* For a discussion of Woolf's sexless plodder, see John Graham, "The 'Caricature Value' of Parody and Fantasy in *Orlando,*" in *Virginia Woolf: A Collection of Essays,* ed. Claire Sprague (Englewood Cliffs, N.J.: Prentice-Hall, 1971), pp. 101–16.

18 See Irving Howe, "The World He Mimicked Was His Own," *New York Times Book Review,* 1 October 1961, p. 34, regarding Schorer's alleged lack of sympathy for Sinclair Lewis. Wade Van Dore begins his emotional review, "Robert Frost: A Memoir and a Remonstrance" (*Journal of Modern Literature,* 2 [November 1972], 554–60), by saying, "Probably the greatest 'tragedy' that ever befell Robert Frost was Lawrance Thompson, and this happened on the day he chose Thompson to be his biographer. Lesley Frost has lamented that Thompson seems to have hated her father rather than loved him the way his family did." See also Marvin Mudrick, "Last Tango in Panoply," *Hudson Review,* 27 (Summer 1974), 303–7; in this wildly sarcastic review of Ellmann's *Golden Codgers,* Mudrick ultimately questions the motives of many authors—including Ellmann, Thompson, Carlos Baker, and Arthur Mizener—whom he shelves under the label "a new breed of literary biographer . . . the squirmy biographers." Finally, John Unterecker, in his *Voyager: A Life of Hart Crane,* carries patience and sympathy with his subject to almost embarrassing extremes, it seems to me. In a letter to Malcolm Cowley (see Notes for Introduction, note 35), Unterecker writes: "Most biographers . . . get tired of their subjects, sometimes come actively to dislike them. That's one reaction I *didn't* have. . . . All the way through my work on the book, I kept feeling: well, this is one man who's worth all this time and trouble."

19 See, e.g., pp. 28–29, 113–14, 206, 254.

20 Richard Ellmann, *Golden Codgers: Biographical Speculations* (New York: Oxford University Press, 1973), p. 6.

Further references to this book will be noted in the text as "GC." Robert S. Newdick, writer of an "interrupted" biography of Robert Frost, had an amazingly similar conversation with his subject; see Lewis P. Simpson, *American Literature*, 49 (May 1977), 279.

21 See, e.g., pp. 250–52, where Jeffrey describes in vivid detail the diverse illnesses—including whiteness of the tongue, diarrhea, constipation, an excess of sugar in the blood, violent headaches, and dizzy spells—which the act of creation causes in the Author; Jeffrey interrupts his narrative to ponder the relationship between *Cartoons* and these physical manifestations of weakness: "And is it possible that a work of art is born not of strength but of weakness, of weakness trying to become strength, of weakness brought to such a pitch of frenzy that it becomes strength?" (Edmund Wilson would, of course, be proud of his fellow critic here.)

22 Michael Rosenthal, "The High Priestess of Bloomsbury," *New York Times Book Review*, 5 November 1972, p. 18.

23 Edgar Johnson, *One Mighty Torrent: The Drama of Biography* (New York: Macmillan, 1955), p. 474.

24 William Gass, "In the Cage," *New York Review of Books*, 10 July 1969, p. 4.

25 Floyd C. Watkins, "Faulkner, Faulkner, Faulkner," *Sewanee Review*, 82 (Summer 1974), 519.

26 John Livingston Lowes, *The Road to Xanadu: A Study in the Ways of the Imagination* (1927; rpt. Boston: Houghton Mifflin, 1955), p. 390. Further quotations from this book will be noted in my text. Jacques Barzun, in an intriguing defense of the uses of biography in criticism ("Biography and Criticism—a Misalliance Disputed," *Critical Inquiry*, 1 [March 1975], 485), seems to echo Lowes: "the act of creation does not take place in a vacuum." But contrast René Wellek and Austin Warren, *Theory of Literature*, 3rd ed. (New York: Harcourt, 1970), pp. 80, 148–50.

27 Malcolm Cowley mentions such interpretation, e.g., in "Hart Crane: The Evidence in the Case," *Sewanee Review*, 78 (1970), 177.

28 There are, of course, noteworthy exceptions here. For example, the extra-literary activities of the "swashbuckling" author (Hemingway, for instance; Carlos Baker's life is discussed briefly in Chapter Three) have obviously attracted biographers and readers alike; but if the author has made any major literary accomplishments, then his primary attraction, it seems to me, will ultimately concern the fact that he created his novels, or poems, or plays. What about the successful biography of the "swashbuckler" who was only a minor writer? This I might call the "*Savage* syndrome" (after Johnson's life of Richard Savage, a minor eighteenth-century poet) and suggest that, aside from the misadventures of the protagonist, the major attraction for the reader is generated by the literary virtuosity of the biographer. By my calculations, modern American literary biography holds exceedingly few examples of the "*Savage* syndrome." For one prominent example, see the end of Chapter Three, p. 145.

29 In addition to the example of Raymond Weaver's biography of Melville (cited in Introduction), see Lynn Marie Zimmerman Bloom, "How Literary Biographers Use Their Subjects' Works: A Study of Biographical Method, 1865–1962," *Dissertation Abstracts*, 24 (1963), 2458 (University of Michigan).

30 John Garraty, *The Nature of Biography* (New York: Alfred A. Knopf, 1957), p. 240.

31 James L. Clifford, *From Puzzles to Portraits: Problems of a Literary Biographer*, (Chapel Hill: University of North Carolina Press, 1970), p. 131.

32 John Cody, *After Great Pain: The Inner Life of Emily Dickinson* (Cambridge: Harvard University Press, 1971), pp. 2–3. Of special interest in Cody's introduction is his helpful explanation, for the skeptical, of both the advantages and the disadvantages of the psychographer versus the psychoanalyst (who can work with a living patient) (pp. 5ff). One recent "lay" literary biographer who seems to have discovered on his own what I have termed Cody's "major guideline" is Douglas Day. See especially pp. 72–73 in Day's *Malcolm Lowry: A Biography* (New York: Oxford University Press, 1973). (For a contrasting view, see Leo F. O'Connor, "Malcolm Lowry and The House of Failure," *Literature and Psychology*, 24 [1974], 167–70.)

33 Quoted in Kendall, p. 34. Kendall's discussion here shows that he agrees whole-heartedly with Maurois; they are both aligned against Leon Edel on the issue.

34 David L. Passler, *Time, Form, and Style in Boswell's*

Life of Johnson (New Haven: Yale University Press, 1971), p. 34.

35 A. O. J. Cockshut, *Truth to Life: The Art of Biography in the Nineteenth Century* (New York: Harcourt, 1974), p. 206.

36 William R. Siebenschuh, *Form and Purpose in Boswell's Biographical Works* (Berkeley: University of California Press, 1972), pp. 71, 9, 80.

37 Passler, pp. 140, 138.

38 The words "form" and structure" are used synonymously in this study and mean, most simply, "shape." I do not attempt to differentiate between them in the manner of Passler (see his p. 52, note 24).

39 Brady, p. 247.

40 See Margaret Church, *Time and Reality: Studies in Contemporary Fiction* (Chapel Hill: The University of North Carolina Press, 1963), pp. 19–20.

41 The major viewpoints here are found represented, again, in the writings of Edel and Kendall. Chapter V of *Literary Biography* is called "Time"; it almost appears that Kendall's whole book is primarily an excuse to present an argument, on pp. 135–43, against the ideas in Edel's chapter. It is perhaps curiously ironic, though, that in their discussions of theory, these two critics both make a small but noteworthy error regarding "clock time": in the early edition of LB, Edel referred to the fact that Henry James attended Ralph Waldo Emerson's funeral in "1883" (p. 146); in the heat of his rather wrong-headed disputation, Kendall (p. 138) repeats this information—although, according to Emerson's biographer, Ralph Rusk (*The Life of Ralph Waldo Emerson* [New York: Columbia University Press, 1964], p. 508), the poet died on 27 April 1882. Edel has not changed the number in his 1973 reprinting of LB, but the date is correct in the third volume of *Henry James*.

42 Besides the neat, three-part structure in *Edwin Mullhouse*, Jeffrey also gives us some other formal conventions of the "scholarly" literary biography. In his case, this means, for example, a long list of "all the books Edwin is known to have owned between the impressionable ages of two and three" (which were "much of a muchness," although "for all practical purposes he was as illiterate as a mouse"); an enormous catalog of the gifts which Edwin gave Rose Dorn (including wax false teeth and a blue-black plastic inkstain); or a complete inventory of the cartoons which Edwin and Jeffrey saw ("A Tail of Two Kitties," "The Brothers KaraMOUSEov," "The Fall of the Mouse of Usher").

43 Maurice Beebe, "'Paris Was Where the Twentieth Century Was': Literary Memoirs of the Twenties," seminar presentation, University of Tulsa, Tulsa, Oklahoma, Summer 1973, pp. 14–15.

44 Passler, p. 143.

45 Vance Bourjaily, "Hemingway on Trial, Judge Baker Presiding," *New York Times Book Review*, 27 April 1969, p. 38.

Chapter Two

1 George Steiner, "The Last Victorian," *New Yorker*, 17 February 1975, pp. 103, 106.

2 A. O. J. Cockshut, *Truth to Life: The Art of Biography in the Nineteenth Century* (New York: Harcourt, 1974), passim.

3 Lawrance Thompson, *Robert Frost: The Early Years: 1874–1915*, *Robert Frost: The Years of Triumph: 1915–1938*, and *Robert Frost: The Later Years: 1938–1963* (New York: Holt, Rinehart and Winston, 1966, 1970, and 1976); and Arthur Mizener, *The Far Side of Paradise: A Biography of F. Scott Fitzgerald* (Boston: Houghton Mifflin, 1951; revised 1965). Although Thompson's biography is used for contrast in this chapter, *Robert Frost* is billed as a "critical and interpretative" biography by its publishers.

David Minter's *William Faulkner: His Life and Work* (Baltimore: Johns Hopkins University Press, 1980), which also uses conventional footnoting, should likewise be contrasted with Blotner's volumes. Minter freely draws on the 1974 biography (he calls it "a storehouse of facts"); but his purpose in this much shorter work is quite different. "My claim to the reader's attention," Minter writes, ". . . stems from the story I try to tell—of deep reciprocities, of relations and revisions, between Faulkner's flawed life and his great art" (p. ix). This biographer deals "simultaneously with [Faulkner's] art and his life, bringing the two into many different juxtapositions and conjunctions" (p. x). At least in his apparent desire to trace the lines of an imagination at work, Minter is similar to Leon Edel and other writers of my third type of literary biography (see my Chapter Four).

4 Carlos Baker, *Ernest Hemingway: A Life Story* (New York: Charles Scribner's Sons, 1969); and John Unterecker, *Voyager: A Life of Hart Crane* (New York: Farrar, Straus, and Giroux, 1969), p. vii.

5 David Levin, *In Defense of Historical Literature* (New York: Hill and Wang, 1967), p. 5.

6 Jay Martin, *Nathanael West: The Art of His Life* (New York: Farrar, Straus, and Giroux, 1970); and Mark Schorer, *Sinclair Lewis: An American Life* (New York: McGraw-Hill, 1961), pp. 807–13. In *Ferber: A Biography of Edna Ferber and Her Circle* (Garden City: Doubleday, 1978), Julie Goldsmith Gilbert uses reverse chronology, beginning with her great-aunt's death and ending with her birth.

7 Joseph Blotner, *Faulkner: A Biography* (New York: Random House, 1974), p. 1807. Subsequent references to this biography will be noted in the text.

8 Elizabeth Nowell, *Thomas Wolfe: A Biography* (New York: Doubleday, 1960).

9 Favorable: Carlos Baker, "From Genesis to Revelation," *Virginia Quarterly Review,* 50 (Summer 1974), 438–40; Terry Heller, *Arizona Quarterly,* 30 (Winter 1974), 355–57; Ilse Dusoir Lind, *Modern Fiction Studies,* 20 (Winter 1974–75), 560–64; and Charles Newman, "An Exemplary Life," *Harper's,* April 1974, p. 98. Unfavorable: William H. Gass, "Mr. Blotner, Mr. Feaster, and Mr. Faulkner," *New York Review of Books,* 27 June 1974, pp. 3–5; Paul Gray, "Footnotes to Genius," *Time,* 25 March 1974, pp. 86–88; Jonathan Yardley, "Everything You Ever Wanted to Know About the Man—Not the Artist." *New York Times Book Review,* 17 March 1974, pp. 1–3; and *New Yorker,* 9 September 1974, pp. 132–33. Mixed: Richard P. Adams, *American Literature,* 46 (November 1974), 392–93; Walter Clemons, "Hunting for Faulkner," *Newsweek,* 25 March 1974, pp. 91–92; Malcolm Cowley, "The Overbrimming Life of a Man of Literary Genius," *Chicago Tribune Book World,* 24 March 1974, pp. 1–2; and Floyd C. Watkins, "Faulkner, Faulkner, Faulkner,"

Sewanee Review, 82 (Summer 1974), 518–27. All subsequent references to these reviews will be made in the text. In her review, Lind notes that "in recognizing its monumental character, one hopes that the biography will not itself *become* a monument" (my italics).

10 Cockshut, p. 101.

11 Robert Craft, "Huxley at Home," *New York Review of Books*, 23 January 1975, p. 12.

12 Cockshut, p. 169.

13 Levin, pp. 6–7.

14 Richard Todd, "'Are You Too Deeply Occupied to Say If My Verse Is Alive?'" *Atlantic*, January 1975, p. 80. The new life of Dickinson is by Richard B. Sewall.

15 See especially Heller, 355–56, and Watkins, 526–27.

16 Quoted in Charles Thomas Samuels, "John Updike: The Art of Fiction, XLIII," *Paris Review*, 45 (Winter 1968), 93.

17 Blotner's decision to present Faulkner's early years, and even his ancestors, in detail should be contrasted to Justin Kaplan's somewhat naive justification (in his preface) for starting *Mr. Clemens and Mark Twain* (New York: Simon and Schuster, 1966) with Twain at age thirty-one: "He was always his own biographer, and the books he wrote about these [early] years are incomparably the best possible accounts, even if they may not always be the truest (and it is possible to argue that Clemens' omissions and reshapings in themselves suggest a kind of truth)."

18 For statements about the importance of future Faulkner biographical material on Faulkner criticism, see Robert Penn Warren, "Introduction: Faulkner: Past and Future," in *Faulkner: A Collection of Critical Essays* (Englewood Cliffs, New Jersey: Prentice-Hall, Inc., 1966), p. 21; and Edmond L. Volpe, "Life and Career," *A Reader's Guide to William Faulkner* (New York: Farrar and Straus, 1964), pp. 5–6.

19 Cockshut, p. 174.

20 Michael Holroyd, "The Revolving Bookstand: Out of Print," *American Scholar*, 39 (Spring 1970), 312.

21 Blotner writes about a part of *The Town*: "... Faulkner used a strategy that Conrad had often employed. He was interested not so much in what had happened as why it had happened, and therefore he gave away suspense to achieve psychological penetration" (p. 426). Generally,

Blotner himself achieves neither suspense nor psychological penetration.

22 It might be worthwhile to compare Faulkner's mythmaking with that of Hemingway (as seen by Baker) and Frost (as seen by Thompson)—and to attempt to see how this mythmaking is related to the creation of the novels and the poetry.

23 Cockshut, p. 87.

24 And beyond these weaknesses, of course, he has failed to examine the quality of his facts themselves. Edward Gibbon divided facts into three classes: "facts that prove nothing but their own existence," "facts that reveal the motives of an action or a trait of character," and "the rarest . . . facts that, prevailing throughout a system, 'move its interior springs'" (see *New Yorker*, 22 September 1975, p. 132).

Charles Newman, in his *Harper's* review, wrote that "Blotner will no doubt be criticized for a kind of academic overkill, as well as for his open, occasionally fawning, admiration for his subject." And then he predicted "that the *New York Review of Books* will reserve one of its finer poodle collars for his [Blotner's] garrote." The "poodle collar" was indeed later created by William H. Gass, and his piece could not be any more enjoyable even if it were less true. Gass writes that "Joseph Blotner's massive Egyptian work is not so much a monument to a supremely gifted writer as it is the great man's grave itself [both Strachey and Virginia Woolf used the grave image to describe biography] . . . ," and then he proceeds to make a very witty attack on Blotner's judgment in selecting his facts. After reading Gass's review, however, the reader is left with some rather large questions: Is literary biography really worth writing at all? If so, have there been any "exemplary" ones? Gass damns even Richard Ellmann's much-admired *James Joyce* (New York: Oxford University Press, 1959).

25 See Yardley, p. 2.

26 Perhaps Joan's letters no longer exist? The use of letters in literary biography has always presented a great problem. Carlos Baker's *Hemingway* suffers considerably because the subject stipulated in his will that none of his letters could be reproduced (see Denis Brian, *Murderers and Other Friendly People* [New York: McGraw-Hill, 1973], p. 17); Baker uses some imagination in presenting his summaries of Hemingway's letters, but he is finally defeated, it seems to me, in his efforts — especially when he attempts to deal with the love letters. By contrast, Unterecker quotes so many letters at such great length in his *Voyager* that the work may conceivably be read as a kind of epistolary novel. Some of Hemingway's letters have now been released for publication by Baker; see James Atlas, "The Private Hemingway," *New York Times Magazine*, 15 February 1981, pp. 23ff.

27 See Shirley Williams, "Ten Years for the Complete Faulkner," *Louisville Courier-Journal and Times*, 1 December 1974, p. E5.

28 Levin, p. 138; ironically, Blotner shows us that he realizes perfectly what Faulkner does in *Absalom, Absalom!* (see p. 1715) — without seeming to realize the need for its application to his biography, to biography in general.

29 Meta Carpenter Wilde and Orin Borsten, *A Loving Gentleman: The Love Story of William Faulkner and Meta Carpenter* (New York: Jove/Harcourt, 1976), photo section following p. 184.

30 Thompson, II, p. xv.

31 Maybe Blotner should have borrowed Boswell's explanation about the effusiveness of his account of his first meeting Dr. Johnson: "My readers will, I trust, excuse me for being thus minutely circumstantial, when it is considered that the acquaintance of Dr. Johnson was to me a most valuable acquisition, and laid the foundation of whatever instruction and entertainment they may receive from my collections concerning the great subject of the work which they are now perusing" (*Life*, Oxford edition, p. 282).

32 Contrast the effectiveness of this one sentence from Lawrance Thompson at the outset of his *Robert Frost:* "The *vicissitudes* of our friendship are suggested by those of his letters to me which were published in *Selected Letters of Robert Frost*, and they may serve as my credentials" (I, p. xxv; my emphasis). For a good example of how the conflict between a subject and the biographer as character in the subject's story may affect the way the biography is written, see John Nathan's *Mishima* (Boston: Little, Brown, 1974).

33 P. 1729; emphasis added. Ironically, it was the present which was finally "de-clutched": facts of *The Mansion* were ultimately changed to match those in *The Hamlet* (see pp. 1724, 1734). See also Victor Strandberg, "Between Truth and Fact: Faulkner's Symbols of Identity," *Modern Fiction Studies*, 21 (Autumn 1975), 445–57.

34 In discussing *A Moveable Feast,* Carlos Baker refers to Hemingway's term "real gen" (*Hemingway: The Artist as Writer* [Princeton: Princeton University Press, 1972], p. 350). One wonders what the "real gen" of Faulkner's memoirs would have been, had he written them. Faulkner said that he never wanted anyone to tell "the Wm. Faulkner story," and he protested that he certainly couldn't ever write it himself, for "I couldn't tell the truth about Faulkner, I'm sure" (pp. 1697, 6). At one point in *Faulkner,* though, Blotner gives us this quotation from a Faulkner letter: "I am thinking about writing my memoirs. That is, it will be a book in the shape of a biography but actually about half fiction, chapters resembling essays about dogs and horses and family niggers and kin, chapters based on actual happenings but 'improved' where fiction would help, which will probably be short stories. I would like to use some photographs. Maybe some of my own drawings. It would probably run about novel length, it will ramble some but will mostly be confined between Rowan Oak, my home in town here, and the farm, Greenfield" (p. 1452).

35 Pp. 1705, 1222, 1312, and 717ff, respectively. This last passage, set off slightly from the rest of the text and beginning "Why did he drink?" is very unusual—and probably Blotner's best piece of speculative writing. It resembles a passage in Constantine FitzGibbon's *The Life of Dylan Thomas* ([Boston: Little, Brown, 1965], pp. 131ff), which begins "Why did he drink so much?" But Blotner has done what FitzGibbon did not do: he has gone to medical authorities for part of his answer (see Blotner's notes, p. 104). See also James L. Clifford, *From Puzzles to Portraits* (Chapel Hill: University of North Carolina Press, 1970), p. 130; and Edward Larkin, "Biographers and Doctors," *Times Literary Supplement*, 22 March 1974, pp. 289–90.

36 Quoted in Williams, p. E5.

37 Marshall Waingrow, "Johnson's *Life of Savage:* Biography as Conjecture," paper read at Seminar 13, Modern Language Association convention, Chicago, December 1973, pp. 9, 11.

38 Faulkner does dedicate *The Mansion* to Phil Stone —but this is, nevertheless, while he is in the proximity of Joseph Blotner's friendship, and it is (as Blotner reminds the reader) "a gesture to the past carried out in spite of the present" (p. 1681), seemingly as much "for consistency" (p. 1727) as for any real gratitude for the special interest and faith which Stone had always had in the trilogy material (see p. 1586).

39 See Joyce Carol Oates, "The Sacred Marriage," in *Marriages and Infidelities* (New York: Vanguard Press, 1972), pp. 3–36.

40 Unterecker, p. 773.

Chapter Three

1 John Leonard, "The Battle of the Books, 1974," *New York Times Book Review*, 1 December 1974, p. 111.

2 Hilton Kramer, "Writing Writers' Lives," *New York Times Book Review*, 8 May 1977, p. 3.

3 Kramer, p. 44.

4 Richard Locke, "Can These Bones Live?" *New York Times Book Review*, 29 January 1978, p. 3.

5 Virginia Woolf, *The Second Common Reader* (New York: Harcourt, 1932), p. 240.

6 Woolf, pp. 238–39.

7 James Dickey, *Self-Interviews* (New York: Dell, 1970), p. 16.

8 Wilfrid Sheed's introduction is reprinted as "More Writers At Work," *New York Times Book Review*, 1 August 1976, pp. 5, 10, and 14. This quotation appears on p. 5.

9 Sheed, p. 14.

10 Quoted in Wade Van Dore, "Robert Frost: A Memoir and a Remonstrance," *Journal of Modern Literature*, 2 (November 1972), 560.

11 William Gass, "Mr. Blotner, Mr. Feaster, and Mr. Faulkner," *New York Review of Books*, 27 June 1974, p. 4.

12 See the section called "Shakespeare's Imagery and the Man," pp. 200–209, in Caroline Spurgeon, *Shakespeare's Imagery, And What It Tells Us* (New York: Macmillan, 1935). But see also S. Schoenbaum, *William Shakespeare: A Com-*

pact Documentary Life (New York: Oxford University Press, 1972), p. viii.

13 Regarding how literary biographers must take special care when they try to make literal and practical applications of Thoreau's theory of how an author's work is linked to personality, see the admonitions in Stephan Ullmann, "Style and Personality," *Review of English Literature*, 6 (1965), 21–31. Ullmann points out that even Leo Spitzer moved in his later lectures to a position which held that " 'psychoanalytical stylistics' [Spitzer's early and celebrated specialty] was merely a special form of the 'biographical fallacy' " (p. 25). In *Style and Stylistics* (London: Routledge and Kegan Paul, 1969), Graham Hough notes that "the naive equation of what a writer reveals in his work with his historic personality is always very uncertain" (p. 45); and in discussing Spitzer's change of mind, Hough writes that the great critic "came to distinguish more clearly between the creative imagination and the historic personality of the author, and between the work of art and the mind of its creator" (pp. 63–64).

14 David Levin, *In Defense of Historical Literature* (New York: Hill and Wang, 1967), p. 13.

15 René Wellek and Austin Warren, *Theory of Literature*, 3rd ed. (New York: Harcourt, 1970), pp. 140–41.

16 Leon Edel, "Biography: A Manifesto," *Biography: An Interdisciplinary Quarterly*, 1 (Winter 1978), 1.

17 I use "so-called" with the phrase "fictional techniques" advisedly. For in a review of a book which treats the nonfiction novel (John Hollowell's *Fact & Fiction*), Chester Eisinger has pointed out that "the use of point of view, dramatic scene, full dialogue, and so on [which presumably includes the elements of style] . . . are not the fundamental distinguishing marks of fiction; and they are characteristics of any kind of narrative—historical, biographical, whatnot. The problem of the differences between fiction and nonfiction, and the similarities, is immensely complex." Eisinger suggests, further, that the real differences are "metaphysical," "theoretical." Eisinger's review appears in *American Literature*, 49 (November 1977), 489. See also Afterword and particularly its note 3.

18 Wellek and Warren, p. 177.

19 George T. Wright, ed., *Seven American Stylists:*

From Poe to Mailer: An Introduction (Minneapolis: University of Minnesota Press, 1973), p. 10.

20 Huntington Brown, *Prose Styles: Five Primary Types* (Minneapolis: University of Minnesota Press, 1966), p. 3.

21 David Passler, *Time, Form, and Style in Boswell's Life of Johnson* (New Haven: Yale University Press, 1971), p. 104. Emphasis added.

22 Richard Poirier, *A World Elsewhere: The Place of Style in American Literature* (New York: Oxford University Press, 1966), p. viii.

23 Nicholas Phillipson, "Intuitions and Interactions," *Times Literary Supplement*, 24 January 1975, p. 90.

24 Hough, p. 43.

25 Northrop Frye, *The Well-Tempered Critic* (Bloomington: Indiana University Press, 1963), p. 60.

26 Frye, pp. 60–61.

27 Virginia Spencer Carr, *The Lonely Hunter: A Biography of Carson McCullers* (New York: Doubleday, 1975); and Matthew J. Bruccoli, *The O'Hara Concern: A Biography of John O'Hara* (New York: Random House, 1976).

28 Tony Tanner, *City of Words* (New York: Harper and Row, 1971), p. 20.

29 Susan Sontag, "On Style," *Partisan Review*, 32 (1965), 548, 549, respectively. The fact that "Miss Sontag has now completely reversed her position" (see Hilton Kramer, "The Evolution of Susan Sontag," *New York Times*, 9 February 1975, sec. 2, p. 31) should in no way affect the aptness of my application of this statement to the situation of literary biography. See also Susan Sontag, "Fascinating Fascism," *New York Review of Books*, 6 February 1975, pp. 23–30.

30 Carlos Baker, *Ernest Hemingway: A Life Story* (New York: Charles Scribner's Sons, 1969), p. x.

31 Baker notes in the preface to the fourth edition of his *Hemingway: The Writer as Artist* (Princeton: Princeton University Press, 1972) that his first two chapters have been "completely revised, incorporating some new material discovered since the publication of my biography in 1969" (p. vii).

32 Seward is quoted in Denis Brian, "The Importance of Knowing Ernest," *Esquire*, February 1972, p. 166.

33 Norman Mailer, "Preface," in Gregory H. Hemingway, *Papa: A Personal Memoir* (New York: Pocket Books, 1977), p. 12.

34 Irving Howe, "The Wounds of All Generations," *Harper's*, May 1969, pp. 96–97.

35 Mailer, p. 11; William White, "Hemingway and Fitzgerald," in *American Literary Scholarship/1968*, ed. J. Albert Robbins (Durham: Duke University Press, 1970), p. 109.

36 Peter Lisca, *Modern Fiction Studies*, 15 (Winter 1969–1970), 561.

37 Scott Donaldson, *By Force of Will: The Life and Art of Ernest Hemingway* (New York: Penguin Books, 1977), p. 243.

38 Richard Ellmann, "The Hemingway Circle," *New Statesman*, 15 August 1969, p. 214.

39 Vance Bourjaily, "Hemingway on Trial, Judge Baker Presiding," *New York Times Book Review*, 27 April 1969, p. 5.

40 Harry Levin, *The Contexts of Criticism* (Cambridge: Harvard University Press, 1958), pp. 144, 163.

41 James Atlas, "Literary Biography," *American Scholar*, 46 (Summer 1976), 453.

42 Denis Brian, *Murderers and Other Friendly People* (New York: McGraw Hill, 1973), pp. 24, 69, and 108. Reynolds Price, "A Son's Soliloquy—Regret, Love, Thanks," *New York Times Book Review*, 30 May 1976, p. 1. The phrase is Price's.

43 Atlas, pp. 456, 458.

44 Atlas writes that "His great familiarity with Joyce prompts Ellmann to call him 'obnoxious' or rebuke him for his intemperate ways." But he later calls such remonstrances "comical asides" (p. 455). Swanberg's are not comical.

45 Quoted in Robert F. Gish's review of biographies of Ronald Firbank and Malcolm Lowry, *Modern Fiction Studies*, 20 (Summer 1974), 260. The statement is from Fitzgerald's notebooks.

46 Here are some other biographies which treat all or part of Fitzgerald's life: Tom Dardis, *Some Time in the Sun* (New York: Scribner's, 1976); Aaron Latham, *Crazy Sundays: F. Scott Fitzgerald in Hollywood* (New York: Pocket Books, 1972); Sara Mayfield, *Exiles from Paradise* (New York: Dell, 1971); Arthur Mizener, *The Far Side of Paradise* (Boston: Houghton Mifflin, 1965 [first edition 1951]); and Henry Dan Piper, *F. Scott Fitzgerald: A Critical Portrait* (Carbondale: Southern Illinois University Press, 1965).

Dardis (p. 5) says, "The Fitzgerald of Latham's pages is . . . the same bleak and despairing man found in the Mizener and Turnbull biographies." Because of a conversation which he had with Anthony Powell (who in turn had talked with Fitzgerald in Hollywood), Dardis wants, he says, to correct errors in fact (Latham) and interpretation (Latham, Mizener, Turnbull). Dardis attacks Turnbull's (and Latham's and Mizener's) "physical descriptions of Fitzgerald" (p. 25). In a recent television interview with Robert Cromie in Chicago, Fitzgerald's daughter, Scottie Smith, expressed concern that all of her father's biographers stressed his "darker" side.

Mayfield makes several "corrections" of Turnbull (pp. 28 and 98, for example), at one point stating, "How Turnbull came by his information, I do not know, for he cites no source for his quotation, and he is now dead" (p. 150).

47 The first quotation is from James Gray, "Troubadour of the Flapper," *Saturday Review*, 10 March 1962, p. 19; the second is from William Barrett, "Two Stricken by the Muse," *Atlantic*, April 1962, p. 158.

48 Andrew Turnbull, *Scott Fitzgerald: A Biography* (New York: Scribner's, 1962), p. 327. Subsequent references to this volume will be noted in the text.

49 F. Scott Fitzgerald, *The Great Gatsby* (New York: Scribner's, 1925), p. 8.

50 See Paul Murray Kendall, *The Art of Biography* (New York: Norton, 1965), pp. 134–35.

51 See, e.g., pp. 5, 13, 24–25, 27, 63, 83, 107, 121, 156, 165, 167, 188, and 296.

52 Pp. 144–45. See Nancy Milford, *Zelda* (New York: Harper and Row, 1970), for a fuller account of Zelda's affair—and for a better spelling of the flyer's name.

53 Burke Wilkinson, "After the Jazz Age, The Crack-Up," *New York Times Book Review*, 11 March 1962, p. 1.

54 James L. Clifford, *From Puzzles to Portraits: Problems of a Literary Biographer* (Chapel Hill: University of North Carolina Press, 1970), p. 132.

55 Ellen Moers, "Hard Times," *New York Review of Books*, 3 June 1965, p. 12. See also Moers's further reactions to and corrections of Swanberg in her book *Two Dreisers* (New York: Viking, 1969), pp. ix, 84, 307, 317, 326, 340, and 344. In *Homage to Theodore Dreiser* (New York: Random House,

1971), p. 171, Robert Penn Warren provides Moers's book with a telling sub-title which it does not possess in its published form (perhaps Warren read a manuscript copy?): "The Man and the Novelist As Revealed in His Two Most Important Works."

56 W. A. Swanberg, *Dreiser* (New York: Scribner's, 1965), p. 531. Subsequent references to this book will be noted in the text.

57 Wilkinson, p. 1.

58 Moers, "Hard Times," p. 11.

59 See, e.g., the sections called "Take Tea With Me" (pp. 234–38) and "Coffee at the Ritz" (pp. 305–8).

60 Moers, "Hard Times," p. 12; my italics.

61 See, e.g., C. Hugh Holman's review (from which this quotation was taken) in *American Literary Scholarship/1965*, ed. James L. Woodress (Durham: Duke University Press, 1967), p. 167.

62 Granville Hicks, "A Liar in Search of the Truth," *Saturday Review*, 24 April 1965, p. 31.

63 Daniel Aaron, "The Unbuttoned Titan," *Reporter*, 3 June 1965, p. 37.

64 Malcolm Cowley, "Genius in the Raw," *Book Week*, 25 April 1965, p. 8.

65 David Levin, p. 11.

66 The secrecy motif appears, e.g., on pp. 270, 284, 298, 495, etc.

67 Saul Bellow, "Dreiser and the Triumph of Art," in *The Stature of Theodore Dreiser*, eds. Alfred Kazin and Charles Shapiro (Bloomington: Indiana University Press, 1955), p. 147.

68 P. 527. For Swanberg's comments on Dreiser's prose style, see pp. 76, 143, 258, 296, and 302–4.

69 David Levin writes: " . . . in histories, as in the novels of a Theodore Dreiser, connoisseurs of style may be too quick to deny all literary merit because the prose is awkward. Conceiving the new truth and finding any words at all that will make it intelligible represent a considerable literary achievement" (p. 10).

70 Poirier, p. 240.

71 Warren, p. 118.

72 Warren, pp. 156–57.

73 Hicks, p. 31.

74 Regarding the "*Savage* syndrome," see notes for Chapter One, note 28.

75 John Leggett, *Ross and Tom: Two American Tragedies* (New York: Simon and Schuster, 1974).

♟ *Chapter Four*

1 Quoted in William Flanagan, "Edward Albee," in *Writers at Work: The Paris Review Interviews: Third Series*, ed. George Plimpton (New York: Viking, 1967), p. 340.

2 Henry James, "The Art of Fiction," in *The Future of the Novel: Essays on the Art of Fiction*, ed. Leon Edel (New York: Vintage, 1956), p. 17.

3 The five volumes of the Edel biography are as follows: *The Untried Years: 1843–1870*, 1953; *The Conquest of London: 1870–1881*, 1962; *The Middle Years: 1882–1895*, 1962; *The Treacherous Years: 1895–1901*, 1969; and *The Master: 1901–1916*, 1972. All were published by Lippincott in New York. Quotations from and references to the biography in my text will be from these editions; I will use, for convenience, roman numerals to indicate volumes, followed by page numbers. Thus "(I, 23)" would refer to *The Untried Years*, the first in the series, page 23, etc.

4 Joseph Epstein, "The Greatest Biography of the Century," *Book World*, 6 February 1972, p. 1.

5 John Aldridge, "The Anatomy of Passion in the Consummate Henry James," *Saturday Review*, 12 February 1972, p. 65.

6 Hilton Kramer, untitled review of *The Master*, *New York Times Book Review*, 6 February 1972, p. 32.

7 Henry James, *Letters: Volume I: 1843–1875*, ed. Leon Edel (Cambridge: Belknap Press of Harvard University Press, 1974), p. xxxv.

8 Rayburn S. Moore, "Henry James, Ltd., and the Chairman of the Board: Leon Edel's Biography," *South Atlantic Quarterly*, 73 (Spring 1974), 264. This essay, one of the few essay-reviews of the whole Edel biography, should be added

to the comprehensive survey of criticism (especially of *The Master*) in William T. Stafford, "Henry James," *American Literary Scholarship/1972*, ed. J. Albert Robbins (Durham: Duke University Press, 1974), pp. 92–98; and Stafford's survey update in *ALS/1973*, ed. James Woodress, pp. 116–18. I have felt it unnecessary to list here previous reviews of the first four volumes of the biography, since I make references to and quote from several notable examples in this chapter.

9 Robert L. Gale, *Modern Fiction Studies*, 16 (Summer 1970), 213.

10 Richard Ellmann, *Golden Codgers: Biographical Speculations* (New York: Oxford University Press, 1973), p. 10; and Stephen Spender, "In Eliot's Cave," *New York Review of Books*, 19 September 1974, p. 18.

11 Mildred Hartsock, "Biography: The Treacherous Art," *Journal of Modern Literature*, 1 (1970), 119; and Joyce Carol Oates, "A Humane and Adventurous Art," *New York Times Book Review*, 13 May 1979, p. 3. The new book which Oates is reviewing is *Telling Lives: The Biographer's Art*, ed. Marc Pachter (Washington: New Republic Books/ National Portrait Gallery, 1979).

12 Edward Mendelson, "Authorized Biography and Its Discontents," in *Studies in Biography (Harvard English Studies 8)*, ed. Daniel Aaron (Cambridge: Harvard University Press, 1978), p. 20; my italics.

13 Frederick J. Hoffman, "The Expense and Power of Greatness: An Essay on Leon Edel's 'James,'" *Virginia Quarterly Review*, 39 (Summer 1963), 518.

14 Robert Garis, "Anti-Literary Biography," *Hudson Review*, 23 (1970), 143–53.

15 Philip Rahv, "Henry James and His Cult," *New York Review of Books*, 10 February 1972, pp. 18–22; and Mark L. Krupnick, "Henry James: The Artist as Emperor," *Novel*, 6 (Spring 1973), 257–65. See also "Digging James," an exchange of letters between Rahv and Adeline R. Tintner, *New York Review of Books*, 6 April 1972, pp. 37–38.

16 Rahv's early praise of James is well-known; Krupnick's generally favorable review of *The Treacherous Years* is "The Sanctuary of Imagination," *Nation*, 14 July 1969, pp. 55–56.

17 Quentin Anderson, "Leon Edel's 'Henry James,'" *Virginia Quarterly Review*, 48 (Autumn 1972), 629–30.

18 Quentin Anderson, "A Master in the Making," *Times Literary Supplement*, 9 May 1975, p. 500.

19 I have transcribed this statement from the taped interview "The Art of Biography," Program No. BC 2295, Pacifica Tape Library, Los Angeles, California, 1975.

20 William Gass, "In the Cage," *New York Review of Books*, 10 July 1969, p. 4. Richard Hall, in a provocative two-part *New Republic* essay, "The Sexuality of Henry James" (Part I, 28 April 1979, pp. 25–29, 30–31; Part II, 5 May 1979, pp. 25–29), has charged that Edel has not been willing enough to take "risks" in dealing with a major element of James's being; there is, consequently, Hall maintains, "a peculiar timidity at the center" of *Henry James* (Part I, p. 25). In attempting to discuss a subject's sexuality, the literary biographer *usually* encounters difficulties—even when verifiable, explicit data are more readily available. See, for example, the discussion in Richard Ellmann's review of Charles Osborne's groundbreaking 1980 biography, *W. H. Auden: The Life of a Poet* ("Getting to Know You," *New York Review of Books*, 23 October 1980, pp. 35–37).

21 V, 381. In *Henry James at Home* (New York: Farrar, Straus & Giroux, 1969), p. 119, H. Montgomery Hyde describes a very similar incident (or the same one?), involving James's killing a *cat*. Hyde's listed source is a diary by Sydney Waterlow. Although Edel mentions Waterlow immediately after this quoted story, and later lists, in the notes for the whole section, an article by himself on Waterlow, one cannot be sure of Edel's exact source.

22 Stuart Hampshire, *Modern Writers and Other Essays* (New York: Knopf, 1970), p. 96.

23 Anderson, "Leon Edel's 'Henry James,'" p. 630; Alfred Kazin, "'Your Lone and Loving Exile,'" *New York Review of Books*, 23 January 1975, p. 12; my italics.

24 A. O. J. Cockshut, *Truth to Life: The Art of Biography in the Nineteenth Century* (New York: Harcourt, 1974), p. 152.

25 Krupnick, "The Artist as Emperor," p. 259; my italics.

26 Unsigned review of *The Master* in *Journal of Modern Literature*, 3 (February 1974), p. 662; and William T. Stafford, *American Literary Scholarship/1972*, p. 97.

27 Leon Edel, "The Biographer's Trip to the Past Is *Déjà*

Vu With a Difference," *New York Times*, 21 January 1973, Travel Section (XX), pp. 1, 13; my italics.

28 Howard Moss, *Instant Lives* (New York: Dutton, 1974), pp. 41–42.

29 And later Edith Wharton managed the same operation for *her* biographer (who was to be R. W. B. Lewis; see *Edith Wharton: A Biography* [New York: Harper & Row, 1975]—although, ironically, her method was *saving* documents, rather than destroying them, in attempting to preserve and transmit the full vision she had of herself. For an illuminating discussion of the biographer's need to discover the "inner myth" of his or her subject, see Edel's essay "The Figure Under the Carpet," *New Republic*, 180 (10 February 1979), 25–29.

30 Geoffrey T. Hellman, "Chairman of the Board," *New Yorker*, 13 March 1971, p. 84.

31 Hellman, p. 72.

32 Millicent Bell, "Henry James: The Man Who Lived," *Massachusetts Review*, 14 (Spring 1973), 392. Incidentally, I believe Bell's other objections to Edel's work are, in general, convincingly stated—but they represent her attempt to condemn what she calls Edel's "speculations" (p. 407) by substituting ones of her own. The main—and good—effect Bell's essay has is that it suggests a further avenue for study: one wants to compare *her* portrait of the James-Wharton relationship, in *Edith Wharton and Henry James: The Story of Their Friendship* (1965), with Edel's—and also with Lewis's.

33 E. M. Forster, *Aspects of the Novel* (New York: Harcourt, 1927), pp. 150–51.

34 Although Swanberg uses the mini-essay pattern in *Dreiser*, one can hardly say that its order is "suitable" for its subject; in choosing the refined pattern, Swanberg violates Dreiser's "mood."

35 Another major charge Bell makes against Edel is that his "approach to James is decidedly unphilosophical and offers no clues to the intellectual roots of his style and aesthetics" (p. 393). This is simply another of the many complaints about the insularity of the work; but if Edel does not investigate the "roots" of James's style, he has certainly examined the style itself—and its changes. For example, he has provided a useful analysis of the changes which dictation brought to the prose style (V, 126–28). And he has given us a totally new James in telling us about Burgess, James's "man," "to whom James wrote as a father to a son, letters of the greatest simplicity and concreteness, in declarative sentences as simple as his characteristic sentences were complex" (V, 521).

36 In light of Edel's life-literature approach, then, the last volume is, in a sense, superfluous? William T. Stafford (*American Literary Scholarship/1972*, p. 96) has written that *The Master* is "in some ways the least engrossing" and "may also be the least dramatic of the five volumes. . . ."

37 Anderson, "Leon Edel's 'Henry James,'" pp. 623, 624.

38 Quoted in Elizabeth Longford, "A Talk With Anthony Powell," *New York Times Book Review*, 11 April 1976, p. 47. Regarding the need for modern biographers to "evolve" with their work, see the opening section of Donald Greene's "'Tis a Pretty Book, Mr. Boswell, But . . . ," *Georgia Review*, 32 (1978), 17–43.

39 See I, 68ff, and V, 549ff. Additional Napoleonic/ Dream references may be found in II, 101; IV, 103; and V, 98, 265, 445. See also Krupnick's discussion of this motif in his *Novel* essay, pp. 560ff.

40 Review of *The Master*, *Journal of Modern Literature*, 3 (February 1974), 661, 662.

41 See, e.g., p. 240, where Edel discusses "success" and his younger brother "desire," and makes a fascinating metaphorical reading of an anecdote involving the young Henry's new summer suit.

42 For more on Edel's attitudes and methods in volume four, see Thelma Shinn's "A Question of Survival: An Analysis of 'The Treacherous Years' of Henry James," *Literature and Psychology*, 23 (1973), 135–48. In *American Literary Scholarship/1973*, pp. 117–18, Stafford labels this "not so much disagreement as supplementation" of Edel and calls it significant because it shows "Edel as model, however different his aims or his conclusions; for Shinn his was obviously a subject and method she found extremely useful for her own illuminating deliberations."

43 Millicent Bell has charged that Edel "breaks into James's literary works as though each, in succession, was a cabinet of clues." "Moreover," she writes, "literary criticism, which should never, I think, abdicate its place in literary biography, tends to be subordinated in Edel's pages to this sort of biographic ransacking of the works" (p. 396). One wonders after reading Bell's essay, though, whether she is not finally complaining because Edel has not, in fact, abdicated biography for criticism. In "Biography and Criticism—A Misalliance Disputed," *Critical Inquiry*, 1 (March 1975), 479–96, Jacques Barzun has discussed provocatively the uses of biography in criticism. But no one, as far as I know, has adequately defined the perfect balance of criticism *in biography*.

44 Richard Poirier, "Robert Frost: The Sound of Love and the Love of Sound," *Atlantic*, April 1974, p. 54.

45 James R. Mellow, *Charmed Circle: Gertrude Stein & Company* (New York: Avon Books, 1974), p. 572.

46 Strother Purdy, untitled review of Mellow's *Charmed Circle*, *Modern Fiction Studies*, 21 (Summer 1975), 289–90.

47 Leon Edel, "A Stone into the Mirror," *American Scholar*, 45 (Winter 1975–76), 828.

⚓ *Afterword*

1 Bernard Malamud, "Dubin's Lives (Part I)," *New Yorker*, 18 April 1977, pp. 46–47. In its later book form, this passage contains slightly different wording; see *Dubin's Lives* (New York: Avon, 1979), pp. 20–21.

As Malamud intimates in this passage, there is a necessary "joining," "marriage," of biographers and their subjects, and these marriages are often filled with struggle. For the biographer grapples with his subject over both the language he uses in re-creating a life and his version of the "truth" of that life. Helen Vendler finds the inherent competition between the biographer and the writer-subject especially fierce when that subject is a poet; she writes, "It is unusual to be able to read the biography of a poet without flinching. Too often the poet's quoted words—apt, beautiful, expressive, original—reduce the biographer's words surrounding them to rubble. The best praise of a literary biographer is to say that his commentary does not disgrace his subject" ("An American Genius," rev. of *Walt Whitman: A Life* by Justin Kaplan, *New*

York Times Book Review, 9 November 1980, p. 29). And Mark Harris, in his curious almost-biography, Saul Bellow: Drumlin Woodchuck (Athens: University of Georgia Press, 1980), demonstrates how the struggle involving a living novelist and his novelist-biographer can be complexly—and often comically—passionate.

2 B. L. Reid, "Practical Biography," Sewanee Review, 83 (Spring 1975), 362, 360. For a perceptive discussion of biography's "own nature," see Peter Nagourney, "The Basic Assumptions of Literary Biography," Biography: An Interdisciplinary Quarterly, 1 (Spring 1978), 86–104.

3 E. L. Doctorow, "False Documents," in American Review 26, ed. Theodore Solotaroff (New York: Bantam, 1977), pp. 228–29, 231. In Ragtime, of course, Doctorow has combined historical and imaginary characters in a manner that makes many readers exceedingly uneasy about his distortion of "truth." Because my central concern in this book is with biography and not with the novel, there is no need to comment directly on this problem. However, in beginning further exploration of the problems involved in attempting to distinguish "history" from "fiction" in modern literature, one might consider Bruce Wardropper's "Don Quixote: Story or History?" (Modern Philology, 63 [August 1965], 1–11) and Leo Braudy's Narrative Form in History and Fiction: Hume, Fielding, and Gibbon (Princeton: Princeton University Press, 1970).

bibliography

Aaron, Daniel. "The Unbuttoned Titan." *Reporter*, 3 June 1965, pp. 37–39.

Adams, Richard P. Rev. of Blotner's *Faulkner*. *American Literature*, 46 (November 1974), 392–93.

Aldridge, John. "The Anatomy of Passion in the Consummate Henry James." *Saturday Review*, 12 February 1972, p. 65.

Altick, Richard. *Lives and Letters: A History of Literary Biography in England and America*. New York: Knopf, 1965.

Anderson, Charles R. *Melville in the South Seas*. New York: Columbia University Press, 1939.

Anderson, Quentin. "Leon Edel's 'Henry James.'" *Virginia Quarterly Review*, 48 (Autumn 1972), 621–30.

———. "A Master in the Making." *Times Literary Supplement*, 9 May 1975, pp. 498–500.

Atlas, James. *Delmore Schwartz: The Life of an American Poet*. New York: Discus/Avon, 1977.

———. "Literary Biography." *American Scholar*, 46 (Summer 1976), 448–60.

———. "The Private Hemingway: From His Unpublished Letters: 1918–1961." *New York Times Magazine*, 15 February 1981, pp. 23–30, 32, 64, 66, 68, 70–71, 83–84, 86–87, 91.

Auden, W. H. *A Certain World: A Commonplace Book*. New York: Viking, 1970.

Baker, Carlos. *Ernest Hemingway: A Life Story*. New York: Scribner's, 1969.

———. "From Genesis to Revelation." *Virginia Quarterly Review*, 50 (Summer 1974), 438–40.

———. *Hemingway: The Writer as Artist*. 4th ed. Princeton: Princeton University Press, 1972.

215

Barrett, William. "Two Stricken by the Muse." *Atlantic*, April 1962, p. 158.

Barzun, Jacques. "Biography and Criticism—a Misalliance Disputed." *Critical Inquiry*, 1 (March 1975), 479–96.

Bedford, Sybille. *Aldous Huxley: A Biography*. New York: Knopf/Harper and Row, 1974.

Beebe, Maurice. "'Paris Was Where the Twentieth Century Was': Literary Memoirs of the Twenties." Seminar presentation. University of Tulsa. Tulsa, Oklahoma, Summer 1973.

Bell, Millicent. "Henry James: The Man Who Lived." *Massachusetts Review*, 14 (Spring 1973), 391–414.

Bell, Quentin. *Virginia Woolf: A Biography*. New York: Harcourt, 1972.

Bellow, Saul. "Dreiser and the Triumph of Art." In *The Stature of Theodore Dreiser*. Eds. Alfred Kazin and Charles Shapiro. Bloomington: Indiana University Press, 1955, pp. 146–48.

Bernstein, Burton. *Thurber*. New York: Ballantine Books, 1975.

Berry, Thomas Elliott, ed. *The Biographer's Craft*. New York: Odyssey Press, 1967.

Bloom, Lynn Marie Zimmerman. "How Literary Biographers Use Their Subjects' Works: A Study of Biographical Method, 1865–1962." *Dissertation Abstracts*, 24 (1963), 2458 (University of Michigan).

Blotner, Joseph. *Faulkner: A Biography*. Two volumes. New York: Random House, 1974.

Boswell, James. *Life of Johnson*. Ed. R. W. Chapman; third edition, corrected by J. D. Fleeman. London: Oxford University Press, 1970.

Bourjaily, Vance. "Hemingway on Trial, Judge Baker Presiding." *New York Times Book Review*, 27 April 1969, pp. 5, 38.

Bowen, Catherine Drinker. *Biography: The Craft and the Calling*. New York: Atlantic-Little, Brown, 1969.

Brady, Frank. "The Strategies of Biography and Some Eighteenth-Century Examples." In *Literary Theory and Structure*. Eds. Frank Brady, John Palmer, and Martin Price. New Haven: Yale University Press, 1973, pp. 245–65.

Braudy, Leo. *Narrative Form in History and Fiction: Hume, Fielding, and Gibbon*. Princeton: Princeton University Press, 1970.

Brian, Denis. "The Importance of Knowing Ernest." *Esquire*, February 1972, pp. 98–101, 164–70.

———. *Murderers and Other Friendly People*. New York: McGraw-Hill, 1973.

"Briefly Noted." Rev. of Blotner's *Faulkner*. *New Yorker*, 9 September 1974, pp. 132–33.

"Briefly Noted." *New Yorker*, 22 September 1975, pp. 131–32.

Brown, Huntington. *Prose Styles: Five Primary Types*. Minneapolis: University of Minnesota Press, 1966.

Bruccoli, Matthew J. *The O'Hara Concern: A Biography of John O'Hara*. New York: Random House, 1976.

Canby, Henry Seidel. *Turn West, Turn East: Mark Twain and Henry James*. 1951; rpt. New York: Houghton Mifflin, 1965.

Carr, Virginia Spencer. *The Lonely Hunter: A Biography of Carson McCullers*. New York: Doubleday, 1975.

Chalfant, Thomas Haight. "The Marriage of Granite and Rainbow: Virginia Woolf as Biographer." *Dissertation Abstracts International*, 32 (1971), 3298A (University of Wisconsin).

Church, Margaret. *Time and Reality: Studies in Contemporary Fiction*. Chapel Hill: University of North Carolina Press, 1963.

Clemons, Walter. "Haunted Exile." *Newsweek*, 9 October 1972, p. 106.

———. "Hunting for Faulkner." *Newsweek*, 25 March 1974, pp. 91–92.

Clifford, James L., ed. *Biography As an Art: Selected Criticism, 1560–1960.* New York: Oxford University Press, 1962.

Clifford, James L. *From Puzzles to Portraits: Problems of a Literary Biographer.* Chapel Hill: University of North Carolina Press, 1971.

————. "How Much Should a Biographer Tell? Some Eighteenth-Century Views." In Daghlian (below), pp. 67–95.

Cockshut, A. O. J. *Truth to Life: The Art of Biography in the Nineteenth Century.* New York: Harcourt, 1974.

Cody, John. *After Great Pain: The Inner Life of Emily Dickinson.* Cambridge: Harvard University Press, 1971.

Connolly, Cyril. *Great English Short Novels.* New York: Dial Press, 1953.

Cowley, Malcolm. "Genius in the Raw." *Book Week,* 25 April 1965, pp. 1, 8.

————. "Hart Crane: The Evidence in the Case." *Sewanee Review,* 78 (1970), 176–84.

————. "The Overbrimming Life of Man of Literary Genius." *Chicago Tribune Book World,* 24 March 1974, pp. 1–2.

Craft, Robert. "Huxley at Home." *New York Review of Books,* 23 January 1975, pp. 9–12.

Daghlian, Philip B., ed. *Essays in Eighteenth-Century Biography.* Bloomington: Indiana University Press, 1968.

Dardis, Tom. *Some Time in the Sun: The Hollywood Years of Fitzgerald, Faulkner, Nathanael West, Aldous Huxley, and James Agee.* New York: Scribner's, 1976.

Davenport, William H., and Ben Siegel, eds., *Biography Past and Present.* New York: Scribner's, 1965.

Day, Douglas. *Malcolm Lowry: A Biography.* New York: Oxford University Press, 1973.

De Sola Pinto, Vivian, ed. *English Biography in the Seventeenth Century.* London: George G. Harrap, 1951.

Dickey, James. *Self-Interviews.* New York: Dell, 1970.

Doctorow, E. L. "False Documents." In *American Review 26*. Ed. Theodore Solotaroff. New York: Bantam, 1977, pp. 215–32.

———. *Ragtime*. New York: Random House, 1975.

Donaldson, Scott. *By Force of Will: The Life and Art of Ernest Hemingway*. New York: Penguin Books, 1977.

Dorsey, T. A., ed. *Latin Biography*. London: Routledge & Kegan Paul, 1967.

Duffy, Martha. "That's All, Folks." *Time*, 25 September 1972, p. ST6.

Dussinger, John. "Style and Intention in Johnson's *Life of Savage*." *Journal of English Literary History*, 37 (1970), 564–80.

Edel, Leon. "The Art of Biography." Taped Program No. BC 2295. Pacifica Tape Library. Los Angeles, California, 1975.

———. "The Biographer's Trip to the Past Is *Déjà Vu* With a Difference." *New York Times*, 21 January 1973, Travel Section (XX), pp. 1, 13.

———. "Biography: A Manifesto." *Biography: An Interdisciplinary Quarterly*, 1 (Winter 1978), 1–3.

———. "Biography and the Narrator." *New Republic*, 152 (6 March 1965), 65.

———. "The Figure Under the Carpet." *New Republic*, 180 (10 February 1979), 25–29. Reprinted in *Telling Lives*, ed. Marc Pachter.

———. "The Final Chord of the Quintet." *New York Times Book Review*, 6 February 1972, pp. 2–3.

———. *Henry James: The Untried Years: 1843–1870*. New York: Lippincott, 1953.

———. *Henry James: The Conquest of London: 1870–1881*. New York: Lippincott, 1962.

———. *Henry James: The Middle Years: 1882–1895*. New York: Lippincott, 1962.

——. *Henry James: The Treacherous Years: 1895–1901.* New York: Lippincott, 1969.

——. *Henry James: The Master: 1901–1916.* New York: Lippincott, 1972.

——. *Literary Biography.* 1959; rpt. Bloomington: Indiana University Press, 1973.

——. "A Stone into the Mirror." *American Scholar,* 45 (Winter 1975–1976), 826–30.

Eisinger, Chester. Rev. of *Fact & Fiction: The New Journalism and the Nonfiction Novel* by John Hollowell. *American Literature,* 49 (November 1977), 488–89.

Ellmann, Richard. "Getting to Know You." Rev. of *W. H. Auden: The Life of a Poet* by Charles Osborne. *New York Review of Books,* 23 October 1980, pp. 35–37.

——. *Golden Codgers: Biographical Speculations.* New York: Oxford University Press, 1973.

——. "The Hemingway Circle." *New Statesman,* 15 August 1969, pp. 213–14.

——. *James Joyce.* New York: Oxford University Press, 1959.

Emerson, Ralph Waldo. *The Journals and Miscellaneous Notebooks.* Ed. William H. Gilman, et al. Cambridge: Belknap Press of Harvard University Press, 1965–

Epstein, Joseph. "The Greatest Biography of the Century." *Book World,* 6 February 1972, p. 1.

"A Few Novels." Rev. of *Edwin Mullhouse* by Steven Millhauser. *New Republic,* 167 (16 September 1972) 30–31.

Fitzgerald, F. Scott. *The Great Gatsby.* New York: Scribner's, 1925.

FitzGibbon, Constantine, *The Life of Dylan Thomas.* Boston: Little, Brown, 1965.

Flanagan, William. "Edward Albee." In *Writers at Work: The Paris Review Interviews: Third Series.* Ed. George Plimpton. New York: Viking, 1967, pp. 321–46.

Forster, E. M. *Aspects of the Novel*. New York: Harcourt, 1927.

Frye, Northrop. *Anatomy of Criticism: Four Essays*. Princeton: Princeton University Press, 1957.

———. *The Well-Tempered Critic*. Bloomington: Indiana University Press, 1963.

Gale, Robert L. Rev. of Edel's *The Treacherous Years*. *Modern Fiction Studies*, 16 (Summer 1970), 213.

Garis, Robert. "Anti-Literary Biography." *Hudson Review*, 23 (1970), 143–53.

Garraty, John A. *The Nature of Biography*. New York: Knopf, 1957.

Gass, William. "In the Cage." *New York Review of Books*, 10 July 1969, pp. 3–5.

———. "Mr. Blotner, Mr. Feaster, and Mr. Faulkner." *New York Review of Books*, 27 June 1974, pp. 3–5.

Gelb, Arthur and Barbara. *O'Neill*. New York: Harper & Row, 1962; enlarged ed. with a new epilogue, 1973.

Gilbert, Julie Goldsmith. *Ferber: A Biography of Edna Ferber and Her Circle*. Garden City: Doubleday, 1978.

Gilman, William H. *Melville's Early Life and Redburn*. New York: New York University Press, 1951.

Gish, Robert F. Rev. of Day's *Malcolm Lowry*. *Modern Fiction Studies*, 20 (Summer 1974), 256–60.

Glover, William. "Doubts Plagued Author of O'Neill Biography." *Indianapolis Star*, 28 July 1974, Section 8, p. 5.

Gray, James. "Troubadour of the Flapper." *Saturday Review*, 10 March 1962, p. 19.

Gray, Paul. "Footnotes to Genius." *Time*, 25 March 1974, pp. 86–88.

Greene, Donald. "'Tis a Pretty Book, Mr. Boswell, But. . . ." *Georgia Review*, 32 (1978), 17–43.

———. "The Uses of Autobiography in the Eighteenth Century." In Daghlian (above), pp. 43–66.

Hall, Richard. "The Sexuality of Henry James: Part I." *New Republic*, 180 (28 April 1979), 25–28, 30–31.

———. "The Sexuality of Henry James: Part II." *New Republic*, 180 (5 May 1979), 25–29.

Hampshire, Stuart. *Modern Writers and Other Essays.* New York: Knopf, 1970.

Harris, Mark. *Saul Bellow: Drumlin Woodchuck.* Athens: University of Georgia Press, 1980.

Hartley, L. P. *The Go-Between:* London: Hamish Hamilton, 1953.

Hartsock, Mildred E. "Biography: The Treacherous Art." *Journal of Modern Literature,* 1 (1970), 116–19.

Haselton, Stephen Jerome. "The Fairest Meed: Biography in America Before 1865." *Dissertation Abstracts,* 20 (September 1959), 1014–15 (Columbia).

Havlice, Patricia Pate. *Index to Literary Biography.* Two volumes. Metuchen, N.J.: The Scarecrow Press, 1975.

Heller, Terry. Rev. of Blotner's *Faulkner. Arizona Quarterly,* 30 (Winter 1974), 355–57.

Hellman, Geoffrey T. "Chairman of the Board." *New Yorker,* 13 March 1971, pp. 43–86. Profile of Leon Edel.

Hicks, Granville. "A Liar in Search of the Truth." *Saturday Review,* 24 April 1965, pp. 31–32.

Highet, Gilbert. *The Anatomy of Satire.* Princeton: Princeton University Press, 1962.

Hjortsberg, William. "Edwin Mullhouse." *New York Times Book Review,* 17 September 1972, p. 2.

Hoffman, Frederick J. "The Expense and Power of Greatness: An Essay on Leon Edel's 'James.'" *Virginia Quarterly Review,* 39 (Summer 1963), 518–28.

Holman, C. Hugh. "Fiction: 1900 to the 1930's." In *American Literary Scholarship/1965.* Ed. James L. Woodress. Durham: Duke University Press, 1967, pp. 162–79.

Holroyd, Michael. *Lytton Strachey: The Years of Achievement,*

1910–1932. New York: Holt, Rinehart and Winston, 1968.

———. "The Revolving Bookstand: Out of Print." *American Scholar,* 39 (Spring 1970), 310–16.

Hough, Graham. *Style and Stylistics.* London: Routledge & Kegan Paul, 1969.

Howard, Leon. *Herman Melville: A Biography.* Berkeley: University of California Press, 1951.

Howe, Irving. "The World He Mimicked Was His Own." *New York Times Book Review,* 1 October 1961, pp. 1, 34.

———. "The Wounds of All Generations." *Harper's,* May 1969, pp. 96–102.

Huxley, Aldous. *Point Counter Point.* 1928; rpt. London: Chatto & Windus, 1963.

Hyde, H. Montgomery. *Henry James at Home.* New York: Farrar, Straus & Giroux, 1969.

James, Henry. "The Art of Fiction." In *The Future of the Novel: Essays on the Art of Fiction.* Ed. Leon Edel. New York: Vintage, 1956, pp. 3–27.

———. *Letters: Volume I: 1843–1875.* Ed. Leon Edel. Cambridge: Belknap Press of Harvard University Press, 1974.

———. *Letters: Volume II: 1875–1883.* Ed. Leon Edel. Cambridge: Belknap Press of Harvard University Press, 1975.

Johnson, Edgar. *One Mighty Torrent: The Drama of Biography.* New York: Macmillan, 1955.

Journal of Modern Literature, 3 (February 1974), 661–62. Rev. of Edel's *The Master.*

Kanon, Joseph. Rev. of *Edwin Mullhouse* by Steven Millhauser. *Saturday Review,* 30 September 1972, p. 78.

Kaplan, Justin. *Mr. Clemens and Mark Twain.* New York: Simon and Schuster, 1966.

Kazin, Alfred. "'Your Lone and Loving Exile.'" *New York Review of Books,* 23 January 1975, pp. 12–13.

Kendall, Paul Murray. *The Art of Biography*. New York: Norton, 1965.

Kramer, Hilton. "The Evolution of Susan Sontag." *New York Times*, 9 February 1975, sec. 2, p. 31.

————. "Writing Writers' Lives." *New York Times Book Review*, 8 May 1977, p. 3.

————. Rev. of Edel's *The Master*. *New York Times Book Review*, 6 Februray 1972, p. 1.

Krupnick, Mark L. "Henry James: The Artist as Emperor." *Novel*, 6 (Spring 1973), 257–65.

————. "The Sanctuary of Imagination." *Nation*, 14 July 1969, pp. 55–56.

Larkin, Edward. "Biography and Doctors." *Times Literary Supplement*, 22 March 1974, pp. 289–90.

Latham, Aaron. *Crazy Sundays: F. Scott Fitzgerald in Hollywood*. New York: Pocket Books, 1972.

Leggett, John. *Ross and Tom: Two American Tragedies*. New York: Simon and Schuster, 1974.

Leonard, John. "The Battle of the Books, 1974." *New York Times Book Review*, 1 December 1974, p. 111.

Levin, David. *In Defense of Historical Literature*. New York: Hill and Wang, 1967.

Levin, Harry. *The Contexts of Criticism*. Cambridge: Harvard University Press, 1958.

Lewis, R. W. B. *Edith Wharton: A Biography*. New York: Harper & Row, 1975.

Leyda, Jay. *The Melville Log: A Documentary Life of Herman Melville, 1819–1891*. Two volumes. New York: Harcourt, 1951.

————. *The Years and Hours of Emily Dickinson*. Two volumes. New Haven: Yale University Press, 1960.

Lind, Ilse Dusoir. Rev. of Blotner's *Faulkner*. *Modern Fiction Studies*, 20 (Winter 1974–75), 560–64.

Lisca, Peter. Rev. of Baker's *Hemingway*. *Modern Fiction Studies*, 15 (Winter 1969–70), 561.

Locke, Richard. "Can These Bones Live?" *New York Times Book Review*, 29 January 1978, p. 3.

Longford, Elizabeth. "A Talk with Anthony Powell." *New York Times Book Review*, 11 April 1976, p. 47.

Lowes, John Livingston. *The Road to Xanadu: A Study in the Ways of the Imagination*. 1927; rpt. Boston: Houghton Mifflin, 1955.

MacCarthy, Desmond. "Lytton Strachey as a Biographer." *Life and Letters*, 8 (March 1932), 90–102.

Mailer, Norman. "Preface." In *Papa: A Personal Memoir* by Gregory H. Hemingway. New York: Pocket Books, 1977.

Malamud, Bernard. "Dubin's Lives (Part I)." *New Yorker*, 18 April 1977, pp. 38–50.

———. "Dubin's Lives (Part II)." *New Yorker*, 25 April 1977, pp. 36–47.

———. *Dubin's Lives*. New York: Avon, 1979.

Martin, Jay. *Nathanael West: The Art of His Life*. New York: Farrar, Straus, and Giroux, 1970.

Matthews, T. S. *Great Tom: Notes Towards the Definition of T. S. Eliot*. New York: Harper & Row, 1974.

Mayfield, Sara. *Exiles from Paradise: Zelda and Scott Fitzgerald*. New York: Dell, Press, 1971.

Mellow, James R. *Charmed Circle: Gertrude Stein & Company*. New York: Avon Books, 1974.

Mendelson, Edward. "Authorized Biography and Its Discontents." In *Studies in Biography (Harvard English Studies 8)*. Ed. Daniel Aaron. Cambridge: Harvard University Press, 1978, pp. 9–26.

Milford, Nancy. *Zelda*. New York: Harper & Row, 1970.

Millhauser, Steven. *Edwin Mullhouse: The Life and Death of an American Writer, 1943–1954, by Jeffrey Cartwright*.

New York: Knopf, 1972. Available since 1978 in an Avon/Bard paperback edition.

Minter, David. *William Faulkner: His Life and Work.* Baltimore: Johns Hopkins University Press, 1980.

Mizener, Arthur. *The Far Side of Paradise: A Biography of F. Scott Fitzgerald.* Revised edition. Boston: Houghton Mifflin, 1965.

Moers, Ellen. "Hard Times." *New York Review of Books,* 3 June 1965, pp. 10–12.

————. *Two Dreisers.* New York: Viking, 1969.

Moore, Rayburn S. "Henry James, Ltd., and the Chairman of the Board: Leon Edel's Biography." *South Atlantic Quarterly,* 73 (Spring 1974), 261–69.

Moss, Howard. *Instant Lives.* New York: Dutton, 1974.

Mudrick, Marvin. "Last Tango in Panoply." *Hudson Review,* 27 (Summer 1974), 303–7.

Nagourney, Peter. "The Basic Assumptions of Literary Biography." *Biography: An Interdisciplinary Quarterly,* 1 (Spring 1978), 86–104.

Nathan, John. *Mishima: A Biography.* Boston: Little, Brown, 1974.

Newman, Charles. "An Exemplary Life." *Harper's,* April 1974, p. 98.

Nicolson, Harold. *The Development of English Biography.* 1928; rpt. London: Hogarth Press, 1968.

Nowell, Elizabeth. *Thomas Wolfe: A Biography.* New York: Doubleday, 1960.

Oates, Joyce Carol. "A Humane and Adventurous Art." Rev. of *Telling Lives,* ed. Marc Pachter. *New York Times Book Review,* 13 May 1979, p. 3.

————. *Marriages and Infidelities.* New York: Vanguard, 1972.

O'Connor, Leo F. "Malcolm Lowry and the House of Failure." *Literature and Psychology,* 24 (1974), 167–70.

O'Neill, Edward Hayes. *A History of American Biography,*

1800–1935. Philadelphia: University of Pennsylvania Press, 1935.

Pachter, Marc., ed. *Telling Lives: The Biographer's Art.* National Portrait Gallery/New Republic Books, 1979.

Pascal, Roy. *Design and Truth in Autobiography.* London: Harvard University Press, 1960.

Passler, David L. *Time, Form, and Style in Boswell's Life of Johnson.* New Haven: Yale University Press, 1971.

Phillipson, Nicholas. "Intuitions and Interactions." *Times Literary Supplement,* 24 January 1975, p. 90.

Piper, Henry Dan. *F. Scott Fitzgerald: A Critical Portrait.* Carbondale: Southern Illinois University Press, 1965.

Plutarch. *Eight Great Lives.* Ed. C. A. Robinson, Jr. The Dryden Translation, revised by Arthur Hugh Clough. New York: Rinehart, 1960.

Poirier, Richard. "Robert Frost: The Sound of Love and the Love of Sound." *Atlantic,* April 1974, pp. 50–55.

―――. *A World Elsewhere: The Place of Style in American Literature.* New York: Oxford University Press, 1966.

Pottle, Frederick A. "*The Life of Johnson:* Art and Authenticity." In *Twentieth Century Views of Boswell's* Life of Johnson. Ed. J. L. Clifford. New York: Prentice-Hall, 1970, pp. 66–73.

Price, Reynolds. "A Son's Soliloquy—Regret, Love, Thanks." *New York Times Book Review,* 30 May 1976, p. 1.

Pritchard, William. "Long Novels and Short Stories." *Hudson Review,* 26 (Spring 1973), 233.

Purdy, Strother. Rev. of *Charmed Circle* by James R. Mellow. *Modern Fiction Studies,* 21 (Summer 1975), 289–90.

Rader, Ralph W. "Literary Form in Factual Narrative: The Example of Boswell's *Johnson.*" In Daghlian (above), pp. 3–42.

Rahv, Philip. "Henry James and His Cult." *New York Review of Books,* 10 February 1972, pp. 18–22.

Rasco, Lavon. "The Biographies of Herman Melville: A Study in Twentieth Century Biography." *Dissertation Abstracts,* 17 (February 1957), 357 (Northwestern).

Reed, Joseph W., Jr. *English Biography in the Early Nineteenth Century: 1801–1838.* New Haven: Yale University Press, 1965.

Reid, B. L. "Practical Biography." *Sewanee Review,* 83 (Spring 1975), 357–63.

Rosenthal, Michael. "The High Priestess of Bloomsbury." *New York Times Book Review,* 5 November 1972, pp. 1, 11–12, 14, 16, 18.

Rusk, Ralph. *The Life of Ralph Waldo Emerson.* 1949; rpt. New York: Columbia University Press, 1964.

Samsell, R. L. "The Falsest of the Arts." In *Fitzgerald/ Hemingway Annual 1971.* Eds. Matthew J. Bruccoli and C. E. F. Clark. Washington, D.C.: NCR/Microcard Editions, 1971, pp. 173–76.

Samuels, Charles Thomas. "John Updike: The Art of Fiction, XLIII." *Paris Review,* 45 (Winter 1968), 85–117.

Schoenbaum, S. *William Shakespeare: A Compact Documentary Life.* New York: Oxford University Press, 1972.

Schorer, Mark. *Sinclair Lewis: An American Life.* New York: McGraw-Hill, 1961.

Sencourt, Robert. *T. S. Eliot: A Memoir.* Ed. Donald Adamson. New York: Dodd, Mead, 1971.

Sheaffer, Louis. *O'Neill: Son and Playwright.* New York: Little, Brown, 1968.

———. *O'Neill: Son and Artist.* New York: Little, Brown, 1973.

Sheed, Wilfrid. "Introduction." *Writers At Work: The Paris Review Interviews: Fourth Series.* Ed. George Plimpton. New York: Penguin Books, 1977, pp. ix–xv.

———. "More Writers at Work." *New York Times Book Review*, 1 August 1976, pp. 5, 10, 14.

Shinn, Thelma J. "A Question of Survival: Analysis of 'The Treacherous Years' of Henry James." *Literature and Psychology*, 23 (1973), 135–48.

Siebenschuh, William R. *Form and Purpose in Boswell's Biographical Works*. Berkeley: University of California Press, 1972.

Simpson, Lewis P. Rev. of Robert S. Newdick's "interrupted biography" of Frost. *American Literature*, 49 (May 1977), 279.

Sontag, Susan. "On- Style." *Partisan Review*, 32 (1965), 543–60.

Spacks, Patricia Meyer. "Some Reflections on Satire." In *Modern Essays in Criticism: Satire*. Ed. Ronald Paulson. Englewood Cliffs, N.J.: Prentice-Hall, 1971, pp. 360–78.

Spender, Stephen. "In Eliot's Cave." *New York Review of Books*, 19 September 1974, pp. 18–19.

Sprague, Claire, ed. *Virginia Woolf: A Collection of Essays*. Englewood Cliffs, N.J.: Prentice-Hall, 1971.

Spurgeon, Caroline. *Shakespeare's Imagery, and What It Tells Us*. New York: Macmillan, 1935.

Stafford, William T. "Henry James." In *American Literary Scholarship/1972*. Ed. J. Albert Robbins. Durham: Duke University Press, 1974, pp. 92–98.

———. "Henry James." In *American Literary Scholarship/ 1973*. Ed. James Woodress. Durham: Duke University Press, 1975, pp. 116–18.

———. "On Movies and Literature: What They Can Do For (And Perhaps To) One Another." Seminar presentation. University of Tulsa Graduate Institute of Modern Letters Colloquium on the Current Critical Scene. Tulsa, Oklahoma, 8 July 1974.

Steiner, George. "The Last Victorian." *New Yorker*, 17 February 1975, pp. 103–6.

Stock, Noel. *The Life of Ezra Pound*. New York: Discus/Avon, 1970.

Strachey, Lytton. *Eminent Victorians*. 1918; rpt. New York: Capricorn Books, 1963.

Strandberg, Victor. "Between Truth and Fact: Faulkner's Symbols of Identity." *Modern Fiction Studies*, 21 (Autumn 1975), 445–57.

Swanberg, W. A. *Dreiser*. New York: Scribner's, 1965.

Tanner, Tony. *City of Words: American Fiction, 1950–1970*. New York: Harper & Row, 1971.

Thompson, Lawrence. *Melville's Quarrel with God*. Princeton: Princeton University Press, 1952.

————. *Robert Frost: The Early Years: 1874–1915*. New York: Holt, Rinehart and Winston, 1966.

————. *Robert Frost: The Years of Triumph: 1915–1938*. New York: Holt, Rinehart and Winston, 1970.

————. *Robert Frost: The Later Years: 1938–1963*. Completed by R. H. Winnick. New York: Holt, Rinehart and Winston, 1976.

Tintner, Adeline R. "Letters: Digging James." *New York Review of Books*, 6 April 1972, pp. 37–38.

Todd, Richard. "'Are You Too Deeply Occupied to Say If My Verse Is Alive?'" *Atlantic*, January 1975, pp. 74, 76–81.

Turnbull, Andrew. *Scott Fitzgerald*. New York: Scribner's, 1962.

————. *Thomas Wolfe*. New York: Scribner's, 1967.

Ullmann, Stephen. "Style and Personality." *Review of English Literature*, 6 (1965), 21–31.

Unterecker, John. *Voyager: A Life of Hart Crane*. New York: Farrar, Straus and Giroux, 1969.

Van Dore, Wade. "Robert Frost: A Memoir and a Remonstrance." *Journal of Modern Literature*, 2 (November 1972), 554–60.

Vendler, Helen. "An American Genius." Rev. of *Walt Whit-*

man: A Life by Justin Kaplan. *New York Times Book Review,* 9 November 1980, pp. 1, 28–30.

Volpe, Edmond L. *A Reader's Guide to William Faulkner.* New York: Farrar and Straus, 1964.

Waingrow, Marshall. "Johnson's *Life of Savage:* Biography as Conjecture." Seminar presentation. Seminar 13, "Eighteenth-Century Biography," MLA Convention, Chicago, Illinois, 27 December 1973.

Wardropper, Bruce. "*Don Quixote:* Story or History?" *Modern Philology,* 63 (August 1965), 1–11.

Warren, Robert Penn, ed. *Faulkner: A Collection of Critical Essays.* Englewood Cliffs, N.J.: Prentice-Hall, 1966.

———. *Homage to Theodore Dreiser.* New York: Random House, 1971.

Watkins, Floyd C. "Faulkner, Faulkner, Faulkner." *Sewanee Review,* 82 (Summer 1974), 518–27.

Weaver, Raymond. *Herman Melville: Mystic and Mariner.* New York: George Doran Co., 1921.

Webb, James Wilson. "Biography in American Literature, 1800–1860." *Dissertation Abstracts,* 19 (March 1959), 2350 (University of North Carolina).

Wellek, René, and Austin Warren. *Theory of Literature.* 3rd ed. New York: Harcourt, 1970.

White, William. "Hemingway and Fitzgerald." In *American Literary Scholarship/1968.* Ed. J. Albert Robbins. Durham: Duke University Press, 1970, pp. 107–17.

Wilde, Meta Carpenter, and Orin Borsten. *A Loving Gentleman: The Love Story of William Faulkner and Meta Carpenter.* New York: Jove/Harcourt, 1976.

Wilkinson, Burke. "After the Jazz Age, the Crack-Up." *New York Times Book Review,* 11 March 1962, pp. 1, 16.

Williams, Shirley. "Ten Years for the Complete Faulkner." *Louisville Courier-Journal and Times,* 1 December 1974, p. E5.

Williams, Tennessee. *Memoirs.* New York: Doubleday, 1975.

Wimsatt, W. K., Jr. *The Verbal Icon.* Lexington: University of Kentucky Press, 1954.

Woolf, Virginia. *Orlando: A Biography.* 1928; rpt. New York: New American Library, 1960.

————. *The Second Common Reader.* New York: Harcourt, 1932.

Wright, George T., ed. *Seven American Stylists: From Poe to Mailer: An Introduction.* Minneapolis: University of Minnesota Press, 1973.

Yardley, Jonathan. "Everything You Ever Wanted to Know About the Man—Not the Artist." *New York Times Book Review,* 17 March 1974, pp. 1–3.

index

M